Canoeing, Kayaking & Hiking
TEMAGAMI

Canoeing, Kayaking & Hiking
TEMAGAMI

Compiled and Illustrated by
HAP WILSON

The BOSTON
MILLS PRESS

*To Stephanie, for hearing the voices in the falls
and for sharing the song of the trail.*

A BOSTON MILLS PRESS BOOK

Published by Boston Mills Press, 2004
132 Main Street, Erin, Ontario N0B 1T0
Tel: 519-833-2407 Fax: 519-833-2195
e-mail: books@bostonmillspress.com
www.bostonmillspress.com

In Canada:
Distributed by Firefly Books Ltd.
66 Leek Crescent
Richmond Hill, Ontario, Canada L4B 1H1

In the United States:
Distributed by Firefly Books (U.S.) Inc.
P.O. Box 1338, Ellicott Station
Buffalo, New York 14205

Copyright © 2004 Hap Wilson

National Library of Canada Cataloguing in Publication

Wilson, Hap, 1951-
Canoeing, kayaking & hiking Temagami / compiled & illustrated by Hap Wilson.

Previously published under title: Temagami canoe routes.
ISBN 1-55046-434-5

1. Canoes and canoeing—Ontario—Temagami, Lake, Region—Guidebooks.
2. Hiking—Ontario—Temagami, Lake, Region—Guidebooks.
3. Temagami, Lake, Region (Ont.)—Guidebooks. I. Wilson, Hap, 1951- .
Temagami canoe routes. II. Title. III. Title: Canoeing, kayaking and hiking Temagami.

GV776.15.O5W54 2004   797.1'22'09713147   C2004-900035-7

Publisher Cataloging-in-Publication Data (U.S.)

Wilson, Hap, 1951-
Canoeing, kayaking & hiking Temagami / compiled and illustrated by Hap Wilson.

[160] p. : photos., ill., maps ; cm.
Includes bibliographical references.
Summary: A guide to canoeing, kayaking and hiking Temagami, Ontario:
with notes on the history and geography of the region, maps, canoe routes, tips on tripping.

ISBN 1-55046-434-5 (pbk.)

1. Canoes and canoeing — Temagami (Ont.) — Guidebooks. 1. Canoes and canoeing — Ontario —
Guidebooks. 3. Temagami (Ont.) — Guidebooks. 4. Temagami (Ont.) — Description and travel. I. Title.

797.1'22'09713 22   GV783.T45.W56 2004

The publisher acknowledges for their financial support of our publishing program,
the Canada Council, the Ontario Arts Council and the Government of Canada
through the Book Publishing Industry Development Program (BPIDP).

We gratefully acknowledge the financial support of the Living Legacy Trust.

This book was printed on paper containing post-consumer waste.

Photography, maps, illustrations by Hap Wilson
Design by Gillian Stead

Printed in Canada

Contents

Foreword

It was obvious that the campsite hadn't been used in some time. The firepit rocks lay undisturbed; dog's tooth lichen, having found purchase among the hearthstones, giving testimony of its abandonment. There was little left within the concavity of rocks, save for a few eroded nuggets of charcoal. Manna grass and coral lichen sprouted from the rubble in small patches. A rusted tin can lay pushed to one side, the identification of which was uncertain except that it had been one man's meal at least half a century ago. From the limb of an archaic jack pine hung a steel fry pan, like an epitaph, almost as if the owner had expected to be back some day to collect it, or they had realized that they had had enough of trail life. There was also the possibility that they may have died right there — it wasn't so unusual fifty years ago — their bones having been picked clean by shrews and ravens and dispersed by wolves so that the only manifestation of their existence was the immutable vessel in which they cooked their last meal, now adorning a wizened tree that stood resolute, overlooking, perhaps, their favourite lake of all.

It sleeps among

the thousand hills

Where no man ever trod,

And only nature's music

fills the silences of God.

Frederick George Scott, 1897, from *The Unnamed Lake*

Stout spruce poles had been cut and stacked against a nearby pine, as was custom, but all that remained now were a few remnant staves, rotted and dismembered, huddled in a disheveled pile like pick-up sticks, at the base of a fallen chicot. The poles would have supported a five-pole pitch, canvas tent, or perhaps a rain tarp or kitchen fly, and after use they would be bundled and propped in the crotch of a limb to keep from deteriorating, to stay dry for someone else's use later on, whoever might be out that way.

It was a melancholy place, resplendent, serendipitous and magnificent. Unchanged for thousands of years, witness to the passing of moccasined feet, host to the same family of loons for many centuries, and decadent in its investiture of ancient pine, whose voices could be heard if you sat and listened long enough. The way into this quiet place was not easy to find. I had been thwarted many times by false beaver "runs" that, although resembling well-trodden footpaths, would eventually fade into the impassable chaos of fallen tree and tag alder after only 100 m. I should have realized that no human foot had marked its way through this territory for decades, and that any traditional portage trail would have by now slipped into oblivion, swallowed up in the blueberry sedge and Labrador tea, the years of windfall and amassed forest duff of leaves and pine needles making any footpath impossible to locate. These trails were all clear at one time or another, kept open by Native hunters, later by forest rangers and possibly by a few individuals escaping from something back home. And that was often the case when a lonely soul would choose the life of a prospector, fire ranger or surveyor; where business on the trail made more sense than a prosaic life in the city.

The lake was indicated on the map but had no name, like a thousand other lakes in the Temagami backcountry. Maybe that was a good thing. Surveyors and politicians had already anglicized many of the Ojibwa place names and replaced them with their own, or the name of a wife or daughter of an earl or Hudson Bay factor. Something drew me to this particular chain of lakes and to this parcel of paradise among the pines. I had found sanctuary. And so long as this lake survives the onslaught of development, I feel that this wilderness will live on. I fear the future because the veneer of hills keeping out the machine is being pared away, layer by layer, tree by tree.

I arranged the stones in the old firepit to my liking, kindled a quick fire and perched my tea pail over the fire irons. Somewhere a loon called. It was early afternoon, but I was in no hurry to go anywhere, not just yet anyway until I got a sense of why I came to this particular place. I braced my back against a pack and looked out over the clear water with its verdant reflections. This is Temagami, I mused, captured in one intensely concentrated scene, a converging of redeeming features, a cachet of perfection. I looked up at the fry pan on the jack pine, its gun-metal sheen long since faded, and had the pervasive notion that I was not alone.

(Taken from journal notes, July 1977)

The Old Canoe

When the sunset gilds the timbered hills
That guard Timagami,
And the moonbeams play on far James Bay
By the brink of the frozen sea,
In phantom guise my Spirit flies
As the dream blades dip and swing
Where the waters flow from the Long Ago
In the spell of the beck'ning spring.

Do the cow-moose call on the Montreal
When the first frost bites the air,
And the mists unfold from the red and gold
That the autumn ridges wear?
When the white falls roar as they did of yore
On the Lady Evelyn,
Do the square-tail leap from the black pools deep
Where the pictured rocks begin?

George Marsh, *Scribner's Magazine,* **October 1908**   ~ **verses 2-3**

Temagami Canoe Country

TEMAGAMI. Even the name conjures up the notion that this is an ancient land once inhabited solely by ancient peoples. "Deep water by the shore," or Te-mee-ay-gaming, as it was known to the local Ojibwa, Lake Temagami formed the core, the body of a giant spider with outstretched legs, with deep bays pointing out to all directions of the compass, its ancient trails leading to lands beyond. The Temagami "wilderness," or backcountry that once formed the intricate travelways of the Anishinabe, was defined by the Montreal River in the north, the Sturgeon and Wanapitei rivers to the west, and the Marten and Ottawa rivers to the south and east. This rather unique geophysical arrangement of waterways covers an area of well over 10,000 sq km. The size alone makes Temagami one of the country's most extensive backcountry canoeing regions — certainly one of the most celebrated and controversial. When someone speaks of Temagami they could be talking about a small village at the eastern terminus of the northeast arm of the lake with the same name, or they could be referring to Temagami as the commonly accepted title of the defined wilderness area. To confuse things further, political boundaries quarter this region into four administrative districts: Temagami, Kirkland Lake, Sudbury and North Bay. This book tries to relieve the confusion by not dissecting routes by arbitrarily drawn boundary lines, even though politics and resource management tend to regulate parcels of this natural region.

The distinction that makes this adventure Shangri-La unique and special could be encapsulated in one night camped beside any one of its clear-water lakes. The sound of the wind in the pines, the crackling of spruce as it burns in the firepit, a circling osprey, the beckoning sound of a cold-water spring on a long portage, a red canoe pulled up on a rocky shore, spring peepers, the smell of wood smoke, camaraderie . . . all meld together to characterize the Temagami experience. There is more, but then there is always more; each time you dip your paddle or line your canoe up the same rapids there is always something you missed the time before. And that's what typifies Temagami — the fact that it grows on you, envelopes your very soul, presents new challenges and reveals new secrets each time you visit.

There are lakes and there are rivers in Temagami, each neatly intertwined into a contiguous web of adventure possibilities. Lake Temagami alone possesses one of the longest undeveloped coastlines in Canada, making it one of the best kayak touring destinations in North America; and with more than 3,500 km of additional canoe and kayak routes, it's one of the largest collections of water trails in Canada. For the hiker, Temagami has some of the finest wilderness trails in the province, certainly the most challenging, as this is the "rooftop" of Ontario. There are over forty backcountry trails and viewpoints, and new trails are constantly being developed.

This new edition of the book contains information on twenty-seven canoe and kayak routes, with at least a dozen additional side or link routes. The first section contains basic canoeing and general interest matter only, and it's recommended that you browse through the bibliography for current publications and websites that keep you up-to-date with conditions, equipment and what's cooking on the environmental front.

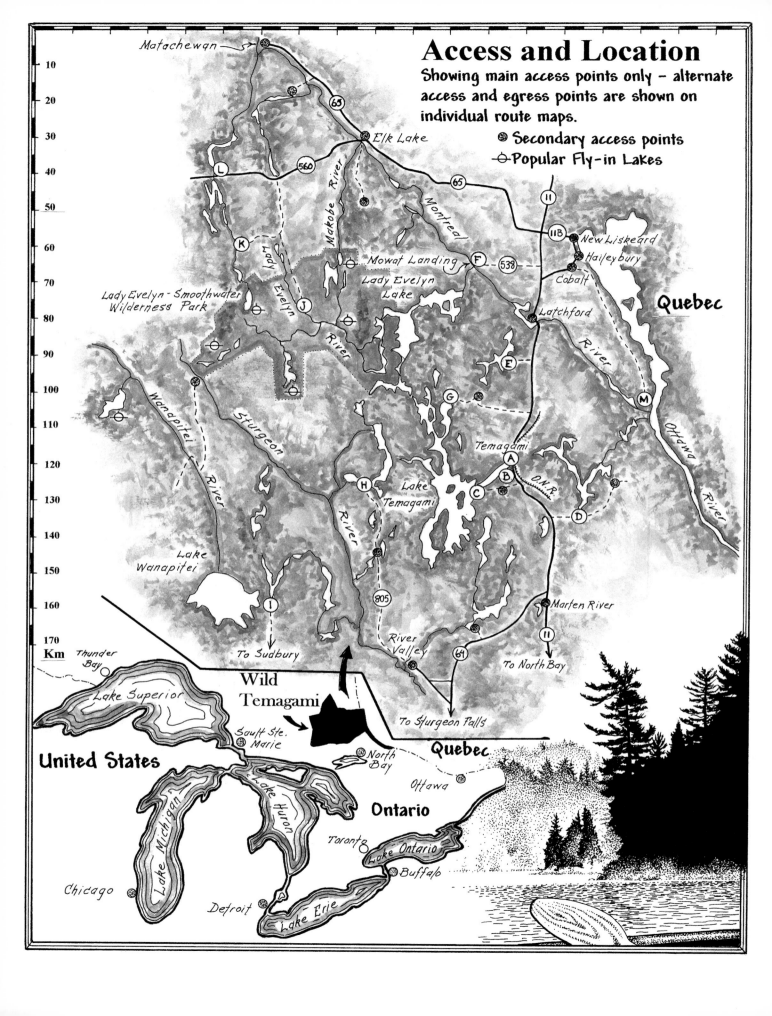

Part One

Temagami
Yesterday and Today

One of the most popular and hallmark vistas in Temagami is the pine shorescape.

N'Daki Menan and the Nastawgan

The Native people of this region were the Te-mee-ah-gamaw anishinawbeg, or "Deep Water People." Primarily nomadic, the Temagami supported a particular lifestyle through hunting, fishing and gathering. There were twelve family groups, each with its own designated territory and family totem or name: White Bear, Pile of Mud, Giant Man and so on. The Anishinawbeg maintained a democratic society and a firm belief that life revolved around the sanctity of the environment around them — birth, life, death and rebirth ensured an ongoing genesis of existence. Resources were managed appropriately for their immediate needs.

Anishinawbeg religion predates Christianity by 20,000 years, believing that humans were an integral part of the cyclical pattern of nature, not above it. They held beliefs in magic, myth and Manitous (spirits) and thought that everything, both animate and inanimate, possessed a spirit. Many sacred sites are found within the district, such as Chee-bay-jing, or what we know as "Maple Mountain." To the Temagami this was a sacred burial ground or "place where the soul spirit dwells." High points in Temagami were used as vision-quest or healing sites. (Vision-quest sites were typically high ridges where the youth were sent to fast and seek their guiding spirit.) Chee-skon-abikong, or "place of the huge rock," within the Wakimika Triangle Trail network, is one of such healing locations still used by the Anishinawbeg today. The people called the world around them N'Daki Menan, or "our land."

Nastawgan are traditional travel routes of the Anishinawbeg. Temagami has one of the world's largest intact collections of Native trails. Numbering upwards of 1,300 winter (bon-ka-nah) and summer (onigum) trails, the Temagami nastawgan have been in constant use for the past 5,000 years. The Temagami maintained the onigum by removing fallen timber and overhanging branches, and often marked trails with axe blazes or rock cairns. Water routes along creeks were also cleared of dead or fallen timber to provide easy passage.

Many creek routes (such as South Lady Evelyn) were used solely as spring routes when the water levels allowed easy paddling. Cedar logs were often placed along "bottomless" trail sections where bog or swamp crossings restricted travel. This metigo-mukana was laid longitudinally in the direction of travel, much the same way as it's done by portage maintenance crews today. The bon-ka-nah were often extensions of summer portages that skirted fast current or falls — longer trails that avoided dangerous ice conditions. Break-up and freeze-up were dangerous times, and the Anishinawbeg often pulled their canoes atop sleighs. When the ice gave way, they simply jumped into the canoe and broke a passageway with an axe or paddle.

Some bon-ka-nah traversed quite a distance, such as the winter route from Maymeen-koba (Willow Island Lake) to Ka-bah-zip-kitay-begaw (Divide or Katherine Lake), following a series of small ponds between the two channels of the Manja-may-gos-sibi (trout streams or Lady Evelyn River). The longest nastawgan route ran 115 km from Smoothwater Lake, following a natural fault line eastward, ending at the Ottawa River. There were a total of fourteen bon-ka-nah located along this particular route.

Until the 1940s, over seventy-five maintained bon-ka-nah existed in the Lake Temagami region. The canoe brigades of the Ontario Forestry Branch during the 1920s to 1940s (read Grey Owl's Men of the Last Frontier) maintained the nastawgan in order to provide quick access to fire towers or for the purpose of combating wildfires in the interior. With the advent of aerial fire suppression techniques, including water-bombing, the trails were left to grow over. It wasn't until 1976, with the initial survey of this book and subsequent years of clearing portages, that these historic routes were reopened for travel. Lake Temagami canoe camps kept a number of these routes open. One, Camp Keewaydin, has been operating on the lake since 1901.

Macominising (Bear Island), Wa-wee-ay-gaming (Wawiagama or Round Lake), Shkim-ska-jeeshing (Florence Lake or Lake that Bends in the Middle), and Non-wakaming (Diamond Lake) were major intersections of the bon-ka-nah.

Today, the Anishinawbeg of Bear Island continue negotiations towards a Treaty of Co-Existence to ensure harmony and certainty for the future of n'Daki Menan, their homeland. However, rifts between factions have divided the band — some want homeland protection through conservation efforts, while others want to exploit the resources for profit. A recent settlement with the Ontario government ceded new lands to the band adjacent to Lake Temagami.

White Interests and Settlement

The Iroquois raids of the mid-1600s brought about the widespread dispersal of many Native groups (Cree, Ojibwa and Algonquin), while almost completely eliminating the Huron culture. This relocation of people, plus the growing use of European trade goods and the fur-trade economy, resulted in a "blending" of groups during this period. The Temagami fought several battles with invading Iroquois in and around the Lake Temagami area.

The Temagami region played only a minor role in local White history, having missed the main trade flow to the south along the Mattawa and French rivers. Fur trading was, however, an important facet of early life on the lake, moving inland from Lake Temiskaming in 1834 when a Hudson's Bay post was established on the south end of Temagami Island. Independent traders took most of the business away from the Hudson's Bay post, but they eventually met their demise as the railway pushed through North Bay and Sturgeon Falls. And by 1890, the Hudson's Bay Company had developed a lucrative sideline — outfitting parties of sportsmen and recreational canoeists.

Business flourished on Lake Temagami, and it soon became a tourist mecca. The rivers and lakes of the region were already famous for their attractions and superb beauty. The T&NO Railway reached Temagami in 1904, bringing with it a burgeoning adventure tourist crowd. Islands were sold to cottagers, while lodges catered to "soft" wilderness seekers. Canoe camps also sprang up throughout the hub of Lake Temagami.

In 1901 and 1903, the Temagami Forest Reserve was established to protect pine resources and to ensure the security of a future forest industry, although logging didn't actually take place within the core Temagami area until after the reserve was disbanded in the mid-1930s. Temagami village boomed until the building of the Mine Road to the hub in 1954. Servicing Copperfield's Mine, this road became the centre stage for lake tourists and Bear Islanders. Both logging and mining peaked in the late 1980s, and with the shutdown of local mills, the economy of Temagami village once again relies on tourism. For a comprehensive history of Temagami, check out www.ottertooth.com.

Tales of the evil Wendigo still permeate the northern forests today: "The most dreaded of all the supernatural beings that are evil or hostile to man is the Wendigo, a personification of the starvation and craving for flesh that so often befell the Ojibwa in the later months of the winter. The Wendigo is a human transformed by cannibalism into a monstrous giant with supernatural powers. A sorcerer through witchcraft may prevent a hunter from killing any game, and reduce his family to such straits that one member, crazed by hunger, kills and eats a brother or sister.

Then the appetite for human flesh becomes insatiable. The cannibal's body swells to the size of a pine tree and becomes hard like stone, impenetrable to arrow or bullet and insensible to cold. Naked save for a loincloth, the monster roves the countryside seeking more victims to devour, its breathing is audible for miles; and its shouting weakens the limbs of the Indian it pursues. It haunts the country only in winter, when it attacks its victims during snow storms or unusually cold weather; with the first melting of the snow it retreats to the north." Jenness, 1935

A Unique Landscape — Vegetation, Topography and Drainage

The Temagami backcountry occurs at the boundary of the boreal forest to the north and the Great Lakes–St. Lawrence forest region to the south, or what is commonly called the transition forest. A small portion of the district bordering the Montreal River in the northeast lies within what is known as the "Little Clay Belt."

Because of the thin, nutrient-poor soils, the flora is not particularly diverse within most of the district. Aside from the Clay Belt, where farming takes place, the highly acidic soil limits the growth of most species and contributes to generally slow forest growth. White pine tends to dominate the canopy along many of the canoe routes; located along the tops of ridges, it forms a treeline image that characterizes the experience. Mixed with white pine are red pine, jack pine and yellow birch. Pockets of hardwoods, including aspen, birch, maple and oak, are scattered throughout the district. Where deep, organic soils are present, white and black spruce, tamarack, black ash and cedar dominate the canopy. Climate also affects the vegetation cover in Temagami, as colder temperatures and lower precipitation exacerbate the adverse growing conditions. The rolling topography of most of Temagami is reflected by the rugged nature of the exposed cliffs, deeply glaciated valleys and bedrock barrens. This fringe boreal forest is primarily a "disturbance" type forest, with frequent disturbances from fire, insect defoliation and wind storms. The government maintains that this forest requires the replication of fire through massive clear-cutting — a procedure vehemently opposed by private biologists and ecologists.

Surficial geology relating to the landforms within the district forms the backbone of the tourist industry. The local Native people built their nastawgan trail network using fault lines and glacially scoured valleys, while high points served well for burial sites and vision-quest ceremonies. Several of the province's highest mountains are found within the Lady Evelyn–Smoothwater Wilderness Park. A number of beautiful beaches are another natural feature within the district.

There are two distinct drainage basins in the area: the Montreal River (including the Lady Evelyn and Makobe rivers) flowing to the Ottawa River; and the Sturgeon (including the Obabika, Temagami and Yorston rivers) flowing south to Lake Nipissing. Break-up on these rivers may occur in early April, although most lakes are still ice-covered until early May. Freeze-up occurs on small ponds and shorelines by late October.

The Last Wild Stand — Three Decades of Environmentalism

Displeasure over how the land was "managed" dates back over one hundred years. The Teme augama anishinabeg claim that they never actually ceded the land to the government during the Huron-Robinson Treaty days. It wasn't until a land caution was implemented by the band in 1973 in a move to stop the government from building a resort on Maple Mountain that there was a more concerted effort to establish home rule and resource management. Intrusive logging in the late 1970s, with subsequent infractions and cutting violations, sparked a move by private citizens to establish a proactive stand against resource mismanagement.

In 1988, the Temagami Wilderness Society (now Earthroots), a non-profit, environmental lobby group based in Toronto, petitioned the government with a proposal to protect a 3,500-sq-km buffer around the existing wilderness park. Its presentation drew international support, and the International Union of the Conservation of Nature put the Lady Evelyn–Smoothwater wilderness on the world's endangered spaces list. The building of the Red Squirrel Road extension through the park, without public consultation, instigated public reaction, demonstrations and road-blocks. At this time, the Temagami Wilderness Society hired its own forest ecologist, Peter Quinby, and it was soon established that Temagami did support an extensive old-growth pine forest. Pressure from environmental and Native groups resulted in major amendments to resource management, including a policy governing "old-growth" forests. New parks were added (Solace, Obabika and Sturgeon Waterway parks), but it was too little too late. Environmental groups still fight to maintain the integrity of the Temagami experience in light of government policy allowing non-conforming park use and recent policy on clear-cut logging. For a detailed look at the chronology of the environmental movement in Temagami, refer to www.ottertooth.com.

Timagami

Far in the grim Northwest beyond the lines
That turn the rivers eastward to the sea,
Set with a thousand islands, crowded with pines,
Lies deep water, wild Timagami:
Wild for the hunters roving, and the use
Of trappers in its dark and trackless vales,
Wild with the trampling of the giant moose,
And the weird magic of old Indian tales.
All day with steady paddles toward the west
Our heavy-laden canoe we pressed:
All day we saw the thunder-traveled sky
Purple with storm in many a trailing tress,
And saw at eve the broken sunset die
In crimson on the silent wilderness.

Archibald Lampman (1861–99)

Lampman, like many others, sought the quietude of Temagami in the 1890s; however, this newfound wilderness paradise almost killed him in the fall of 1896 when he suffered a cardiac relapse as a result of the physical strain of camping and portaging. (Temagami was officially spelled Timagami until 1968, when the Names Authority was persuaded to accept the preferred local spelling.)

Part Two

Things
You Should Know

Things You Should Know

Preparation — Key Points

Because you are on your own in an undeveloped region, it is essential to plan your trip well. You must foresee every need and equip yourself according to trip demands, keeping in mind that weight should be minimal for portaging. You must also pursue a style of camping that "leaves no trace." By doing so, you will help preserve this unique place for future generations. Most of the routes are "user-maintained," which means doing the little extras to keep campsites and trails clean and clear for the next party. Choice of route and schedule are important, so allow ample time in case of delays. Inform someone of your plans so that authorities can be notified if you are overdue. And before you set out on your trip, learn the basic skills of canoeing.

Reading Whitewater — River Grading

It is unsafe to attempt the running of rapids unless you are experienced in reading fast-water conditions, have the appropriate equipment, and can control the movements of the canoe at all times. The river routes in this book indicate rapids that can be run under optimal conditions only, which vary greatly with water flow and seasonal fluctuations. It is important that you know your own skill level, based on experience, and apply it to current conditions. It is the responsibility of each individual to beach their canoe well above the rapids, walk to a point where the entire river flow can be observed, and determine whether or not the run can be made safely. When in doubt, portage!

Be aware that variations in water level can have a number of effects on navigation: logjams and "sweepers" (fallen trees) may impede water flow; beaver dams may flood portage trails and alter stream direction; and entire river channels may shift as a result of heavy spring run-off. The routes are graded according to required skill level and difficulty. Choose a route that best suits your abilities.

No-Trace Camping

Since the late 1980s, after the Ontario government disbanded the Crown Land Recreation Maintenance Program, the Temagami backcountry has been under a user-maintained system of stewardship. However, this doesn't work well in most cases, especially since there are several areas in the district that fall into the multiple-use category. That puts the onus for care on the individual camper.

The most important thing to remember while tripping in Temagami is to leave no mark on the trails or campsites. This rules out destructive practices such as cutting spruce boughs for bedding, mutilating live trees or clearing tent space over new ground. If you have planned your menu wisely, you should have little or no unburnable garbage; if there is any, it should be packed out in a litter bag. Avoid burning leftover food in the firepit — there's nothing worse than arriving at a campsite to find partly scorched globs of oatmeal adhering to the rocks of the firepit! Dishes should be washed away from the shoreline and grey water dumped well back from the water.

Latrines

We still can't get it right when it comes to taking a dump in the woods. This primary bodily function is the scourge of the north country, and campers continue to despoil the sanctity of wild places with their sewage. The thin soils of Temagami require careful planning of latrines, well back from campsites, shoreline or trails. Scrape or dig a shallow pit in the ground and bury all fecal matter. Toilet paper can be discretely burned in the firepit, or packed out in a bag specifically designated for this use.

Try to leave your campsite cleaner than when you arrived, make sure your campfire is extinguished, and take a last look around for forgotten items and any garbage left on the site. Care should also be taken while walking along portage or hiking trails; take the time to pick up any garbage found along the way.

Nature Observation

Our appreciation and enjoyment of the outdoors matures through experience. That experience allows us to acquaint ourselves with the fundamental principles and ethical values of wilderness travel, values that are not always respected. To understand the nature of Mother Nature, on her own terms, there needs to be an abrupt shift in our perception of how things work. As we urban creatures evolve, or distance ourselves from nature, we lose that ability to gel with the environment, or to understand its peculiarities, nuances or patterns. We then begin to presume that wildlife within the political boundaries, say, of a provincial park, will be lined up along the shore waiting serenely for their pictures to be taken at our convenience. Our disappointment that the forest is now devoid of all life forms may then prompt the notion that we are, in reality, not familiar with the program.

Being knowledgeable and respectful about wildlife traits and habitat is essential for successful outdoor photography and observation. Methods of approach, wind direction, seasonal variations, time of day, even the way in which you handle a canoe or paddle are considerations. So, next time your group is happily singing "Stairway to Heaven" and loudly banging those gunwales, think of the effect it may have on the wildlife populations. What is the key to successful nature observation? Perseverance, patience, an understanding of your surroundings, and early and silent departures will all help in your personal quest.

Nuisance Animals

There's really no such thing as a nuisance animal; it's their territory and we are simply subject to temporary travels within their jurisdiction. In order to avoid any potentially unpleasant confrontation with a bear (or skunk) there are simple rules and precautions that can be exercised. A bear has poor eyesight, but he can smell traces of food left on clothing or in packs no matter how well secured. If you conceal food in the tent or under the canoe, there is a chance a bear may destroy either to get at what it wants. Hoisting your food pack in a tree won't work if it's done wrong — bears are smart, and these piñatas can be figured out eventually by a wily bruin. Sometimes it's best to avoid well-used campsites in key areas such as Hobart Lake or Diamond Lake; human excrement, garbage or fish remains left around a campsite will attract bears and skunks. If you have a chance encounter with a bear at a campsite, loud noises (pot banging or air horns) will generally do the trick to get rid of them. Sometimes nothing will work, then it's time to move to a new site. It gets trickier if it's dark and some campers have had to stay up through the night dealing with particularly motivated bears. Luckily, in Temagami there are few instances of what one might call "bad" situations, as compared with parks such as Algonquin, but they still happen. Be cautious around female bears and moose if they have young with them. If you encounter either while on the water, remember that a swimming bear or moose may swamp a canoe if you paddle in front of them.

Other campsite critters to be wary of are snowshoe hares in spring (eating of leather straps on packs), and mice, squirrels and chipmunks (eating their way into a pack that conceals goodies such as nuts or gorp mix). I seldom hang my food pack, relying on keeping the site and gear clean and the victuals packed in tight containers or barrels, propped under the kitchen fly. Pots and dishes go on top, so if an animal disturbs the packs the ensuing noise of the pots clanging on the bedrock is usually enough to have them scampering for cover. Deterrents such as bear spray or bear bangers can be taken along as a precaution, but there is generally no need for them in Temagami.

potassium and high on citrus; avoid dark clothing, especially blue-jean material; pack a bug jacket; avoid strong fragrances and scented lotions; and carry a live chicken under your arm (a traditional folk answer to pest control). The added weight of a mosquito awning is an insignificant compromise for group or family peace. I've used one for years and it's kept the morale at a high level through the worst of conditions. Shave off half the weight by leaving the poles at home and string the awning up using guy lines.

For wildlife viewing, fishing and whitewater paddling, you can't beat the early part of the season, and with a little forethought, there's no reason to avoid traveling during this time of year because of the bugs.

Insect Pests

Mosquitoes, blackflies, sand flies, horse flies and deer flies all have their appropriate place in the Temagami ecosystem, and their presence shouldn't interfere, or depreciate, a planned excursion during the bug season. And as at any other Canadian Shield destination, bug season can last most of the summer. After the lakes are clear of ice (April 28 to May 8, on average), there is a buffer of about two weeks before the blackfly season. If rain persists through June, though, this may push their reign well into July. Mosquitoes follow close on the heels of the black fly, followed again by the other biting scourges. Aside from a brand of biting house fly, Temagami is virtually fly free in late summer and September, although fall rains can bring a short onslaught of black flies. Chapters could be written about dealing with insect pests, but I do have a few suggestions that work well and may help you keep your self respect and composure when the bugs descend upon your campsite.

Gear has evolved since I started canoe camping. That means good tent screening that will keep out sand flies and a design that will guarantee excellent air flow. Avoid repellents with a DEET fixative — anything that melts plastic is not doing your body any favours. Choose a natural-base repellent and rely on a diet low in

Fishing

All interior travelers are required to have a current fishing licence; these can be purchased at local retail outlets in the area. Temagami is home to many sport fish (northern pike, lake and brook trout, walleye and smallmouth bass). Anglers are encouraged to pack lightweight fishing kits that break down easily, and to carry needle-nose pliers to extricate embedded hooks. Catch-and-release ethics, as well as the use of barbless hooks, is encouraged. The cleaning of fish at campsites is not recommended.

Camping Permits

Permits for non-residents traveling into the interior are required before setting out. Local outfitters and retail outlets can assist in the planning of your trip and ensuring that you have the appropriate permits. Additional interior park user-fees are now a requirement.

Weather

Warm days and cool nights are typical in this "warm" boreal environment. Prevailing winds are from the southwest but may swing to the northwest during the spring and late fall. The daily mean temperature throughout the paddling and hiking season is 14 C (60 F), and the mean rainfall is about 7.5 cm per month. Break-up time varies, so before heading out, check conditions with local outfitters. Freeze-up of small lakes and connecting streams occurs in late October. Special care must be taken during any buffer-season expedition due to inclement weather and the cold-water factor. Immersion in ice water for any more than a few minutes could be hazardous.

Temagami experiences severe thunder and "push" storms, sometimes with tornado effects on the ground. These storms can move in quickly and create dangerous traveling conditions. Keep a sharp eye on weather patterns, especially building storm clouds on humid days, and head for protected shelter at the first sign of trouble. But these storms and the strong winds that accompany them often last only a short while. Make sure canoes are secured and tied, and pitch the tent away from tall, outstanding or dead trees during a wind storm.

Water temperature warms quickly after break-up, and swimming is generally at the comfort level from mid-June to mid-September (18–20 C).

First Aid and Evacuation

The best first aid is prevention. It is unwise to take unnecessary risks because help may be a long way off. Someone in your group should be familiar with the basics of first aid. If not, take a course. Your first-aid kit should include a first-aid booklet, Band-Aids and blister patches, adhesive waterproof tape, compresses, gauze dressings, triangular bandages (a bandana works well), tweezers, scissors, needles, safety pins, thread, disinfectant, burn ointment, suntan lotion, painkillers, antihistamines and personal medications. Persons with specific ailments should make these known to other members of the party. Everyone should know the inherent dangers of hypo- and hyperthermia, know how to recognize the signs and be able to deal with the problem.

Know your route and familiarize yourself with all evacuation points.

Take care of the small stuff. In over thirty-five years of canoe tripping and guiding I have never experienced an evacuation because of a serious accident but I have often had someone enjoy the experience less because they ignored a small discomfort that turned ugly — blisters, cuts, burns, aches, slivers, bites . . . take them seriously before they become serious.

WALLY SCHABER, TRAILHEAD

USE OF CELL AND SATELLITE PHONES: Cell phones have limited power in Temagami, and only within a relatively close proximity to the Highway 11 corridor. Three-watt bag phones work well using a Yagi antenna. Satellite phones are now relatively inexpensive if you use them only for emergency purposes.

LOST OR INJURED In this techno-age it is virtually impossible to get lost. If you carry your maps and compass and know where you are at all times, the chance of getting turned around is quite slim. But it happens. Some trails within the district are non-existent or poorly marked, and with a canoe over your head it's quite easy to lose sight of the path and stray. The most important advice is to remain calm. Avoid panic, sit down, collect your thoughts and think about where you might have gone wrong. Quite often you can trace your way back by watching signs of ground disturbance or familiar landmarks. If this doesn't work, stay put; try whistling to someone else in your group or call out in low tones (deep sounds carry farther than high, shrill screams). If you're alone, don't travel far; pitch a camp at a lake shore or clearing and remain there. If an aircraft comes directly into sight, you can signal for help with three signals of any kind (flashes from a light or mirror, circling in a canoe, or building a smoky fire using green vegetation to cause a smudge. One of the best distress signals is to build three smoky fires at the points of a triangle on a beach or rocky point.

USE OF GPS, PLBS AND ELTS The use of personal locating beacons or emergency locating beacons is not recommended. The use of satellite phones and global positioning systems is recommended; however, do not totally rely on their use, since these devices are subject to malfunction if they get wet or damp. GPS units are handy for reference, determining speed and distance, and locating your whereabouts on the 1:50,000 topographical maps in case you get confused as to exact location. During an emergency, if you have a phone then you can give the rescue authorities an exact location for pick-up.

Misty morning campfire — a typical Temagami scene.

Part Three

Tips on Equipment and Technique

Tips on Equipment and Technique

General Note   The information and advice given here is particularly related to the Temagami environment. There often exists a strong traditional element — the use of cedar-and-canvas canoes and wannigans, for instance, is still preferred by some of the local canoe camps. Because of the rugged nature of the backcountry and the difficulty of portaging, canoeists must weigh the advantages of lightweight gear and equipment against the aesthetic character of traditional, oftentimes heavier, canoes and packs.

EQUIPMENT

Choice of Canoe, Paddle and Lifejacket

In 1969, when I first arrived in Temagami, it was unlikely that you would see anything other than a cedar-and-canvas boat anywhere. Fibreglass canoes were just making their debut, while aluminum boats had been put into service by the Forestry Department. Canoe camps dictated which routes were commonly used, and some, like the lower Temagami River, were avoided because of the inherent risk of damaging equipment. Today, you have several choices to make depending on personal preference and how you want your boat to perform. After being in the outfitting business for years and watching new Kevlar canoes come back to the shop in varied states of annihilation, I have come to the conclusion that you require more than one canoe for the Temagami wilds. Here are my suggestions.

Canoes come in five basic types: canvas-covered cedar, aluminum, fibreglass, Kevlar and plastic (RPF, ABS or Royalex). You get what you pay for. Lightweight Kevlar (under 25 kg) has become the popular choice for routes requiring a lot of carrying. Be careful though, because Kevlar has been overrated as an indestructible phenomenon — these canoes are susceptible to tearing on sharp rocks. Stick to flat-water routes, secure your boat when you come to shore, and portage most rock-littered rapids. ABS, although heavy, is less likely to be damaged if you ride up on a rock. Most whitewaterists prefer Royalex canoes for their forgiving qualities. Make sure you have a comfortable carrying yoke set-up and strong track-lines, as the weight of the ABS tends to

suggest other options to canoeists while river running, i.e., to avoid portaging, paddlers often run or line down bigger rapids.

Paddles vary considerably in size, shape and material. If you are unsure what to purchase, have someone knowledgeable recommend something that suits your needs. Carry a spare paddle in each canoe in case one is lost or broken. Also choose an approved, comfortable personal flotation device (PFD), and wear it at all times while canoeing or lining.

Packs and Packing

There have been many improvements to canoe packs since I first wrote this section twenty-five years ago. At that time, the traditional canvas Deluth pack was the favourite among paddlers, and to stiffen it up you could insert a varnished cardboard box. As Anne and Bill Ostrom, makers of Ostrom packs, explain: "Traditional canoe packs provide very little support, and are great for lighter loads of soft gear. However, an internal-frame canoe pack (one with a rigid back and a hip belt) will transfer the weight to your hips, and is far superior for food packs and other heavy gear."

A good pack, carefully chosen and well-organized, contributes a great deal to the enjoyment of the trip. Many canoeists tend to overload packs so that lumps form in inappropriate places and put undue strain on the back. Internal-frame packs are best, and these can be lined with waterproof stuff bags to ensure that everything stays dry. Small plastic containers or mini olive barrels can be used to separate meal or gear items. Distribute the weight properly by putting heavier items near the top of the pack. Waterproof barrel packs are very popular today, and it's easy to organize your menu and gear so that things you need during the day are close at hand. Dry bags are essential for keeping your gear waterproof, and these come in various sizes, with or without carrying harnesses. Avoid carrying loose articles in your canoe, and don't hang stuff off your packs or it will drive you crazy after awhile. Keep a small day pack handy for such things as snacks, camera, water bottle, sunscreen and rain suit. Because of the air trapped inside dry bags, in the event of an upset your packs will float; remember not to tie in packs to your thwarts — in Temagami there is no need to do this on any river or lake trip. It is difficult to extricate or rescue a boat when packs are secured to the gunnels.

The Canoe Pack

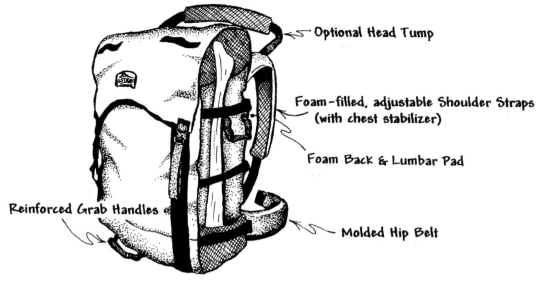

- Optional Head Tump
- Foam-filled, adjustable Shoulder Straps (with chest stabilizer)
- Foam Back & Lumbar Pad
- Reinforced Grab Handles
- Molded Hip Belt

Barrel Packs

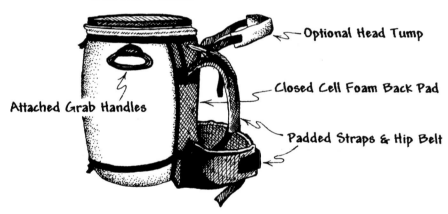

- Optional Head Tump
- Closed Cell Foam Back Pad
- Attached Grab Handles
- Padded Straps & Hip Belt

Best Pack Design:
Ostrom Packs
Eureka/Johnson Outdoors
Knudsen (EZ-Tripper)

Canoe packs come in many styles. Signs of quality include seams with eight to ten stitches per inch; heavily reinforced shoulder straps; and bound edges to prevent fraying of seams, etc If choosing an internal frame canoe pack (one with a rigid back panel), it is critical that the hip belt, shoulder straps, and length of the frame fit your body shape.

Bill Ostrom, Ostrom Outdoors

Clothing and Footwear

Personal risk increases should you decide to travel in the off-season months (May to June and September to October). Temperatures vary considerably, and it's not unusual to have snow in May or October. More people succumb to hypothermia in temperatures 5 to 10 degrees C above freezing than during temperatures that range much colder. Add rain and wind and you have a formula for disaster if not properly attired. Whether it's a freak snowfall or blazing sun, your clothes must not only be comfortable, but must protect you from the extremes of weather and biting insects. "Preparing for the worst" is wise council.

Select clothes for roominess and durability. Avoid fashionable tightness. Have an outfitter explain the benefits of clothing that wicks moisture and dries quickly. Take at least one complete change of clothes and pack it in a dry bag. Invest in a quality, two-piece Gore-Tex rain suit. For cold weather, pack wet suits, gloves, fleece-lined shell and pants, and wool hat. Don't pack too much stuff, just make sure it's the right stuff. Footwear should include one "wet" and one "dry" pair of shoes or boots. If there is a lot of river work such as lining, then I do recommend the L. L. Bean boot (rubber bottoms and leather tops) for the best grip on loose and slippery rocks. Hiking boots are good for easy portaging and hiking but are generally too stiff for scrambling over Temagami rocks. Waterproof canoe "booties" are great for wading in rivers with a sandy bottom, but are not recommended for portaging or working on rock surfaces. Sandals are only appropriate for lounging around the campsite — I've seen too many badly mangled ankles and "Teva toes," and that can seriously affect the success of your trip. A bandana or hat should be worn during sunny days in order to prevent hyperthermia (heatstroke).

Sleeping Gear

There are numerous types of quality sleeping bags on the market. Regardless of material composition (down or feather or synthetic), your bag must be securely waterproofed. Bags filled with synthetic material will dry much more quickly than bags filled with down. Bags should be aired frequently and dry cleaned before departure. Clean bags "breathe" better and expel moisture. Self-inflating ground mats are popular and come with non-skid fabric — important if you end up sleeping on a slope. Pads can also be linked and sleeping bags zipped together to form a double bed. We actually use a pair of easily washed sheets and a comforter and make a "family bed" — great if you have toddlers — at least until your kids graduate to their own tent.

Water Purity and Personal Hygiene

Although much of the Temagami backwater is clean enough to drink by dipping a cup over the gunwales, for peace of mind I highly recommend filtering all of your personal drinking water and boiling all other water used for cooking. The risk of contracting illness due to giardia, cysts, viruses and evil forms of bacteria is present regardless of location. Boiling water for at least five minutes is sometimes inconvenient, but necessary if you don't pack a purifier. There are several commercial filters available that effectively remove the microorganisms that may cause you grief. More cases of giardia get transferred via the old gorp plunge into the communal goody bag than you might think. It is essential that all people practice clean habits and thoroughly wash hands before preparing food.

Food Preparation

Voyageurs of yesterday, even the canoe rangers who patrolled Temagami at the turn of the century, depended on such simple fare as salted pork and dried beans. Fish and game were procured along the way; the bowsman always had a shotgun at easy reach. They would be amazed at the variety of fine, lightweight foods available today. Freeze-dried or dehydrated pre-packaged foods are expensive, but convenient. Personally, I find the flatulence caused by consuming a heavy diet of this type of food a trifle objectionable, so I tend to travel heavy, baking much of my food in a reflector oven and making up my provisions with whatever I can select from grocery-store shelves. Dried foods can be labeled and packed in Zip-lock bags and categorized according to meal, while messy items such as jam, honey or butter can be packed in plastic Nalgene bottles. Glass bottles and tin cans should not be taken along.

Canoeing, kayaking and hiking produce hearty appetites; even on easy-cruise days you will be burning over 3,000 calories. Heavy slugging against wind or grueling portage work will have you burning up to 750 calories an hour. Unless you purposely want to lose weight, it makes good sense to calculate food according to the difficulty of the trip — the harder the trip, the more high-energy food should be packed. Local outfitters can supply a well-planned menu for your group at a reasonable price. Check out the recipe section at the back of the book.

Stoves and Cooking

The use of a lightweight pack stove is recommended, although not mandatory unless a fire ban is instituted (usually for a short duration anywhere from mid-May to mid-August depending on days without rainfall). There is an ongoing debate as to which fossil fuel is harder on the environment, the use of gas or the burning of wood, as a contributor to the greenhouse effect on the atmosphere. The use of stoves is preferable as it does not deplete available firewood and conforms to no-trace camping codes. Stoves should be used out of the wind and sheltered in the firepit. If you do have a campfire, please conform to the precautions and ethical codes as listed below. Food scraps should be composted well back of the campsite and buried under at least 10 cm of ground cover, or packed out. Do not leave scraps of food at the campsite!

Campfires

If you build a campfire, please observe the following precautions:

- Use only deadwood collected at least 1 km away from the campsite. Good hardwood can be gleaned from the tops of abandoned beaver lodges. Refrain from cutting deadwood where the cut stumps can be seen from offshore.
- Light a fire in a safe, established fireplace only (one per campsite). If no fireplace exists, build one on solid rock or mineral soil, digging as necessary to remove all combustible materials within a 2m radius. Do not use rocks that have been submerged in water, as they may explode when they heat up.
- Keep your campfire small and your cooking irons or grill at a low level to the fire.
- Never leave a fire unattended, and always have some water handy for dousing. There's nothing worse than finding someone's melted globs of sock or running shoe pasted to the campfire rocks.
- Keep scraping the embers together during the last stages of the fire so that charcoal will burn down to ash. Refrain from throwing the last bits of toilet paper or gum wrapper in the fire at this stage because they usually won't burn.
- When extinguishing your fire, soak, stir and then soak again. Make sure that the rocks surrounding the fire are well drenched. Leave it for five minutes then come back and check it once more.
- Good camping ethics suggest that a bundle of firewood be left for the next party.

BUILDING A FIRE

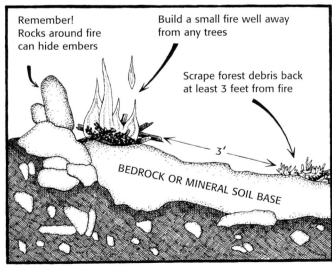

Remember! Rocks around fire can hide embers

Build a small fire well away from any trees

Scrape forest debris back at least 3 feet from fire

3'

BEDROCK OR MINERAL SOIL BASE

RIGHT

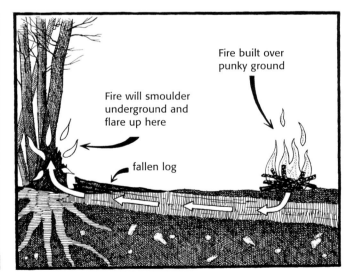

Fire built over punky ground

Fire will smoulder underground and flare up here

fallen log

WRONG

An easy and pretty accurate rule of thumb for paddle sizing is to hold the paddle horizontally over your head like a weight lifter, with one hand on the grip and the other at the throat (where the shaft meets the blade); your elbows should be bent at 90 degrees for a proper fit. However, an inch or two either way won't make much of a difference.

Jodie-Marc Lalonde, Turtle Paddle Works

Use of Axe and Saw

Stove use is great for the summer season, but when the cool winds blow and the temperature drops to just above freezing then it's sure nice to be able to sit around a warm campfire. In Temagami, the campfire is still a strong part of the tradition, and I hope that it always will be. Lighting a campfire is a lost art these days, and becomes particularly difficult if it's been raining for a couple of days. Personal well-being is a concern in the off-

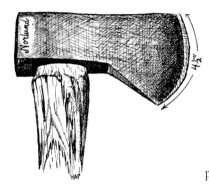

Hudson's Bay style camp axe

season, and one tends to be more mindful of environmental conditions and safety. The proper use of a camp axe is fundamental, and the splitting of wood need not be done with a full and dangerous swing. Some canoeists bring either an axe or a saw. I suggest you bring both. Leave hatchets and machetes at home. Saw your wood into the required lengths (using nothing thicker than the size of your calf) and then split these pieces over a hard surface using light, downward thrusts.

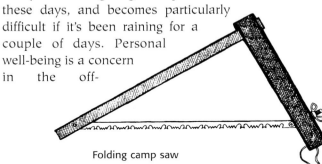

Folding camp saw

> *We have forgotten the use of axes and saws, forgotten the joy of doing physical work. How few know the feel of an axe as it bites into a log, the solid feel of it going into the resin, the clean break of a chunk splitting in the cold. How many know how to saw — that one must not ride the saw on its return, only pull. These things have been forgotten, along with walking, paddling, and carrying loads.* Sigurd F. Olsen, *Runes of the North*, 1963

Suggested Gear Essentials

Aside from major gear items like canoe, tent and pack, a complete miscellaneous item checklist may look something like this:

- waterproof matches
- flashlight and extra batteries
- insect repellent, bug shirts
- kitchen tarp and guy lines
- pocket or belt knife
- sewing kit
- multi-tool
- biodegradable soap and toiletries
- topo maps and this book (waterproofed)
- camera, film, extra battery (in a waterproof case or bag)
- sunglasses and case, sunscreen, skin cream
- a roll of 5cm duct tape
- bolts or self-tapping screws (canoe repairs)
- a tube of waterproof epoxy

- throw or rescue bag
- whistle
- two coils of waterproof nylon rope
- compass or GPS
- first-aid kit
- emergency rations
- extra plastic bags or Zip-locks
- pot gloves
- fire irons or grill
- knee pads
- fishing gear
- sketch pad, journal and pens
- required permits
- nesting pot set (stainless steel) and related cookwear and utensils
- cleaning sac (biodegradable dish soap, cloth, scrubber, towel)
- plastic wash basin

TECHNIQUES

Loading the Canoe and Getting In

I remember watching in absolute horror as two canoeists dragged their fully loaded Kevlar canoe over the rocks along a portage, cursing all the way. Little did they expect to see three days later on a Lady Evelyn River portage the person who had rented them the canoe. Before the advent of the indestructible "rubber" canoe, paddlers using cedar-and-canvas boats knew that allowing their craft to bump a rock was tantamount to severe humiliation. We pound new-age canoes with wild abandon down chutes and rapids that were once portaged around, and are no kinder when it comes to loading and unloading at the trail landings. The canoe should always be lowered gently into the water so that it's fully afloat, then it's appropriate to load it, with one person steadying the canoe while the other places the packs neatly below the gunwale line. Balance out the load so that it sits a little higher in the bow. Take into consideration the different weight of the paddlers and compensate by shifting heavier packs fore or aft. Get in the water if there are shore rocks to contend with, and load or unload your canoe from there. Please do not block the portage trail landing with your gear or canoe. Be considerate of others using the trail, and wait until the other party is fully loaded and departing before taking over the landing.

> *If you get blisters on your grip hand during long trips, try sanding the varnish off and polish the grip with tung and teak oil — actually sand the oil into the grip with a high-grit wet-dry sandpaper — over time the grip is baby-smooth and less likely to give you blisters.*
>
> Jodie-Marc Lalonde, Turtle Paddle Works

Paddling

You don't have to be uncomfortable while paddling — it is not required that you kneel in the canoe at all times. You do have to shift or lower your centre of gravity when conditions become intense (wind or whitewater), but there are several ways to "lounge" while paddling. For most casual or calm conditions you can sit with legs crossed and knees pushing lightly against the gunwales for stability, making sure that your knees are not pointing skyward. Allow your waist to pivot, your lower body moving with the boat while the upper body remains vertically centred over the keel line. The bow person sets a comfortable pace for both paddlers while paddling on the opposite side. Switch often so you won't tire as quickly. The stern paddler employs the use of a J or steering stroke (there are four different J strokes) while the bow paddler keeps a sharp eye for what's ahead. In whitewater, the bow paddler must know the various steering strokes to assist the stern paddler in manoeuvreing the boat through safely. Before heading out, make sure that you know the basic strokes and keep in control at all times.

Lining and Wading

Many sections of shallow water or rapids can be navigated through if the canoe is guided by use of "track" lines (painters). These ropes should be secured low to the bow or stern, or slightly under the hull, in order to gain optimum control. Life jackets should be worn at all times; there have been many accidents and canoes lost by canoeists who do not employ proper technique while lining. Be particularly cautious while lining over ledges, as the hydraulics will pull the boat back and into an uncontrolled roll. The canoe must be pulled forward using the bow line. One person can handle both lines, although it is easier for two paddlers to guide a canoe while walking along the shore rocks. Wading is necessary in the summer when water levels diminish. Proper footwear is essential. Do not step out on the downstream side of the canoe in rapids, as you may end up getting pinned.

Liftovers

At beaver dams and other narrow obstacles such as fallen trees, it's easier to lift over than to portage. Care must be taken not to damage the bottom of the canoe on a sharp knot or stick. Here, the bow person gets out first, followed by the passenger and/or stern paddler. Two people take a central position on each side of the canoe and hand-over-hand gunnel pull over the obstacle while lifting gently.

Beaching and Landing Safely

Improper beaching and unloading causes needless damage to the canoe, or can tie up the trail for others. Approach the shore carefully, either parallel to shore rocks or bow first over beach sand. Assist each other and help unload the packs, putting them in a neat pile off the trail. Secure the canoe by lifting it well out of the current, tying it off and making sure the wind doesn't pick it up (flipped-over Kevlar canoes are easily blown by even the slightest breeze).

Repairs

Make sure that you have the appropriate tools, patch kit, nuts and bolts to do canoe repairs in the field. Duct tape is universally accepted as the best and most important quick-fire emergency repair item. Tighten all seat and thwart bolts securely before leaving on your trip — these bolts often loosen to the breaking point if not looked after early. An ounce of prevention is worth a pound of cure.

Portaging

If done properly and with the right frame of mind, portaging can be enjoyable. When traveling over new ground, carry your packs over first and get a view of where the trail goes; portage paths sometimes are hard to distinguish while walking with a canoe. Keep your group together on the first hike over the trail and make sure that you keep the landings clear. To avoid back strain, get someone to help lift a heavy pack onto your back. Avoid carrying packs over your chest, as this restricts your view of the trail. Practice lifting and carrying the canoe; this should be done by one person only. Two-person carry methods are often difficult over the tougher portages, although this method is often used by younger paddlers. Make sure that you have a comfortable, padded yoke that won't dig into your neck while carrying the canoe. Walking in the bush is one of those recondite skills people often disregard. Knowing where and what to step on will eliminate a nasty fall or getting stuck in waist-deep bog.

Pitching Camp

For some people, the hours spent at a campsite are certainly the most memorable. During the busy summer season it is recommended that you start looking for a campsite by mid-afternoon, certainly no later than two hours before sunset. A good campsite is open to the wind (during bug season), or protected from the wind if storms approach. The site should be well drained and away from trees suspect of falling or being struck by lightning. Make sure to keep the site cleaner than when you found it! Keep track of your gear and where you put it, and before leaving the site do a gear check to ensure that everything has been cleaned, the fire is dead out, and you've left nothing behind.

Autumn morning on Katherine (Divide) Lake.

Part Four

General Information

General Information

Outfitting Services and Guided Tours

Area outfitters provide a variety of services, from food and lodging to completely outfitted expedition packages. They can also tell you what the current conditions are on specific routes; this could include water level, campsite cleanliness, ease of portaging and spring break-up. They also stock camping supplies, maps and licences, and a variety of equipment and canoes suited to the rigors of the Temagami experience. For first-time visitors I would highly recommend joining a guided tour or clinic offered by one of the several professional companies in the district — see the listing of outfitters and tour companies at the back of the book.

Fly-In and Shuttle Services

Flying into the interior in a fifty-year-old de Havilland Beaver can be part of the adventure and intrigue, and it's not as expensive as you might think. The best thing about flying in is that you avoid busy access points and gain access to a remote area within forty-five minutes. And, if you arrange your destination to take advantage of downstream travel and paddling with the prevailing winds, you'll quickly appreciate the expense of flying in.

Air charters should be made well in advance. When you arrive at the float-plane base, make sure your gear is tightly packed and all miscellaneous lines and gadgets are removed from the canoe. Get there at least one-half hour before departure time, and be prepared for delays because of weather conditions. Float planes are restricted to one tie-down (canoe strapped to pontoon) per trip, plus passengers and their gear. If flying in a Beaver aircraft, the weight or length of canoe is not a consideration; however, both Cessna 180 and 185s usually limit gear weight to 80 kg (excluding passengers and canoe), and will not fly a canoe over 16 feet in length (varies with air service). Flight costs vary and are charged by calculating distance per kilometre to your destination and back. There is an additional charge for external loads.

No matter where you park your personal vehicle in the Temagami backcountry, there is the chance of vandalism and theft. It's not a big problem, but it does happen occasionally. And a dead battery on a back road, 80 km from the nearest service station, is no way to end your trip. Local outfitters offer shuttle services to and from many of the access points listed on the access map. They will also jockey your own vehicle for a nominal fee.

The Temagami Tourist Area

Accommodation, restaurants, tourist lodges and cross-country ski facilities all comprise part of the Temagami experience. You may decide to rest and relax at one of many tourist lodges or visit the many scenic attractions or historic displays along the Highway 11 corridor. The Ontario Northland rail and bus service stops at Temagami village every day. North Bay International Airport is located one hour south from Temagami, and shuttles can be arranged through Temagami area lodges or outfitters.

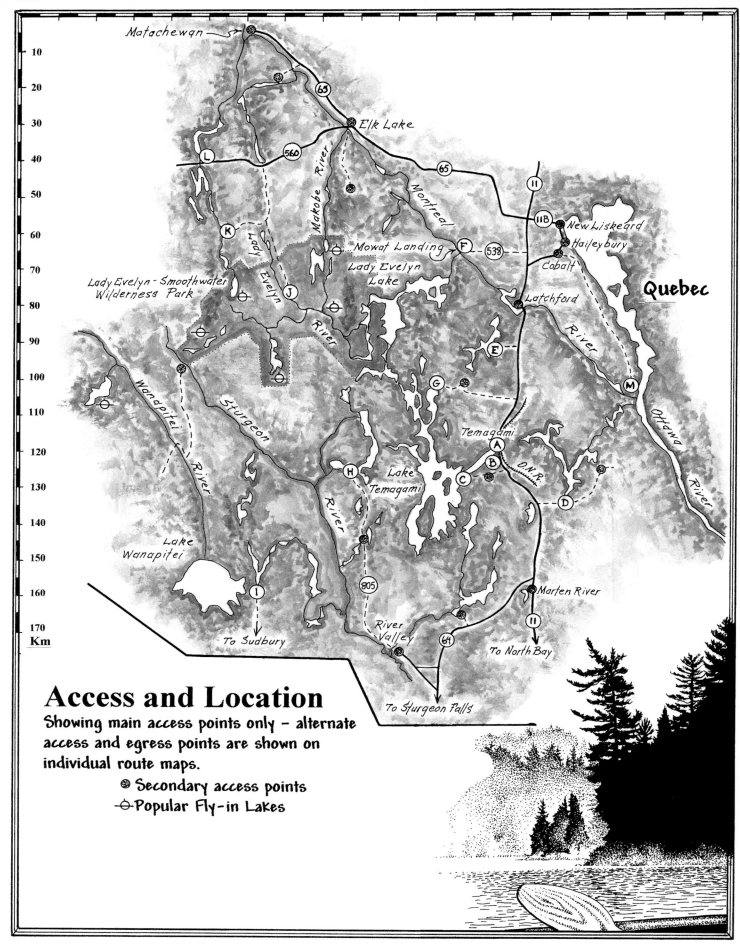

Access and Location

Showing main access points only — alternate access and egress points are shown on individual route maps.

- ⊛ Secondary access points
- ⊖ Popular Fly-in Lakes

Regional Access Points and Overview

The map on the facing page illustrates the Temagami adventure region in a provincial context and in a regional setting. In comparison, the Temagami backcountry comprises an area more than twice the size of Algonquin Provincial Park. Access points, as shown on the accompanying map, are divided into three categories — primary, secondary and fly-in. Only the primary access points are explained below, as per letter designation. Secondary access points and fly-in destination points are shown on individual route maps.

Primary Access Points

A   Town of Temagami   There are three points of access: (1) Finlayson Point Provincial Park, (2) the government dock beside Temagami Outfitting Company, and (3) Snake Island Lake (Rabbit Lake).

B   Strathcona Public Access Road   Located 1.5 km south of the town of Temagami and west off Highway 11, provides a public boat launch and parking.

C   Central Lake Temagami Access Road   Once known as the "Mine Road," built to service the Copperfield's Mine in the 1960s, this good gravel road runs west from Highway 11, about 6.5 km south of the town of Temagami. The road is 18 km long, and is serviced by a private marina (boat taxi) and two public landings. Parking is unlimited. This is a very busy access point from late June to Labour Day weekend.

D   Rabbit Lake Public Access Road   Located about 20 km south of Temagami, this good gravel road runs east off Highway 11 to a short lane (8 km in) and north to a public access point on Rabbit Lake.

E   Anima Nipissing Lake   This good gravel road runs 10 km west off Highway 11 just south of Latchford. There is a public launch and limited parking area.

F   Mowat Landing   Located 20 km west of Highway 11. Take Highway 558 (16 km north of Latchford) over a good, partly paved, mostly gravel road to the public launch at the very end. There is a small lodge and outfitting base here. Parking is unlimited, but busy during peak season.

G   Sandy Inlet   About 9.5 km north of the town of Temagami on Highway 11, the Red Squirrel Road runs west to Red Squirrel Lake (mileage 29) and Sandy Inlet at Camp Wanapitei (mileage 35). The gravel road is only in fair shape and is heavily used by logging trucks, so care must be taken at all times. Watch for signs to Camp Wanapitei and turn south (left) off Red Squirrel Road onto a packed dirt trail through jack pine stands to a limited parking lot. There is a 300 m trail to Sandy Inlet.

H   Obabika Lake and Wawiagama Lake   From the village of River Valley, follow Highway 805 (partly paved but mostly good gravel), 58 km to the gate, where unlimited parking is available at the old lumber camp. You can portage 250 m to Wawiagama Lake, or 1 km to Obabika Lake from here.

I   Matagamasi Lake   Located about 27 km north of Highway 17 on Kukagami Lake Road. Parking here is limited.

J   Gamble Lake and Lady Evelyn River   West of Elk Lake, on Highway 560, take Beauty Lake Road south from Longpoint. Make sure you take the left fork at Beauty (Isabel) Lake. The road is in good shape to Beauty Lake and then deteriorates from there. It is in generally poor condition, especially after break-up in May, and culverts often wash out. Check conditions first. You can drive to Gamble Lake (26 km) located 250 m off the main road on a canopied jack-pine lane (follow your topo map carefully), or travel an additional 12 km to the Lady Evelyn River gate. Parking at Gamble is not recommended unless you're staying at the campsite. The gate at Lady Evelyn is closed from late June to mid-September, and it is a 300 m carry to the river. Parking is unlimited, with campsites available.

K   Montreal River   Take the Beauty Lake Road but veer right at the split and drive 10.5 km southwest of Beauty Lake to Montreal River. There is a public boat launch and there are parking facilities here, as well as limited, poor camping.

L   Edith Lake   Located 2.5 km north of Gowganda on Highway 560, with good parking facilities.

M   Matabitchuan River and Beaver Mountain   South from North Cobalt, 38 km on Highway 567, to the Lower Notch Hydro Dam. There are several points of access, depending on what you want to do. You can put in below the dam, or drive farther on to the power house on the Matabitchuan River. This is a good, very picturesque road.

Secondary Access Points

These points, commonly used for drop-off or pick-up only, are listed as follows: Iceland Lake and South Tetapaga River on Central Lake Temagami Road; Anima Nipissing River Bridge on Red Squirrel Road; Thieving Bear Bridge on Red Squirrel Road; Ross and Glassford lakes on Rabbit Lake Road; Mountain Lodge off Highway 64 (Marten River); Marten River village; River Valley; Manitou Lake on Highway 805; Latchford (Montreal River); tri-towns (Cobalt, Haileybury, New Liskeard); Cooke Lake, south of Elk Lake village; Elk Lake (Makobe pick-up); Sydney Lake access point off Highway 65; Matachewan village; Sturgeon River (85 km north of Capreol and Highway 545).

Popular Fly-In Lakes

From West to East: Welcome Lake, Paul Lake, Scarecrow Lake, Smoothwater Lake, Florence Lake, Banks Lake, MacPherson Lake, Katherine Lake, and Hobart Lake (see directory for air services in Azilda, Longpoint, North Bay and Temagami).

Viewpoints and Hiking Trails — Reference Guide

Viewpoints and hiking trails are listed under the following four categories:

A   **Maintained Trail Network** — semi-remote or remote system with the main feature being a unique forest ecosystem.

1. White Bear Forest Trails: Road or canoe accessible; interpretive guide available from earthroots.org. See Routes 3, 4, 7, 8 and 10.
2. Temagami Island Old-Growth Trails: Canoe or boat accessible; interpretive trail guide available from earthroots.org. See Routes 1, 2, 3, 4 and 5.
3. Obabika Lake (Wakimika Triangle) Trails: Canoe accessible only; interpretive guide available from earthroots.org. See Routes 6 and 11.
4. Blueberry Lake Trails: Canoe accessible only; interpretive guide available from earthroots.org. See Route 10.
5. Smoothwater Cross-Country Ski Trails: Road accessible and private. Contact temagami@onlink.net.

B   **Historical Trail** — semi-remote, with main feature highlighting historic, non-Native use.

1. Burns Trail: Vehicle, boat or canoe accessible; trail information available from nastawgantrails.com.
2. Coleman Trail: Vehicle, boat or canoe accessible; trail information available from nastawgantrails.com.
3. Grand Campment Bay: Vehicle, boat or canoe accessible; trail information available from nastawgantrails.com.

C   **Lookout or Viewpoint with Established Trail** — semi-remote or remote trail with casually maintained trail.

1. Caribou Mountain Lookout Tower: Boat or canoe accessible. See Routes 3, 4, 7, 8 and 10.
2. Maple Mountain Fire Tower: Canoe accessible only. See Routes 12 and 14.
3. Ishpatina Ridge Fire Tower (highest point in Ontario): Canoe accessible only. See Route 21.
4. Bear River Lookout Tower: Road accessible only. Refer to Route 12 and Muir's Discovering Wild Temiskaming.
5. Anima Nipissing Fire Tower: Road and canoe accessible. Refer to Routes 7 and 13.
6. Beaver Mountain Viewpoint: Road and canoe accessible. Refer to Route 10 and Muir's.
7. Ferguson Mountain Viewpoint: Road, boat and canoe accessible. Information is available from nastawgantrails.com. See Routes 4, 6, 7, 9 and 13.
8. Napoleon Mountain Viewpoint: Boat and canoe accessible. See Routes 4, 6, 7, 9 and 13.
9. Point Opimica Lookout: Road, boat, kayak and canoe accessible. Information is available from nastawgantrails.com. Refer to Route 26.
10. Dry Lake Ridge: Canoe accessible only. See Routes 2 and 12.
11. Triangle Hill: Road accessible only. Information is available in Muir's Discovering Wild Temiskaming. Drive 11 km west of Highway 11 on Highway 65 (to Elk Lake).
12. Florence Mountain: Canoe accessible only. See Route 2.
13. High Rock Lookout: Boat and canoe accessible. See Routes 1, 3, 4 and 5.
14. Devil Mountain: Boat and canoe accessible. See Routes 4 and 6.
15. Devil Rock: Road, boat and canoe accessible. See Route 26.

*Geesh pin geesh ka
nawha teegook mahne
gegoom dunebo we gook
sech gwe gwe shuk weh deen.
(If you [clear] cut the
timber, all forms of life
will die in that area.)
Pita wan kwun —
coming of the clouds.*

Alex Mathias,
Obabika Lake, 2002

*Grandmother and Grandfather Rock —
Obabika Lake offerings are still left here by
the Teme augama anishnabek.*

16. Lynn's Lookout: Road, boat, kayak and canoe accessible. Information is available from nastawgantrails.com. See Route 26.
17. Mattawa Mountain: Boat, kayak and canoe accessible. See Route 26.

D   **Viewpoint** — remote setting with no established trail, but accessible. Trails are proposed.

1. "The Gate": On the Sturgeon River. Canoe accessible only. See Route 21.
2. Macpherson Knoll: Canoe accessible only. See Routes 2 and 12.
3. Pinetorch Fire Tower: Canoe accessible only. See Route 11.
4. Duff Lake Viewpoints: Canoe accessible only. See Routes 2 and 19.
5. Smoothwater Lake Ridge: Canoe accessible only. See Route 19.
6. Eagle Lake Ridge: Canoe accessible only. See Route 9.
7. Ma-heen-gun Mountain: Canoe accessible only. See Route 23.
8. Shed Lake Ridge: Canoe accessible only. See Route 23.

9. White Mountain: Canoe accessible only. See Route 23.
10. Kwa-pwa-say-ga Viewpoint: Canoe accessible only. See Route 11.
11. Nasmith Overlook: Canoe accessible only. See Route 11.
12. Pinetorch Fire Tower: Canoe accessible only. See Route 11.
13. Devil's Face: Boat and canoe accessible only. See Route 1.
14. Helen Falls Viewpoint: Canoe accessible only. See Route 12.
15. Sucker Gut Ridge: Boat and canoe accessible. See Route 12.
16. Indian Head Rock: Boat, kayak and canoe accessible. See Route 26.
17. Mount Antoine: Boat, kayak and canoe accessible. See Route 26.

Note about Spiritual Sites

Most of the highpoint lookouts in Temagami are also religious or spiritual sites, having been used for vision questing, conjuring or other cultural purposes. Some of these sites are still in use by the Teme augama anishnabe. Please respect these sacred places — leave tobacco only and walk quietly.

December freeze-up below Cabin Falls,
South Channel of the Lady Evelyn River.

Part Five

How to Use
This Book

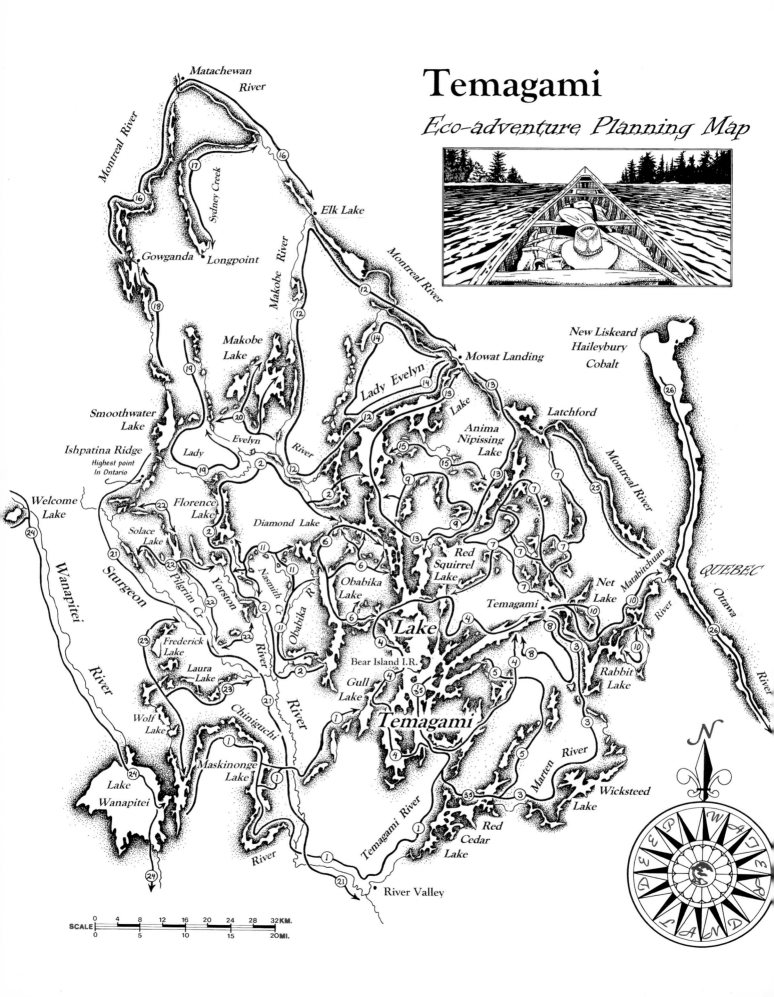

Temagami

Eco-adventure Planning Map

Matachewan River

Montreal River

Sydney Creek

Elk Lake

Gowganda • Longpoint

Makobe River

Montreal River

New Liskeard
Haileybury
Cobalt

Makobe Lake

Lady Evelyn

Mowat Landing

Lady Evelyn Lake

Latchford

Smoothwater Lake

Evelyn

Lady

River

Anima Nipissing Lake

Montreal River

Ishpatina Ridge
Highest point
In Ontario

Welcome Lake

Florence Lake

Diamond Lake

Red Squirrel Lake

QUEBEC

Solace Lake

Wanapitei

Sturgeon

Pilgrim Cr.

Yorston

Nasmith Cr.

Obabika R.

Obabika Lake

Lake

Net Lake

Temagami

Matabitchuan

Ottawa

River

Frederick Lake

River

Bear Island I.R.

Rabbit Lake

Laura Lake

Gull Lake

Temagami

Wolf Lake

Chiniguchi

Lake Wanapitei

Maskinonge Lake

Marten River

Wicksteed Lake

N

Temagami River

Red Cedar Lake

River

River Valley

SCALE
0 4 8 12 16 20 24 28 32 KM.
0   5   10   15   20 MI.

How to Use this Book

About the Maps

Route maps have been drawn using various cartographic scales, from 1:50,000 (as found on most detailed "inset" maps and some smaller route systems) to the larger 1:250,000 scale (as used for some longer routes such as the Ottawa River). Where applicable, I have detailed the more important information using the 1:50,000 scale maps, or illustrated exact field calculations to estimated field research at the site (rapids diagrams). Circled numbers 1 through 27 on the map at left refer to Routes 1 through 27 that begin on page 52.

Although these maps are as accurately compiled as possible, I still encourage travelers to use the standard 1:50,000 topographical maps for navigation purposes. Information from the book can easily be transferred to the field maps; this book should be taken for reference only. You can save on purchasing the actual topographical maps by using SoftMap Ontario topo50™ Vol. 2, Upper Ontario East software, usually available at outfitting stores. You can then isolate the section of route that you want and transfer information from this book onto the created trip program and print it off.

Rapids diagrams are not intended to make the running of whitewater easier for the inexperienced paddler. It is important to remember that navigable channels may vary considerably with each season. The Sturgeon River, for example, flows almost 2 m above normal summer levels just after break-up in early May. Rapids classification has been calculated at moderate flow levels, neither high nor low, but at flow rates canoeists are likely to confront during the normal season, mid-June to mid-October. Those who paddle far outside of this period should rely less on the information about rapids provided in this book and more on their own skill at reading extreme conditions.

Using Topographic Maps with this Book

There are acquired skills for wilderness navigation, and being able to read a topographic map is one of them. Plotting where you are on a two-dimensional map while bobbing around in a canoe among an archipelago of islands is not always an easy task. And canoeists often relax into their trip, relying on someone else to do the navigating until they get into a fix and forget where they are in their surroundings. This creates momentary panic and disorientation, which may lead to extra hours of work locating a specific portage or dealing with inclement weather while searching for a campsite. The use of a GPS can relieve some of the pressure, but not everyone is inclined to use one, nor are they entirely reliable as the only navigational aid, in case of battery failure or submersion in water.

You should always know where you are, and if traveling in a group, at least one person should be assigned the duty of map reading. You should also have two sets of maps in waterproof pouches. When looking for portages, remember, many Temagami trails are not signed. This conforms to a long-standing tradition and non-signage policy. Most nastawgan were established on the premise that the best place to carry was the shortest distance between two lakes. In some places you will see yellow plastic P signs, but on most remote routes you will find nothing obvious to mark the trail. Some landings may be grown over; however, there are always telltale signs such as rock cairns or axe blazes to indicate their presence.

General Note about Adventure Travel, Temagami-Style

Although this book is essentially a paddling guide, I have included places to hike or get off the beaten path. Temagami has over forty hiking trails and viewpoints on high ridges. That in itself makes the Temagami experience appealing. As with any outdoor activity there exist inherent risks. But without some uncertainty and danger, life would be quite prosaic! Hiking and nature observation, on their own, pose little threat to life and limb, barring any sudden urge to free-climb the face of Devil Rock. Water sports, on the other hand, require at least a basic understanding of the skills required to travel safely and knowledge of environmental conditions.

Whitewater paddling and open-water kayaking can be dangerous fun. Attempting to run rapids or cross wide expanses of open water is foolhardy if you don't possess the skills to do so safely. Rescue and survival training is not something that can be picked up without some guidance. I highly recommend joining a guided expedition or paddling clinic before you head out on your first wilderness adventure.

Rating River Difficulty & Skill Level

The difficulty of a river or route is determined by risk factor and overall stamina to complete the trip safely. Variables such as weather, wind and water levels are unpredictable and should be considered when choosing a route. For example, the time spent travelling against a strong headwind or navigating rapids during unusually high water levels may suddenly change the general classification of a route. Specific rating factors for these routes include the number and difficulty of technical rapids, gradient or elevation drop per kilometre, length and difficulty of portages and their degree of maintenance, and any unusual characteristics. Individual rapids are graded in accordance with the International River Grading System and apply to stock, recreational canoes only. Out of a total grading of six on the IRGS scale, only the first three grades apply to open boats, or those canoes that are not seriously modified for extreme whitewater sport.

Know Your Skill Level

A growing number of well-geared canoeists have trouble admitting that they are, in fact, novice paddlers, and quite often will attempt running a particular rapid or route far beyond their capability. The mounting number of derelict canoes that decorate rogue boulders on our northern rivers attest to this grim fact. People have perished on Temagami rivers. *If you do not have the compulsory skills, do not whitewater paddle.* You should either sign up for a clinic or join a guided expedition where you can learn the basic strokes, after which you can assess your personal level of skill and apply it to a route of comparative grading. Being able to read whitewater is an acquired skill that takes years to develop.

Skill Classifications

The following skill level categories are predicated upon the paddlers' ability to safely handle a stock recreational open canoe. Each classification indicates the necessary skills required, route characteristics, and type of difficulty or hazard one may encounter.

Novice or Beginner

Skills Required
Canoeists have little or no experience or knowledge of whitewater techniques but do have primary flat-water skills. Capable but not proficient at navigating easy Class I rapids or swifts only, while all technical rapids are avoided. May attempt next grade if accompanied by higher skilled paddler.

Route Characteristics
Predominantly flat-water with some river or creek links that may have swifts or very minor rapids with the option to portage. Portages are not excessively difficult and water temperature exceeds 16 C (60 F) from June through August.

Hazards
High wind on larger lakes and possible cold weather and water during buffer season paddling, or a sudden rise in water levels.

Experienced Novice

Skills Required
Canoeists have basic whitewater skills and are proficient at safely navigating Class I and Class I technical rapids. Class II rapids and higher are portaged. Some basic lining skills (roping canoe on rapids); may attempt next grade if accompanied by higher skilled paddler.

Route Characteristics
River gradient is generally consistent and gradual with sporadic drops exceeding 1.5 metres/kilometre. Predominantly Class I rapids interspersed with more technical rapids that can be portaged. Portages are generally easy, but with a few classic steep climbs, bogs, or long hauls (over 1 km). Water temperatures are above 16 C (60 F) during the summer months.

Hazards
Same as novice with the addition of potential for capsize in easy grade rapids located above or close to dangerous chutes, falls or continued rapids.

Intermediate

Skills Required

Canoeists are proficient whitewater paddlers and are able to safely navigate up to Class II technical rapids without difficulty. Class III rapids are carefully scrutinized and run only with safety and rescue precautions in place and/or accompanied by an advanced paddler. Eddy turns and cross-ferries are fully understood and implemented. Canoe extrication and rescue techniques are mandatory.

Route Characteristics

River gradient is often steep-pitched with at least 50 percent Class II rapids or greater. Some longer Class I and II rapids may not have portages but lining is possible during lower water level conditions. Water temperatures may be lower than 16 C (60 F) during off-season paddling. Portages could be precipitous, longer than 2 km, and may be partially obstructed or overgrown. Environmental conditions are generally moderate.

Hazards

Cold weather and water risk during buffer season trips, and the greater risk of capsize in larger rapids. Temptation to run the more difficult rapids is greater.

Advanced or Expert

Skills Required

Canoeists have extensive whitewater experience and high-level skills. Ability to safely navigate Class III rapids or greater (with specialized gear). Paddling skills include all technical rescue and extrication procedures. High level of stamina and endurance under duress.

Route Characteristics

River gradient has long, steep-pitched drops with a high proportion of technical rapids. Longer rapids may not have portages, and lining may not be possible. Water temperatures may be lower than 16 C (60 F) as with early "polar bear" runs during high flow periods. Portages extremely difficult or even nonexistent. Environmental conditions may be extreme.

Hazards

Cold weather and water risk is much higher, as is the possibility of capsize in larger rapids in cold water. Wet- or dry-suits, added flotation to canoes, and spray covers are mandatory for high flow and cold-water navigation on long sets of rapids.

Rapid Classification

This classification of rapids conforms to the International River Grading System (IGRS), which includes a total of six classifications. Since Class or Grade III rapids are considered the maximum safe rating for open, stock recreational canoes, not modified for whitewater, only the first three grades are listed. Each class is defined, including "technical" ratings. This information will enable you to assess your own skills and experience and apply them to the routes described in this book.

CI: Definite deep water, clear channel with well-defined downstream V, small regular waves to 1/3 metre. Beginner's level.

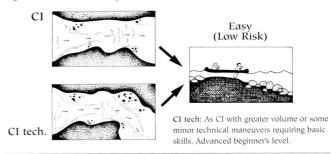

CI tech: As CI with greater volume or some minor technical maneuvers requiring basic skills. Advanced beginner's level.

CII: Definite main channel with optional secondary channels visible in high water. Rock gardens, ledges present with standing waves to 2/3 metre. Technical moves such as eddy turns and ferrying are required. Intermediate level paddler.

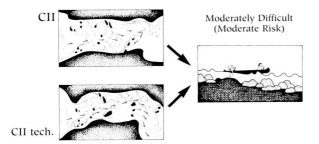

CII tech: As above with greater volume and larger waves, rock gardens with indefinite main channel; may be clogged with sweepers, snags, logjams or larger boulders. Low-profile canoes may swamp. Experienced intermediate level paddler.

CIII: Maximum for open canoes – spray deck optional for rockered whitewater canoes but recommended for low-profile designs. Definite main channel with high volume, often narrow, steep-pitched V ending in an hydraulic/souse. Less reaction time. Boulder gardens, high ledges present with waves to one metre or more. Scouting and rescue spotters mandatory. Advanced level only.

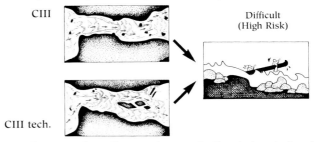

CIII tech or CIV: As above with greater volume, questionable main channels often split; tight passages and steep drops with serious aerated holes present. Specialized whitewater equipment/canoes required. Playboats with flotation or decked canoes only. Scouting and safety teams required. Expert level only.

Provincial Parks, Reserves and Protected Areas

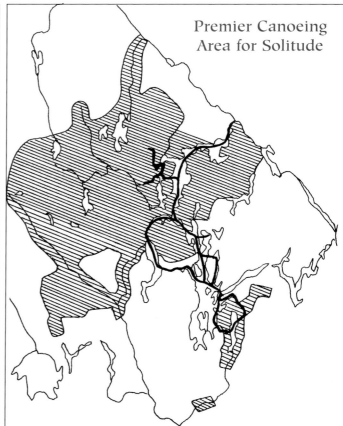

Premier Canoeing Area for Solitude

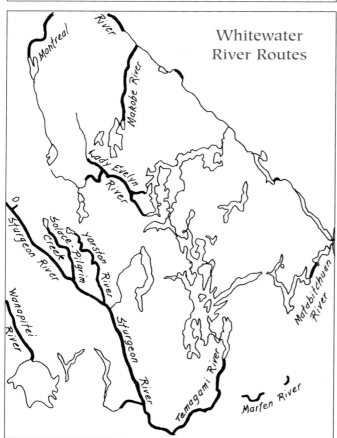

Whitewater River Routes

Montreal River
Makobe River
Lady Evelyn River
Solace-Pilgrim Creek
Yorston River
Sturgeon River
Wanapitei River
Temagami River
Marten River
Matabitchuan River

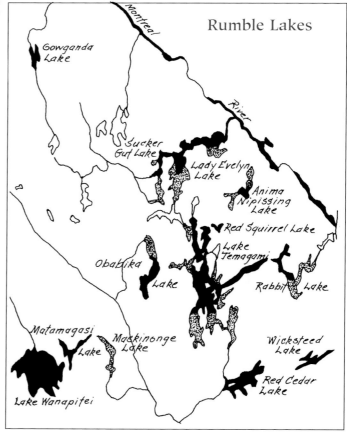

Rumble Lakes

Montreal River
Gowganda Lake
Sucker Gut Lake
Lady Evelyn Lake
Anima Nipissing Lake
Red Squirrel Lake
Obabika Lake
Lake Temagami
Rabbit Lake
Matamagasi Lake
Maskinonge Lake
Wicksteed Lake
Red Cedar Lake
Lake Wanapitei

Provincial Parks, Reserves and Protected Areas

Although controversial, the actual amount of protection allotted to these areas seems to be ever-changing and insignificant. One hopes that wise stewardship will prevail. The research in this book pays little attention to any politically assigned lands, although for information I've listed the primary areas designated under the Ontario government parks system. For detailed information contact the Ontario Ministry of Natural Resources Information Centre, 300 Water Street, P.O. Box 7000, Peterborough, Ontario, K9J 8M5. General Inquiry: 1-800-667-1940.
Renseignements en francais: 1-800-667-1840
Fax: 705-755-1677

PARKS AS LISTED ON THE MAP
A   Lady Evelyn–Smoothwater Provincial Wilderness Park
B   Makobe River Waterway Park and Conservation Reserve
C   Sturgeon River Waterway Park and Sand Dunes Natural Heritage Park
D   Solace Lake Waterway Park
E   Obabika River Waterway Park
F   North Yorston Conservation Reserve
G   Pinetorch Conservation Reserve
H   Bob Lake Conservation Reserve
I   North Chiniguchi Recreation Park
J   Chiniguchi River Waterway Park
K   West Montreal River Waterway Park
L   W. B. Greenwood Provincial Park
M   Marten River Recreation Park
N   Holdridge Creek Conservation Reserve
O   Temagami River Waterway Park
P   Lake Temagami Shoreline Conservation Reserve
Q   Wolf Lake Old-Growth Forest Reserve
R   Big Spring Lake Conservation Reserve
S   Lake Wanapitei Provincial Park
T   North Muskego Conservation Reserve
U   Ottawa River Waterway Park
V   Rib Lake Conservation Reserve
W   Finlayson Point Provincial Park
X   White Bear Forest Conservation Reserve
Y   Rabbit Lake Conservation Reserve
Z   Marten River Provincial Park

Premier Canoeing Area for Solitude

For most of the summer (July and August), routes within this area are generally not congested. You may encounter some remote fly-in activity and small motorboat traffic, but this is restricted to only a few popular fishing lakes, mostly in the southwest section of the district. Black bands show routes that are heavily used in July and August. Avoid areas near access points on weekends in July and August. Outside of the summer months, the area of solitude expands greatly, and there are no congested routes.

Whitewater River Routes

This map illustrates all rivers that offer Class I to Class III rapids for stock, recreational canoeing. Refer to the River Grading Chart or each specific route for more information.

Rumble Lakes

These lakes possess good road access, cottages and lodges, so you can expect motorboat traffic throughout the general canoeing season. The dark areas show heavy motorboat use during peak times (late June through to Labour Day). Shaded areas show moderate traffic flow at peak times. Because of the size of some of these lakes and the absence of shore development, it is not difficult to stay out of the main rumble areas. Plan your canoe route to avoid these areas, or travel in the off season.

Natural Environment Codes

Each route is assigned a vegetation site code, found under the Features and Ecology sub-heading. These codes are explained below, describing the forest and plant species common to the route. Site types are a categorization of vegetation types and microclimate factors such as temperature, moisture regime and soil characteristics.

1 **Upland Coniferous Forest (UCF)** Very dry, well-drained rock, sand or gravel conditions with thin soil and poor nutrient availability. Look for jack pine, red pine, white pine (dominant species) and mountain alder. Sheep laurel, northern bush honeysuckle and velvetleaf blueberry are common understory shrubs. Limited ground flora includes dogbane, bluebead lily (berry not to be confused with the blueberry), pink lady's slipper, bracken fern, starflower, wild lily of the valley, bunchberry and bristly sarsaparilla.

2 **Upland Mixed Forest (UMF)** The most common site type in Temagami, this forest is generally found on dry to mesic sand and gravel sites in average microclimates. There may be a thin layer of humus soil, and the canopy cover ranges from almost pure deciduous to coniferous species. Red pine, jack pine, white pine, white and black spruce, white and yellow birch and trembling aspen are the dominant species. Mountain alder, hazelnut, northern bush honeysuckle and velvetleaf blueberry are the common understory shrubs. The ground flora is relatively diverse, and includes bristly sarsaparilla, bluebead lily, twinflower, wild lily of the valley, rose twistedstalk, large-leaved aster, bunchberry, ground pine, bracken fern and starflower.

3 **Upland Deciduous Forest (UDF)** Typical of mesic (not too dry or wet) loam soils in average to warmer-than-average microclimate sites. Thicker humus soils are present. White birch, poplar and sugar maple are the dominant tree species. Common understory shrubs are hazelnut, mountain maple and northern bush honeysuckle. Ground flora varies at particular sites, but includes bluebead lily, rose twistedstalk, wild lily of the valley, bunchberry, starflower, bracken fern and ground pine.

4 **Thicket Swamp (TS)** Very common in Temagami, these sites are found on wet peat and alluvium (river-deposited soil) sites in cool or average temperature environments, predominantly as shoreline ecosystems. Scattered occurrences of black ash, white cedar and tamarack form the shore canopy; understory shrubs include sweet gale, meadowsweet and mountain holly. The ground flora is quite diverse and includes purple-stemmed aster, dwarf raspberry, Canada manna grass, Canada bluejoint, marsh St. John's-wort, wild iris and beaked sedge.

5 **Shoreline Meadow (SM)** Relatively common sites throughout Temagami, they occur on sand, gravel and alluvial shores that are mesic to extremely wet, in all microclimate types. (Microclimate refers to atmospheric conditions prevailing within a small space, usually close to the ground level.) Shoreline meadows are common as a narrow band along waterways and may be dominated by low shrubs such as sweet gale and meadowsweet. Herbaceous plants such as Canada bluejoint and wool grass (cotton grass) are also seen. These are very diverse ecosystems, varying in local plant distribution but usually including bog aster, yellow sedge, beaked sedge, northern bugleweed, marsh St. John's-wort, Canada bluejoint, woolly sedge, three-way sedge and cotton grass.

6 **Meadow Marsh (MM)** These diverse sites are commonly found on abandoned beaver floodways. Dominated by herbaceous species, they usually include Canada bluejoint, various sedges and willows.

7 **Aquatic Community (AC)** These are commonly found in shallow water over sand, silt or alluvium in all microclimate sites (Dry Lake). They occur as small zones or occasionally extensive areas of shallow lakes and lagoons. Some species, such as subterminal club-rush or slender water milfoil, remain submersed, while others, such as bullhead lily and emersed pondweed, grow chiefly at or above the surface. The most common community association is dominated by bullhead lily and fragrant water lily. Also common are water shield, pipewort, narrow-leaved bur-reed, water horsetail, water lobelia, great bulrush and common bladderwort.

8 **Rock Barren (RB):** Found on bare, exposed rock, which is very dry in all microclimate types. These are occasional features scattered within coniferous or

deciduous zones. Scant soil is found in the rock crevices or depressions only. Various lichens predominate, while scattered, wind-sculpted and dwarfed tree species include jack pine, red pine, white pine, white or black spruce, maple or oak. Common shrubs may include sheep laurel, velvetleaf blueberry and low blueberry. Typical ground flora includes pink lady's slipper, wild lily of the valley, bracken fern, wavy hair grass and cow-wheat.

9 **Cliff** (C) Similar to RB, these environments are found on exposed, very dry rock in all microclimates. Sparse sand deposits are found in fissures only. The most common type occurs on sandstone, which is very resistant to erosion. Flora on these cliff faces is not diverse. Cliffs of diabase (dolerite, dark-coloured igneous rock streaked with quartz) may support a more diverse flora community. These sites may contain: wavy hair grass, rock polypody, velvetleaf blueberry, low blueberry and wild lily of the valley. Examples of these sites are found along the west coast of Lake Temiskaming and east central shore of Lake Temagami, with several other scattered locations throughout Temagami.

GENERAL MAP DETAILS

Access/take-out point	Ⓐ
Viewpoint (with or without trail)	Ⓥ
Portage in meters	
Rapids (classified swifts to CI-CIII)	
Roads (generally paved)	
Bush Roads (gravel-based or seasonal)	- - - - - -
Campsite (size indicated in route write-up)	▲
Scale in Kilometers	

RAPIDS DETAIL

Running Channel (optimum conditions)	
Ferry (side maneuver)	
Deepwater "V" entry-point	
Standing Waves (deep in spring/rocky in summer)	
Ledge or Rock	
Rapids Classification (CI-CIII)	

Sunrise on Diamond Lake — a moment of calm.

CANOEING, KAYAKING & HIKING TEMAGAMI

Part Six

Canoe & Kayak Routes

Hiking Trails & Viewpoints

ROUTE

1

TEMAGAMI *to* LAKE WANAPITEI LOOP

Canoeists paddling Temagami River only require a shuttle drop and pick-up. These can easily be arranged personally, with two vehicles, or through an outfitting service in Temagami. Distance is 64 km (4–5 days), intermediate classification.

Paddlers tackling this loop should start at central Lake Temagami; it can also be done as a straight run to the pick-up point at Kukagami Lake Road. Canoeists may also do a loop from this access point and take advantage of a shorter trip down the Chiniguchi and return via the Sturgeon, then hop over to Colin and Gold link back the start point. Because of the strong current and long rapids on the Temagami River, upstream travel is not recommended.

LOOP ROUTE **SECTION 1**

Cross Lake, Temagami River, Sturgeon River, Chiniguchi River.

This route is considered the best full-season whitewater run in the district. Depending on water levels, a total of twenty CI to CIII rapids can be negotiated. Remember, do not attempt this river unless you have the acquired skills to do so safely!

CLASSIFICATION intermediate

DISTANCE 220 km

TIME 12–14 days

PORTAGES 39 (14 km)

MAPS 1 I/16, 41 I/9, 41 I/15, 31 L/12, 31 L/13

FEATURES & ECOLOGY Temagami River Provincial Waterway Park, with its bedrock prominence, gorges, whitewater play and heavily forested pine shores, makes this section quite remarkable. Chiniguchi Waterway Provincial Park, extending from the south of Maskinonge Lake to Matagamasi Lake and west to Donald, provides a variety of glacial and geophysical landscape features, rolling hills and bedrock troughs, and rich Native history (pictographs and ancient travelways). Take your time. In fact, you'll regret missing the Temagami Island old-growth pine trail, High Rock Lookout, or resplendent beauty of the south lake environs. As you move away from the bustle of the central hub, the quiet bays of Cross Lake beckon. Vegetation Site Code: UCF, UMF, RB, UDF (lower Temagami River, Sturgeon River).

Cross Lake Dam On the east bank above the dam is a clearing; here the portage follows a bush road to the right, then down sharply along a trail to the top of the rapids. This CI rapid is easily run keeping centre and is a good primer — a play spot for tuning up skills. You might consider carrying your gear a further 225 m to the bottom of the rapids and running the canoes down empty. The amount of water flowing out through the holding dam will give you a good indication of the flow below.

Temagami River Proceed south past a low bridge. The next set of CII to CIII rapids (Keel Hauler) should be scouted. Flow will determine grade and ease of manoeuvreing. The bottom is particularly gnarly in low water and could be lined. The following CII rapids (Short and Sweet) change drastically with flow, so check before you run. Heron's Leg Campsite is a great spot for an overnight, free float and water play with the canoes. Check out the narrow chute before running; there is a submerged and very sharp-edged rock right where you don't want it to be. Finally, the last two sets of rapids are easily run out to Red Cedar.

Red Cedar Lake Keeping to the southwest extremity of this flooded lake, continue to the dam and portage along the east side to Thistle (Island) Lake. Thistle has few, if any, decent campsites, so it is advised that you either camp at the dam, or paddle on to the first rapids out of the lake.

Temagami River You'll notice the current picking up, and you'll have to avoid sharp rocks through three sets of swifts before stopping to check over Thistle Chutes. I used Triple Play as a teaching zone for whitewater; it has a couple of great campsites, three runs (two good ones), and an easy carry back over for replay. These rapids provide good water play when high but can get bony when the levels drop. A is the preferred channel, B is the second choice, and C tends to be unrunnable at most times.

Route # 1

Temagami to Lake Wanapitei Loop
(Temagami River and Lower Sturgeon River detail)

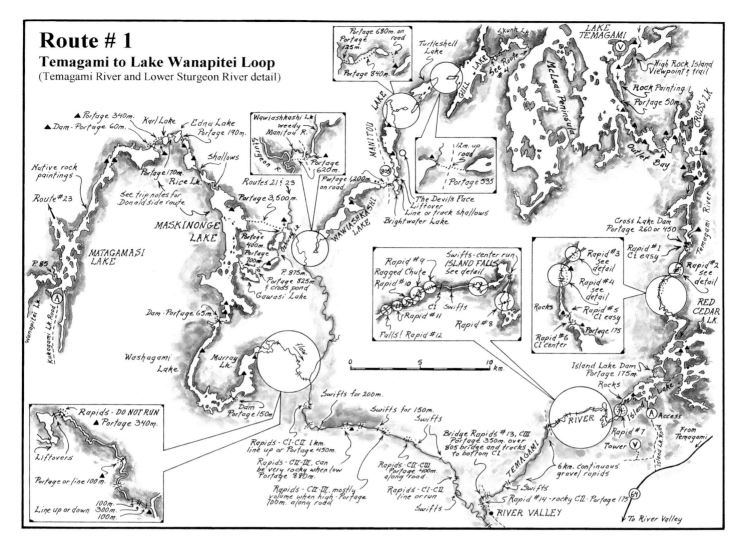

Island Portage & Falls Here you have two options, depending on water flow and your inherent skills. Take the portage, or follow A carefully, playing the right side of the top rapids, and keep right to reach the campsite. Line B and carefully cross the pool above curtain falls (C) and lift over the rock ledge to the bass pool. It's a bony CI ride out from there. Check out the falls here — you can climb in behind the curtain of water spilling over the gneissic ledge. This is a wonderful spot for exploring, there's plenty of history here and there was at least one death during the log-drive days. The river is tight, dark and mysterious here, the current tugging at the canoe as the river begins a rather precipitous drop. There is a set of swifts and an easily run CI (keep right) to the rock beach landing before Canyon Rapids. You really need to get out and scout this one. There is so much variety here it's easy to spend a whole weekend. The runs are not easy, and you'd best have spotters at the appropriate locations. A is an easy but tense play — you don't want to spill here. B is a hefty 2 m drop and plunge, and if you don't come up with the open side to the sky, then it's a long, hard swim. C is a vicious CIII with a split channel, and when the flow is high it's a veritable roller coaster.

Ragged Chutes Some have tried to run this but it's not a pretty sight. Carry over and put in, watching the outflow from the chutes as it backs against the rock ledge (A) on your left. It could pull you into a spin, especially if the water is heavily aerated. Portage around the next chutes (B), and like the last falls, don't get any grandiose ideas that you're anything more than a mortal human.

Double Bend This is what whitewater canoeing is all about. A is a passive CI that leads to a wily CII to III drop, and if you don't hit B in the right slot, the current will push you up and over the rock ledge where everybody is standing with their cameras waiting for you to mess up. Portage across the grassy clearing and down an ATV trail to the bottom, where you can play the easier CIs to the top of Railroader.

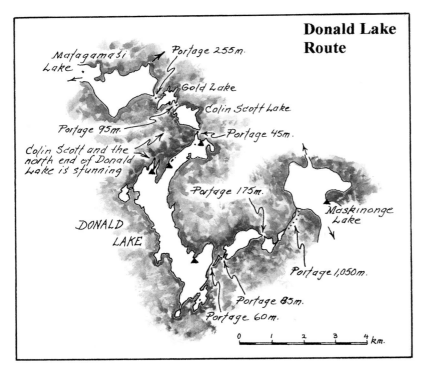

Donald Lake Route

Map labels: Malagamasi Lake, Portage 255m., Gold Lake, Colin Scott Lake, Portage 45m., Portage 95m., Colin Scott and the north end of Donald Lake is stunning, DONALD LAKE, Portage 175m., Maskinonge Lake, Portage 1,050m., Portage 85m., Portage 60m., 0 1 2 3 4 km.

rough trail to a road. Turn left and follow on to an open campsite above the rapids.

Murray Lake There is a short liftover before entering the north end of the lake and another before an old log dam that has been removed. Just past the grassy narrows is a good, sandy beach campsite. At the southwest end of the lake you'll have to carry around a dam beside a lodge. This will take you to Washagami Lake. Keep a sharp eye for osprey here.

Washagami Lake Paddle to the north end and carry around the dam to Maskinonge Lake.

Maskinonge Lake Canoeists traveling on to Lake Wanapitei may proceed north to Rice Lake, or have the option to return to Lake Temagami by way of the two routes leaving Maskinonge along the east shore as indicated on the map.

Rice Lake Be mindful of the rocks that litter the shallows at both ends of the lake.

Lower Matagamasi Lake Take the portage into Edna Lake on the west side of the shallow rapids.

Edna Lake Portage just left of a pretty, cascading rapid located at the west end of the lake.

Karl Lake Paddle on to the northwest end of the lake to the next portage, which is located on the north side of the river inlet, and carry over a rocky trail. There are two good campsites on the trail and one additional site across the river at the upper end of the portage. This section of the route is quite pretty, and you won't have any trouble eating up your film supply halfway through this route. Proceed up the narrows to the wooden dam and carry over on the right. One of the dam outlets is a natural, smooth-rock sluice, where it is possible to slide down the fast current on your butt cheeks.

Matagamasi Lake This is an incredibly beautiful lake with clear, cool water. The pictographs along here are still evident, although damaged by thoughtless people. They should not be touched in any way. It is advisable to approach with reverence and to leave a plug of tobacco as an offering. The portage into Lake Wanapitei is located in the west bay past Goalscap Island and runs beside an old cabin, across a road and on to Boucher Lake, which connects directly to Wanapitei Lake.

Donald Lake Side Route This long-used and loved side route has been a favourite of youth camps for decades. See additional map for details.

Railroader A bony CII or a vicious CIII with unforgiving qualities; either line on river right and run the bottom, or count your rosaries and take your best shot. Valley Chutes should not be run, so carry below the chutes and run the final CII out to the pool. From here to the 805 bridge it's a cakewalk — the current is fast for the first 7 km, river speed averaging 10–12 kph. To the bridge, it's a quiet paddle through pastoral farmland.

River Valley Aside from having one of the best bluegrass festivals, River Valley has one of the best and most challenging rapids in the district — Bridge Rapids is a powerful CIII, just look over the highway bridge and see for yourself. Watch the bottom, because you can't see the falls around the bend. It's runnable, but you have to keep your wits about you and a clean pair of underwear ready to change into. Below here it's an easy cruise, but bumpy, out to the Sturgeon.

Sturgeon River (up or downstream) Upstream travelers will find the current fairly strong. Keep to the shore where you can take advantage of back eddies, and all rapids can be lined up or portaged around using the 805 gravel road. Stick to the map notes and you'll do fine whether paddling up or downstream.

Chiniguchi River There are three sets of very shallow rapids that can be lined up or down. Just north of the log bridge is a small island with rocky rapids. Line the canoe on the left or portage the 100 m across the clearing. Proceed about 3 km to the base of the next rapids and beach on the right bank; here you'll find a

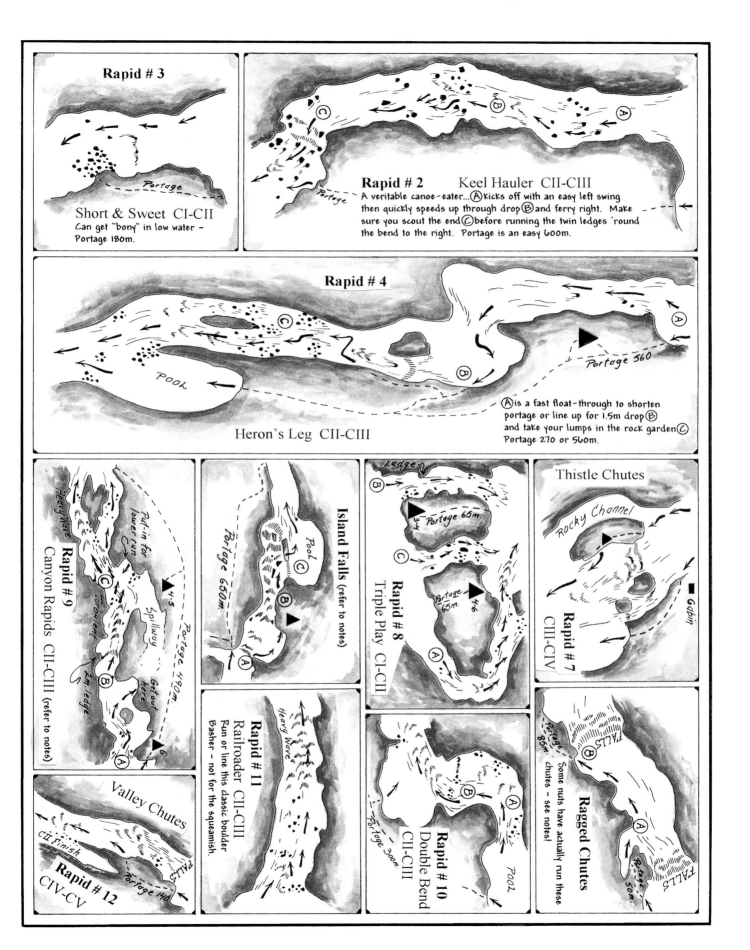

LOOP ROUTE **SECTION 2**

There are two routes back to Lake Temagami through Maskinonge and the Sturgeon River.

Route One   Portage 3.5 km from the most easterly bay in the north central section of Maskinonge, beginning at an old mine site. This well-used trail runs directly through to the old homestead of Kelly's Farm, on the banks of the Sturgeon. Here you could camp and still pick fresh rhubarb and berries from the abandoned gardens.

Route Two   From the east bay in the south central section of Maskinonge, portage over a rocky trail to Gowasi Lake. From there, continue to the northeast bay and carry over to Gamagowong Lake, making a short paddle across Gagnon Lake. Paddle to the northern extremity of Gamagowong and portage over to Ozhway Lake. The south end of the lake can be boggy, requiring some deft pushing and shoving. Proceed to the north end and carry, starting just left of the creek outlet. This trail, too, passes through Kelly's Farm and to the Sturgeon River.

Sturgeon River   About 5 km down from Kelly's Farm you will notice the Manitou River flowing into the Sturgeon on the east side. The portage begins just inside the river mouth, following a good trail to a campsite on Wawiashkashi (Grassy) Lake.

Wawiashkashi Lake   Paddle north through the grassy narrows to the north end of the lake. The portage begins at the lodge above the river. From the beach, follow the road and cross over the Highway 805 bridge. Keep left and obey the signs, where a short trail will guide you to Brightwater Lake. There are a few liftovers before reaching Manitou Lake.

Manitou (Devil's) Lake   There is a naturally formed face on a cliff located a third of the way up the lake on the east side, across from the government campsite. The portage leaving Manitou is located 1.5 km south of the north end of the lake, on the east shore by a small creek. The trail crosses this creek three times before you reach a small pond. Cross the pond to a rocky trail and carry over to the next pond. At the east side of this pond is a bush road; follow this road, keeping left, to a campsite on Turtleshell Lake.

Turtleshell Lake   Paddle to the northeast end to the next portage, located directly across from some old log buildings. Turn north and walk up the bush road, when you reach it, for about 15 m, then hang right to catch the trail again to Gull lake.

Gull Lake   See Route 4 for the description from Gull to Skunk and Lake Temagami.

Old cross at Island portage. Replaced in 1986.

FLORENCE LAKE LOOP

Including Yorston and Lady Evelyn Rivers

This route can be done either way. No matter what the flow, you'll have to contend with upstream travel one way or the other. The Obabika River has a powerful current in the spring, and so, too, does the Yorston, so you may prefer to take the Lady Evelyn upstream when water levels are extreme. The Yorston gets extremely shallow by mid-summer and is dependent on summer rains to maintain a modicum of flow. This is a classic, wild Temagami tour, and you won't be disappointed.

CLASSIFICATION   intermediate (long, strenuous
   portages, heavy current, isolation)

DISTANCE   200 km

TIME   12–14 days

PORTAGES   39 (14.5 km)

MAPS   41 P/1, 41 P/2, 41 P/7, 41 P/8, 41 I/16

FEATURES & ECOLOGY   In Obabika Waterway Provincial Park, the Obabika River shows its power along its lower course as it drains into the Sturgeon. Clear, cool water emanates from the highlands around Obabika Lake, and paddlers will find treasures around each gentle meander. This route takes in several smaller river environments (Obabika, Yorston and Lady Evelyn), all with special features indicative of their own personal character. On the more isolated trips you can be sure to see moose, bear, otter, mink, beaver, osprey, heron, and possibly golden eagle. There are many isolated stands of old-growth pine (marten, pileated woodpecker) and second growth of jack pine over previously burned sites. Lady Evelyn–Smoothwater Provincial Wilderness Park is one of the most scenic and rugged canoe routes through "rock-knob uplands," areas of glacially scoured escarpments, spectacular waterfalls and a long history of Native use. Vegetation Site Code: UMF, UCF, RB, C (Duff Lake), UDF (Obabika and Sturgeon River), SM and TS (South Lady Evelyn River), AC (Dry Lake).

Lake Temagami   Start from the central lake access point across from the Temagami Island hiking trails. Head northeast to Obabika Inlet; here you'll notice the second growth from the 1977 fire. Blueberries are quite

exceptional anywhere along the old burn, especially along the upper south slopes in Obabika Inlet. There is a choice of two portage routes to Obabika; the long carry is along an old skid road.

Obabika Lake   As you head south you may want to hug the west shore to stay out of the prevailing winds. The portage into Wawiagama is pretty obvious and is lined with huge red pines. The trail crosses directly over the Goulard Road.

Wawiagama Lake & River   Round Lake provides fine camping on sloped bedrock sites and excellent pike fishing near the outlet bluffs. Enter the river through the weedy shallows (bittern, red-winged blackbirds), and you'll notice that the Wawiagama is nothing more than a glorified ditch. It's an easy go while the water levels are high, but by mid-summer there will be several log liftovers necessary.

Obabika River   From here, the Obabika is generally free of log-jams. Don't miss the Sturgeon portage, located at an old lumber camp clearing (now overgrown, but there is an old shed visible by the shore). The trail is level and easy, but drops suddenly at the end where the bank has recently been undercut by spring flooding. There is a magnificent chute just off the trail where logs were flumed in the '40s.

Sturgeon River   Paddle upstream and line up the rapids on the left side to access the Upper Goose Falls portage (camping possible). It's a short distance to the Yorston River mouth; don't expect to see anything more than a creek.

Yorston River   The first 5 km up the river can be quite shallow, where lining and wading may be required during extreme low-water conditions. Follow the route map closely to Linger Lake; waterplay varies with flow, and upstream travel requires wading and lining along open but broken rock shoreline, while running downstream can provide some exciting CI–II play through tight channels.

Linger Lake   Starting from a small bay to the right of the river, the trail crosses an ATV trail halfway along.

Seagram Lake   You'll find two good campsites on the south shore. Head west and past a picturesque falls, through an old burn to the next wide section of river. Paddle to the end of this pond and carry over to the next small lake (watch the rocks shortly after putting

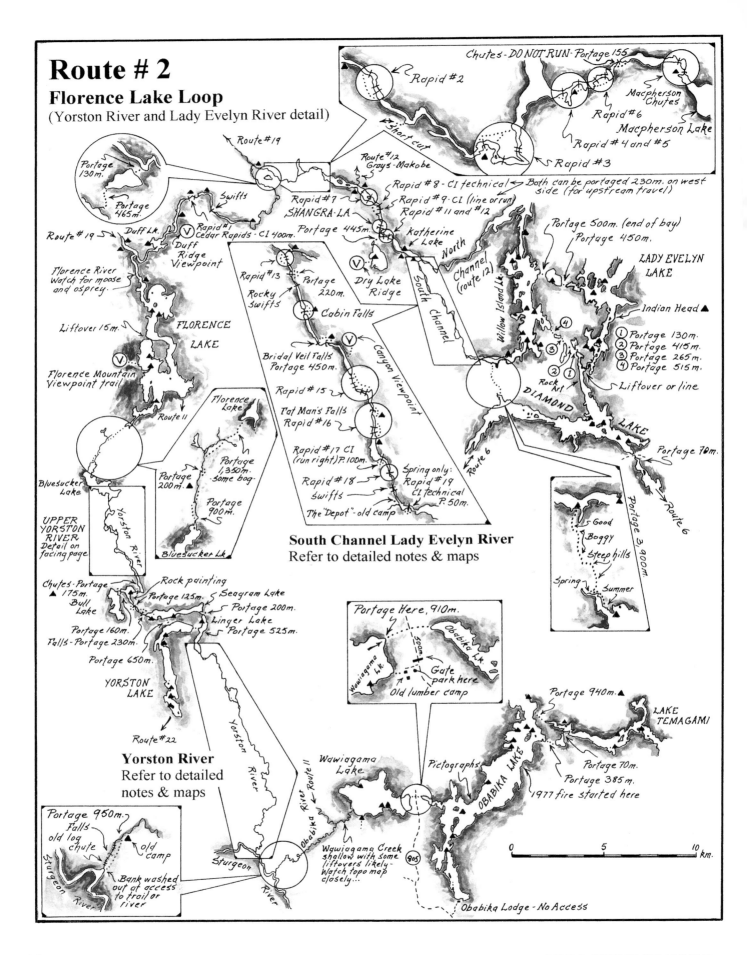

Route # 2
Florence Lake Loop
(Yorston River and Lady Evelyn River detail)

Chutes - DO NOT RUN - Portage 155

Rapid #2

Macpherson Chutes

Rapid #6

Macpherson Lake

Rapid #4 and #5

Rapid #3

Short cut

Route #19

Route #12 Grays-Makobe

Portage 130 m.

Portage 465 m.

Rapid #8 - CI technical

Both can be portaged 230 m. on west side (for upstream travel)

Rapid #9 - CI (line or run)

Rapid #7

SHANGRA-LA

Rapid #11 and #12

Portage 445 m.

Katherine Lake

Portage 500 m. (end of bay)

Portage 450 m.

LADY EVELYN LAKE

Route #19

Swifts

Rapid #1
Cedar Rapids - C1 400 m.

Duff Ridge Viewpoint

Duff Lk.

North Channel (route 12)

Rapid #13

Portage 220 m.

Dry Lake Ridge

Indian Head

South Channel

Willow Island Lk.

Florence River
Watch for moose and osprey.

Rocky Swifts

Cabin Falls

① Portage 130 m.
② Portage 415 m.
③ Portage 265 m.
④ Portage 515 m.

Liftover 15 m.

FLORENCE LAKE

Rock Art

Liftover or line

Florence Mountain Viewpoint trail

Bridal Veil Falls
Portage 450 m.

Canyon Viewpoint

DIAMOND LAKE

Route 11

Rapid #15

Florence Lake

Portage 70 m.

Fat Man's Falls
Rapid #16

Portage 200 m.

Portage 1,350 m. some bog.

Route 6

Portage 3,900 m.

Rapid #17 CI
(run right) P.100 m.

Spring only:
Rapid #19
CI technical
P. 50 m.

Route 6

Bluesucker Lake

Portage 900 m.

Rapid #18
Swifts

The "Depot" - old camp

Good

UPPER YORSTON RIVER
Detail on facing page

Yorston River

Bluesucker Lk.

South Channel Lady Evelyn River
Refer to detailed notes & maps

Boggy

Steep hills

Spring

Summer

Chutes - Portage 175 m.
Bull Lake

Rock painting

Portage 125 m.

Seagram Lake

Portage 200 m.

Portage Here, 910 m.

Portage 160 m.

Linger Lake

Portage 525 m.

Wawiagama Lk.

500 m.

Obabika Lk.

Falls - Portage 230 m.

Portage 650 m.

Gate park here

Portage 940 m.

LAKE TEMAGAMI

YORSTON LAKE

Old lumber camp

Pictographs

Portage 70 m.

Route #22

Yorston River

Wawiagama Lake

Portage 385 m.

1977 fire started here

OBABIKA LAKE

Yorston River
Refer to detailed notes & maps

Obabika River Route 11

Portage 950 m.
Falls
old log chute

old camp

Sturgeon River

Bank washed out at access to trail or river

Sturgeon River

Wawiagama Creek
shallow with some liftovers likely -
Watch topo map closely...

905

0   5   10 km.

Obabika Lodge - No Access

in). The next portage bypasses a shaded falls. Spend some time here exploring the lichen and moss-covered crags and boulders. Follow the route map closely for detail north as you approach Bluesucker Lake.

Bluesucker Lake There is a large campsite on the point as you enter the lake. Proceed to the north bay and you'll see the next portage located left of the creek mouth. Allow enough time to reach Florence; if you do get stuck for time, camping is possible at the small falls along the short portage. The 1,350m portage to Florence is a Temagami classic, throwing just about everything at the porteur from rock ledge to fathomless bog. Persevere: Florence is worth the extra slugging!

Florence Lake Shkim-ska-jeeshing, or "lake that bends in the middle," is surrounded by beautiful hills and towering pine — no wonder the Teme augama preferred this lake as a sanctuary. There is a rough trail to a viewpoint up Florence Mountain, which rises almost as high as Maple Mountain and offers a superb view east and north. Don't hurry. Spend at least one day marveling at the clarity of the water (see to a depth of 20 m), play on one of the

The author relaxing at his favourite campsite on Florence Lake. Stephanie Aykroyd

sand beaches or simply explore the shoreline. Head north and carry over a sand isthmus by an old log cabin (or take the long way around).

Florence River Shallow, clogged with maiden hair waving slowly with the gentle current, walled in by huge white pine, the Florence River exudes a sense of primal esteem, old wisdom that is somewhat haunting. Osprey love this place of quiet seclusion. Painted turtles sit basking in the sun on fallen cedars that line the shore, flipping off their perches as you paddle by.

South Lady Evelyn River Speckled trout fishing is worth a try, below the rapids just upstream of the Florence–Lady Evelyn junction. From here through Duff Lake the landscape is impressive, encapsulating the quiet meanders of the river below in a rather extensive, narrow wetland. There is a viewpoint without a trail overlooking the Duff Lake "elbow," certainly worth the hour to climb. The campsite just past here, located on a high rock ledge, sports a cool spring through most of the early summer. The long CI

rapids pose no problem for running or lining any time throughout the paddling season. There is a shortcut, or pond hop that bypasses the junction with the main branch, as indicated on the route map.

Main Branch Follow the route map carefully here; you can wade, line or run many of the rapids throughout most of the season. At the second rapids and falls you'll notice that the area is recovering from a forest fire that raced through here in 1993, set intentionally by disgruntled folk still angry about the formation of the park in 1984. The rapids above Macpherson Chutes can be lined (poor channel) carefully, taking out close to the right side of the falls. There is a good vantage point here and excellent blueberries.

Macpherson Lake This can be used as an optional float-plane access point. There are five good campsites on this pretty lake. Heron, mergansers, loons and moose are often seen here, so keep a lookout for resident wildlife as you approach the weed beds. Rapids can be negotiated from here as far as Shangri La Falls, just follow the map descriptions. Shangri La is a popular camp-over and rendezvous site for canoeists passing through. Ledge cascades, rapids, erratic boulders, caves and scattered jack pine make it particularly favourable for easy exploration.

Dry Lake Ridge The trail is rather rough but worth the day excursion from Shangra La campsite. There is a rough trail (under construction) from the campsite marked on the map to the summit, which rises over 500 vertical feet above the shallow lake.

Katherine (Divide) Lake There are four excellent campsites on the lake. The south narrows site is backed by a scrabble of huge boulders, forming natural caves large enough for a small party to sit in to get out of the rain.

South Branch Lady Evelyn River This is the downstream leg of the popular Lady Evelyn circuit trip, most groups preferring to paddle up the north branch and take advantage of the rapid play on the south branch. The river drops significantly here, plunging over three falls (Cabin Falls, Bridal Veil and Fat Man's Chutes, respectively). Unique features include: Hap Wilson's

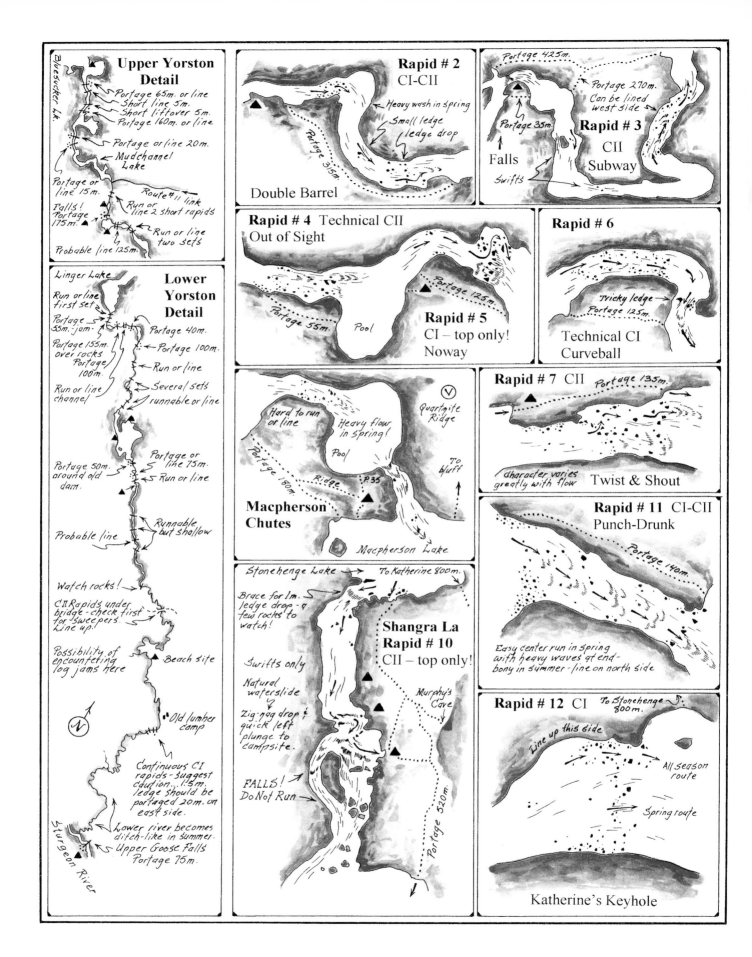

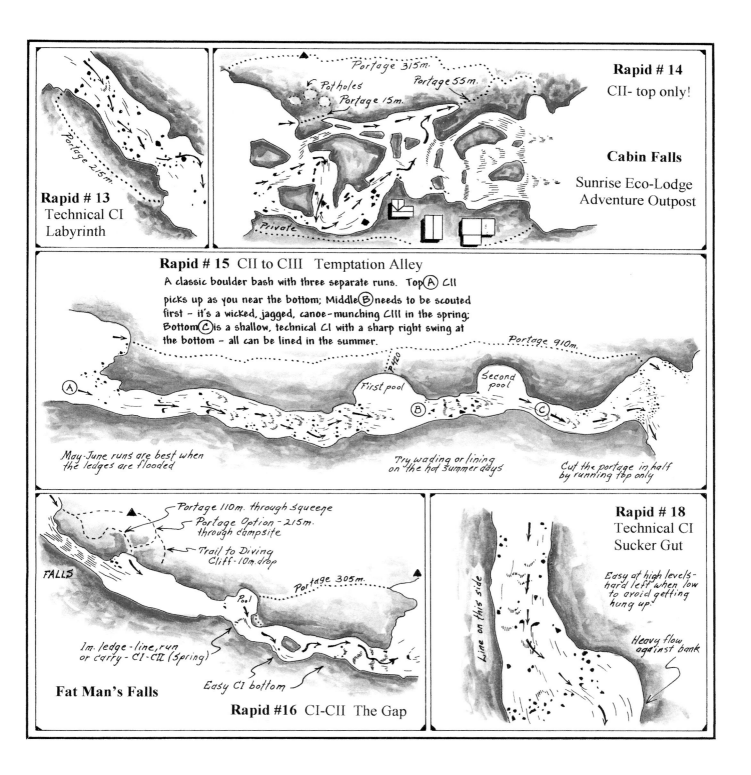

Bridal Veil Falls, South Channel, Lady Evelyn River.

CANOEING, KAYAKING & HIKING TEMAGAMI

eco-lodge at Cabin Falls (tripper's journal located here and safety depot with phone); the canyon (eastern cougar sighted here); and several sets of runnable rapids and choice campsites at which to while away the evenings. Trails are steep and strenuous, and it is suggested that you employ a spotter at Fat Man's, both at the squeeze and at the landing, which is located in fast water beside the chutes (spring caution!). Spring flow also makes it difficult to put in at the bottom without someone securing hold of the canoe at all times. The rapids below Fat Man's can be run (after the first line over the ledge) right past the old Depot lumber camp, which was used in the 1950s. Walleye and pike fishing is excellent here, especially out in the wider river, where you'll notice deadheads along the shore.

Route Variation Canoeists have the option to paddle north up Willow Island to cross the small lake route to Lady Evelyn Lake or take their lumps on the long portage south to Diamond Lake.

Portage to Diamond Lake Also known as the "Two Miler" or "Dead Man's March," the trail is easily spotted as a grassy campsite. The trail can be divided almost equally into four sections:

Easy Going: about 800 m in length, slightly rolling and not at all intimidating. That's a good thing, because it starts to get tough from here.

The Bog: rain or spring thaw can mire you down here, and it's a 1 km balancing act over slippery logs, ducking alder and climbing over fallen cedar.

High Country: rock terraces among young pine, dips and easy climbs for about 1,100 m until you hit the marsh opening at Diamond. If you're lucky, and the water on Diamond is extremely high in the spring, you can get access to a deep channel at this point.

Marsh Walk: you'll most likely have to carry an additional 500–750 m to deep water, if traveling in the summer. This section skirts a wet bog that moose frequent.

Diamond Lake: There are more campsites on this lake than you could count (as long as canoeists cease to burn them out!). Walleye, bass and lake trout provide fair fishing throughout, and there's good blueberry

*Fat Man's Squeeze,
Lady Evelyn River.*

HAP WILSON

picking in the summer months. There are actually several routes you could take back to Lake Temagami from here; no matter what you choose, you won't regret your decision.

MARTEN RIVER *to* WICKSTEAD LAKE LOOP

This loop offers a variety of experiences, from intermediate whitewater on the Temagami River to the tranquility of the deep bays of Rabbit, Cedar and Cross lakes. Before embarking, paddlers should feel comfortable with their whitewater skills, or should be prepared to portage around all dangerous rapids.

CLASSIFICATION experienced novice to intermediate
DISTANCE 152 km
TIME 8 days
PORTAGES 20 (total 5.7 km)
MAPS 31 L/12, 31 L/13, 41 I/9, 41 I/16, 31 M/4
FEATURES & ECOLOGY The Wicksteed–Boyce Lake area is ideal for viewing moose, not surprising since much of this route travels through the Nipissing Crown Game Preserve, where hunting is restricted. Landscapes change often, typifying the warm boreal ecosystem of mixed pine and hardwood forests and lush ground cover of blueberry and Labrador tea, interspersed with shoreline fen communities. Earth science features include the Marten River kame field — domes of gravel and boulders left behind by retreating glaciers and ice melt. Temagami community trails (Caribou Mountain and White Bear), central hub trails (Temagami Island and High Rock), and the opportunity to take a side trip to Blueberry Lake trails are all important features of this route. Vegetation Site Code: UMF, UCF, UDF (Wicksteed Lake), SM and TS (Marten River).

Lake Temagami There are two optional routes to Cross Lake, as indicated on Routes 4 and 5 maps. The Iceland route may be attractive to those wishing to bypass boat traffic on the northeast arm; from Wasaksina, you could take Shiningwood Bay back to the hub in order to take in the old-growth trails on Temagami Island. Refer to Route 1 for details on Cross Lake and the Temagami River. An optional start point could also be the central lake access.

Red Cedar Lake The effects of flooding are evident in the amount of deadwood piled along the shores of the lake. This is a high-use fishing lake, so you may prefer to camp off the main body away from the noise and bothersome boat wake. There are two small sites at the mouth of Loon Bay, and one excellent site at the mouth of the Marten River, near the narrows. This level, grassy site is situated on a high bank, accessible by a plank ladder.

Marten River The river environment includes shore communities of spruce and cedar, with several marsh offshoots and shallow duck ponds. For about 1 km upriver from the campsite there are four sections of rocky shallows. The dark colour of the jagged rocks makes them hard to spot under poor light, unless they're already blessed with a coating of canoe paint. Follow the route map carefully to Marten River Provincial Park. Supplies can be purchased locally. There are few campsites available past the park until Wicksteed Lake.

Wicksteed Lake Wicksteed is a shallow pike and walleye lake, infested with below-surface deadheads. Camping is generally good, and prevailing winds may be in your favour as you head northeast. Enter a marshy narrows at the far end and turn north alongside the railroad tracks. Keep to the main left channel here, as it may be a little confusing.

Marten River Line the canoe up where the river narrows to a rocky channel. There may be a beaver dam to lift over shortly past this spot. Around the bend you'll come to a small falls and a shallow rapids above, where the portage on the right will carry you to Boyce Lake.

Boyce Lake Boyce is a beautiful lake with many hidden bays and channels. There are three good campsites on the lake — the best site is perched on the central island. Continue on to the west shore to a small inlet that runs north (you'll see a rock that looks like a whale guarding the channel).

Marten River During high water, bypass the portage to the left and follow the river up to a shallows, where you will have to lift over rocks for about 30 m. During the normal canoeing season you can simply take the portage to avoid logjams and obstructions. About 1 km past the portage it may be necessary to line or wade through shallows, followed by a 10-m liftover to wider channels. Keep right before the next narrows, and take the portage to Chokecherry Lake.

Route # 3
Marten River to Wicksteed Lake Loop

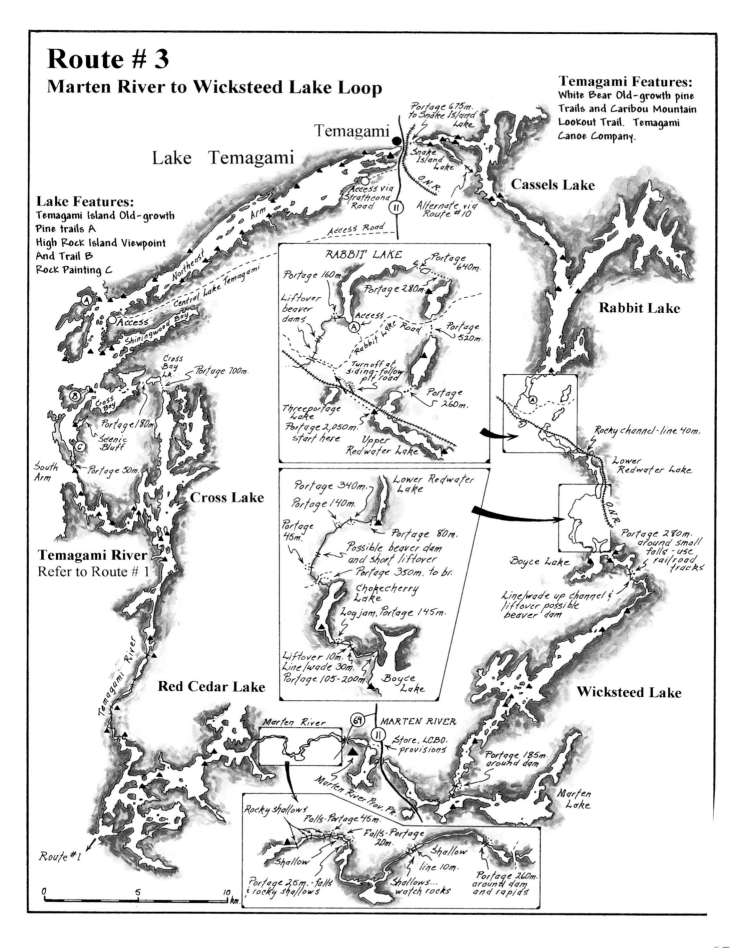

Temagami Features:
White Bear Old-growth pine
Trails and Caribou Mountain
Lookout Trail. Temagami
Canoe Company.

Temagami

Lake Temagami

Cassels Lake

Portage 675m.
to Snake Island
Lake

Snake
Island
Lake

Access via
Strathcona
Road

O.N.R.

Alternate via
Route #10

Lake Features:
Temagami Island Old-growth
Pine trails A
High Rock Island Viewpoint
And Trail B
Rock Painting C

Northeast Arm

Access Road

Central Lake Temagami

Shiningwood Bay

Rabbit Lake

RABBIT LAKE
Portage 640m.
Portage 160m.
Portage 280m.
Liftover
beaver
dams
Access
Rabbit Lake Road
Portage 520m.
Turn off at
siding-follow
pit road
Portage 260m.
Threeportage
Lake
Portage 2,050m.
start here
Upper
Redwater Lake

Access

Cross
Bay
Lk.
Portage 700m.

Cross Bay

Portage 180m.
Scenic Bluff

South Arm
Portage 50m.

Cross Lake

Rocky channel-line 40m.

Lower
Redwater Lake

Lower Redwater
Lake
Portage 340m.
Portage 140m.
Portage 45m.
Portage 80m.
Possible beaver dam
and short liftover
Portage 350m. to br.
Chokecherry
Lake
Log jam, Portage 145m.
Liftover 10m.
Line/wade 30m.
Portage 105-200m.

Boyce Lake

Boyce
Lake

Portage 280m.
around small
falls - use
railroad
tracks

Line/wade up channel &
liftover possible
beaver dam

Temagami River
Refer to Route # 1

Wicksteed Lake

Red Cedar Lake

Marten River

MARTEN RIVER
Store, LCBO,
provisions

Marten River Prov. Pk.

Portage 185m.
around dam

Marten
Lake

Route #1

Rocky shallows
Falls-Portage 45m.
Falls-Portage
20m.
Shallow
line 10m.
Shallow
Portage 25m. - falls
& rocky shallows
Shallows...
watch rocks
Portage 260m.
around dam
and rapids

0   5   10
km.

A familiar encounter in Temagami.

Chokecherry Lake There is one very nice but small campsite on the island on Chokecherry. Continue north and enter the mouth of the river once again.

Marten River In low water you may have a bit of a struggle to gain access to the portage on the right bank. Portage 350 m to a bush road and put in on the far side of the bridge. On the opposite side of the river here you'll see an old portage to Frances Lake. Head north a short distance until you come to steep cliffs on the right and a rock-and-log obstruction in the river. Portage on the left side. The next 200 m is very shallow, with required liftovers and wading. Portage 140 m on the left around the next obstruction. This trail is rather strenuous and steep, edging along a high embankment. Wading or portaging is required, with one final carry-out to a campsite on Lower Redwater Lake.

Lower and Upper Redwater Lake Paddle north about 2 km, keeping left of the tracks, and line the canoe up the narrow, rocky channel 40 m into Upper Redwater Lake. There is only one, rather poor campsite here, located on a point about one third of the way up the lake on the north shore. From here you have two options to access Rabbit Lake — following Rabbit Creek, or a chain of lakes connected to Redwater via the north bay. The creek route begins at the tracks then right into a gravel pit. Follow the gravel pit road to the Rabbit Lake access road and hang a left and follow it until you reach the bridge over Rabbit Creek.

Rabbit Creek The height of water and ease of paddling depend on the activity of beaver and the number of dams along the way. It's a pretty creek, flanked by a high, rocky ridge to the east.

Rabbit Lake From here there are two routes back to Lake Temagami, depending on where you started your trip. Take Rabbit north to the site of the town, or take Route 8 as a slight diversion.

LAKE TEMAGAMI CIRCLE LOOP

Lake Temagami hub area can get pretty busy during the summer. What makes this tour unique is the fact that the route avoids most of the congested areas of the lake and takes in some fine scenery and back-route environments. The main lake can also get rough — another good feature about this circle loop because it sticks primarily to smaller lakes. This route can be done in either direction.

CLASSIFICATION experienced novice
        (some hefty portages)

DISTANCE 135 km

TIME 6–8 days

PORTAGES 24 (total: 10.5 km)

MAPS 41 I/16, 41 P/1, 31 L/13, 31 M/4

FEATURES & ECOLOGY There is plenty to do on this trek, starting with the White Bear Forest trails located close to the town of Temagami. Other trails and lookouts are too numerous to mention but listed on the route map. Lake Temagami Skyline Waterway Park is a relatively new designation to further protect, or classify, the lake environs after the Ontario government settlement of lands with the Teme augama anishnabe in 2002. The original Skyline Reserve was created in 1935 in a hand-shake deal between the government and local logging companies. It protected a thin band of old-growth timber from logging, cottage development and road building. It did not prohibit mining. The new reserve will extend back to include most of the skyline "past the first ridge," as originally established. Although some question the validity of the Waterway Park designation because it doesn't afford much in the way of protection, the establishment of a green belt now connects the town of Temagami all the way to the Lady Evelyn–Smoothwater Wilderness Park. There exist the variety of wildlife communities typical of small lakes and ponds. Of particular importance is the variety of warblers found throughout. Vegetation Site Code: UMF, UDF, RB, C.

Lake Temagami, Northeast Arm Begin the tour from the town of Temagami or from the Strathcona public access point, and paddle down the arm. If it's windy past Axe Narrows, then take shelter above the islands along the north shore as far as the Hay Lake portage. East of the creek you'll find the well-worn trail to Hay. Optional loop start is Sandy Inlet on Ferguson Bay.

Hay Lake No campsites, but you'll find a lot of bog at the next portage entrance (canoeists have dropped down logs for ease of landing). After the initial ooze, the trail levels out and crosses a creek about two thirds of the way along, ending at another small creek that runs into Command Lake.

Command Lake Paddle to the southwest bay and look for the trail entrance located just south of the creek. The trail is rocky, with one small, wet section, but not difficult.

McLaren Lake Still no established campsites but a very pretty cruise to the next portage carry. This trail is located at the extreme southwest notch, and if you're stuck for a campsite, you'll find one at the end of the portage.

Spawning Lake Paddle to the southwest end of the lake and stay east of the creek where you'll find a smooth, well-trodden path leading to Spawning Bay on Lake Temagami.

Spawning Bay There are a couple of campsites located in this quiet bay. It wasn't so quiet back in 1969 when a tornado ripped through here, taking out the fire tower on Bear Island.

Kokoko Bay & Lake "Owl" Lake and Bay remains one of Lake Temagami's choice camping zones, with several prime sites to choose from. Clear water and resident pine forests are hallmarks of Kokoko; especially noticeable are the huge white pines lining the trail back to Devil Bay on Lake Temagami.

Lake Temagami Anishnabe lookout during the Iroquois wars, vision-quest site — stories of remarkable legends emanate from the archives of the rock precipice of Devil Lookout. The trail is located back of the campsite at the foot of the mountain. Head north to Sandy Inlet, Mount Ferguson (site of an old fire-tower lookout), and then east to the portage into Whitefish Bay. Mind the winds as you travel south on the approach to Devil Bay, one of the windiest stretches of open water on the lake. There is a good trail through second-growth poplar and birch to Eye Lake on Obabika Inlet.

Route # 4
Lake Temagami Circle Loop
(Kokoko, Gull and Cross Lake detail)

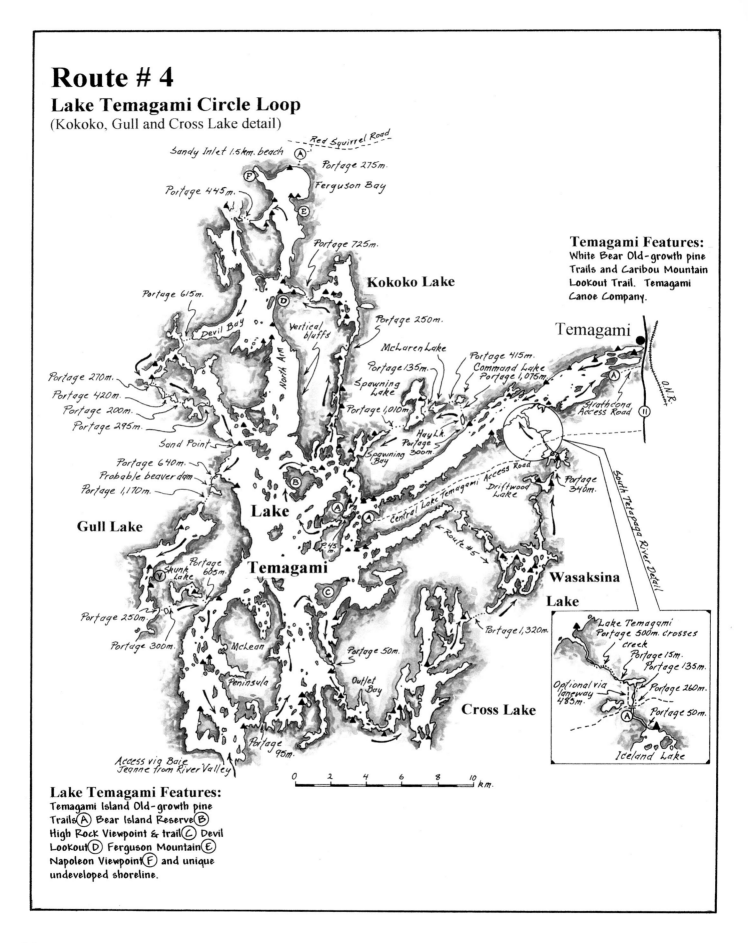

Red Squirrel Road

Sandy Inlet 1.5 km. beach
Ⓐ
Portage 275 m.
Ferguson Bay
Ⓕ
Portage 445 m.
Ⓔ
Portage 725 m.

Kokoko Lake

Portage 615 m.
Ⓓ
Portage 250 m.
Devil Bay
Vertical bluffs
McLaren Lake
Portage 135 m.
North Arm
Spawning Lake

Portage 270 m.
Portage 420 m.
Portage 200 m.
Portage 295 m.
Sand Point
Portage 640 m.
Probable beaver dam
Portage 1,170 m.

Portage 1,010 m.
Hay Lk.
Portage 300 m.
Spawning Bay

Portage 415 m.
Command Lake
Portage 1,075 m.

Temagami

Strathcona Access Road

O.N.R.
11

Temagami Features:
White Bear Old-growth pine
Trails and Caribou Mountain
Lookout Trail. Temagami
Canoe Company.

Gull Lake

Ⓑ
Lake
Ⓐ
Ⓐ
Central Lake Temagami Access Road
Driftwood Lake
Portage 340 m.

Temagami

Route #5

South Tetapaga River Detail

Ⓨ
Skunk Lake
Portage 605 m.
P. 45 m.

Wasaksina Lake

Portage 250 m.
Ⓓ
Portage 300 m.
Ⓒ
Portage 1,320 m.

McLean
Portage 50 m.

Peninsula
Outlet Bay

Cross Lake

Portage 95 m.
Access via Baie
Jeanne from River Valley

0   2   4   6   8   10 km.

Lake Temagami
Portage 500 m. crosses creek
Portage 15 m.
Portage 135 m.
Optional via laneway 485 m.
Portage 260 m.
Ⓐ
Portage 50 m.
Iceland Lake

Lake Temagami Features:
Temagami Island Old-growth pine
Trails Ⓐ Bear Island Reserve Ⓑ
High Rock Viewpoint & trail Ⓒ Devil
Lookout Ⓓ Ferguson Mountain Ⓔ
Napoleon Viewpoint Ⓕ and unique
undeveloped shoreline.

Jumping Cat Lake Route Proceed to a small bay at the south section of Obabika Inlet. The trail is located here, following an old bush road to the right for 140 m then branching left the remainder of the distance to Banana Lake. The next trail is easily spotted on the east shore, two thirds of the way down the lake. It's an easy carry to Jumping Cat, followed by another short trail that takes you to the final pond before dropping back to Lake Temagami.

Lake Temagami You'll probably see houseboats moored at Sand Point during the summer; if it's vacant, you'll find a couple of nice beach campsites here. The trail to Herbert follows an old skid road uphill and crosses the creek at the top. Put in at a marshy area on the west side of this creek and proceed to the Gull Lake portage.

Gull Lake The trail is located at the southwest end of Herbert, and is fairly strenuous, with one wet spot near the Gull end. Featured on Gull are pine-clad campsites clustered near the spectacular cliffs. There is a viewpoint without a trail from the summit of the cliff that offers an unrestricted view west. A short distance south of the narrows, follow the bay and put in right (south) of the creek. Don't take the logging trail north of the creek. The trail takes you to a small pond and on to the next portage to Skunk Lake.

Skunk Lake There are four good campsites on Skunk. The trail back to Lake Temagami is well-worn and downhill.

Lake Temagami The islands of the southwest arm offer not only shelter from the winds but a chance to catch some of the resident walleye that lurk off the rocky points in the evening. There is a short 95-m portage across the McLean Peninsula and no shortage of campsites as you head down Outlet Bay to Cross Lake.

Cross Lake This lake boasts many, large, pine-covered campsites and no development — a good place for a well-earned rest day. The trail to Wasaksina is well-used and slightly uphill.

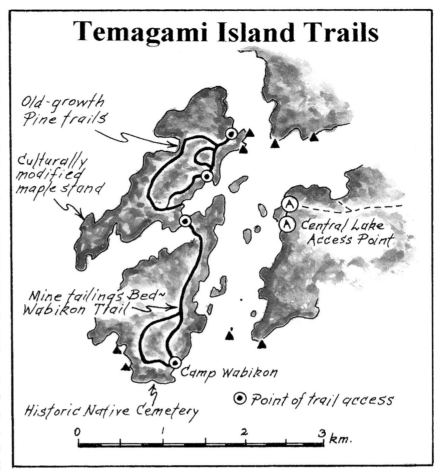

Wasaksina Lake From here there are two routes back to Temagami Route 5, or continue on this route north to Driftwood and Iceland. Wasaksina is one of the most beautiful lakes in the area. Fishing is still good and campsites are plentiful. Continue north through a long, narrow pond and enter the cedar-lined channel into Driftwood Lake. Continue northeast through the narrows and access the portage into Iceland.

Iceland Lake & South Tetapaga River Believe it or not, it's easy to get turned around on this lake because of its many outstretched arms. This is a shallow lake with three prime campsites. Once on the river you'll eventually hit the Central Lake Temagami access road, where you have two options for carrying past the obstructions blocking the river. Follow the instructions on the route map out to Lake Temagami, where you'll have about two hours' paddle left back to the village.

Route # 5
Red Cedar to Jumping Cariboo Lake Loop

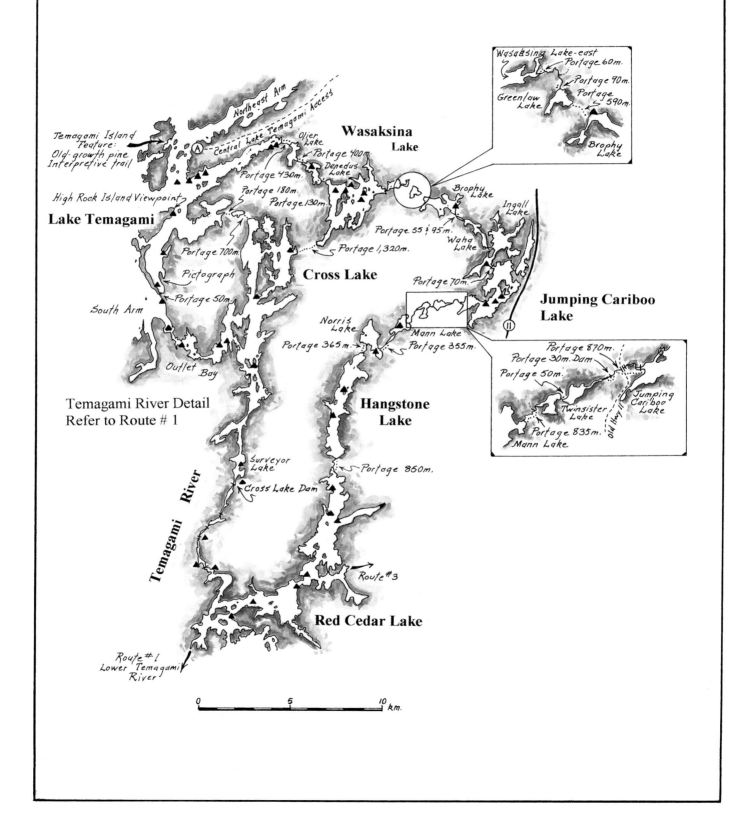

Northeast Arm

Temagami Island Feature: Old-growth pine Interpretive trail

Central Lake Temagami Access

A

Olier Lake

Portage 400m.

Denedus Lake

Wasaksina Lake

Wasaksina Lake-east

Portage 60m.

Portage 90m.

Portage 590m.

Greenlaw Lake

Brophy Lake

High Rock Island Viewpoint

Lake Temagami

Portage 430m.

Portage 180m.

Portage 130m.

Brophy Lake

Ingall Lake

Portage 55 & 95m.

Waha Lake

Portage 700m.

Portage 1,320m.

Pictograph

Cross Lake

Portage 70m.

Jumping Cariboo Lake

Portage 50m.

South Arm

Norris Lake

Portage 365m.

Mann Lake

Portage 355m.

11

Portage 870m.

Portage 30m. Dam

Portage 50m.

Outlet Bay

Hangstone Lake

Twinsister Lake

Jumping Cariboo Lake

Temagami River Detail Refer to Route # 1

Portage 835m.

Mann Lake

Old Hwy 11

Surveyor Lake

Portage 850m.

Cross Lake Dam

Temagami River

Route #3

Route #1 Lower Temagami River

Red Cedar Lake

0   5   10 km.

RED CEDAR *to* JUMPING CARIBOO LAKE LOOP

This loop offers the paddler just about everything — whitewater play on the upper Temagami, small-lake travel, great campsites and fishing, and a choice of three routes back to the start point from beautiful Wasaksina Lake.

CLASSIFICATION experienced novice
        (intermediate if rapids are run)

DISTANCE 100 km

TIME 5–6 days

PORTAGES 21 (total: 6 km)

MAPS 31 L/12, 31 L/13, 41 I/9, 41 I/16

FEATURES & ECOLOGY Temagami Island old-growth pine hiking trails are located near the start point of this loop and should not be missed. Since Cross and Red Cedar lakes are flooded lakes, natural shoreline communities have been disrupted and altered. It has in no way depreciated the aesthetics of this route, but it does offer a look at the changes taking place along riparian environments. Wasaksina Lake typifies the Temagami geological and natural phenomenon in its resident floral growth, pine shores and rock outcrops — a photographer's paradise. Vegetation Site Code: UMF, UCF, UDF (Red Cedar Lake).

Lake Temagami & Cross Lake This loop begins at the central Lake Temagami access point; alternate staging points could be the town of Temagami or Angus Lake on Highway 11. From central lake, paddle south to Outlet Bay and enter Cross Lake. There is a shortcut to South Cross Lake, through the islands, located just past the point campsite. This wide, log-cluttered bay is an excellent spot to view moose, heron and related marsh wildlife and plants. Lifting over submerged logs may be required in low water.

Temagami River Refer to Route 1 for detailed information.

Red Cedar Lake Once on Red Cedar Lake, paddle eastward to the narrows. This lake often becomes busy with fishing boats, and good campsites are few and far between, so chart out your route accordingly. The best site, large enough for three or four tents, is located on the peninsula on the west shore near the north end of the lake. Continue north for 1.5 km and keep east (right) of the north bay, which is jammed with logs. You'll find a good trail to Hangstone. The portage is east of the creek, hilly, and crosses a road at the far end.

Hangstone Lake There are two good campsites on the lake: one medium-sized site is located past the narrows on the west shore, the other site is located on the north end of the large island. Paddle north and enter a small, grassy narrows to gain access to the next portage. Keep slightly right on this smooth trail as you cross the bush road through an opening and then continue on to Norris Lake.

Norris Lake Paddle to the creek across from the island at the southeast end. On the island you'll find a small, exposed campsite. The Mann portage is located directly across from the island. This trail climbs a small hill and crosses a bush road and trail alongside a cabin.

Mann Lake Continue northeast to the extreme east bay and put in at the road. When the water is high enough, the creek may be the logical choice, although several liftovers would be necessary. At the road you can portage left and turn off the road opposite a "private road" sign and access a trail to the right. This will bring you out to the open section of the creek and the south end of Twinsister Lake.

Twinsister Lake At the narrows where the creek passes through an old logjam, portage to the left up a steep bank 50 m to gain access to the east section of the lake. Continue northeast to the narrows and portage 30 m around the right side of the dam. Paddle up the creek for about 200 m, lining or wading where necessary, until you come to a small rapid and pipeline clearing. Follow it for about 400 m, crossing old Highway 11, and continue on a track uphill and catch the trail to the left to Jumping Cariboo Lake. Do not follow the creek to the lake.

Jumping Cariboo Lake This is a pretty lake with three campsites. Paddle to the northwest end of the lake and portage into Ingall Lake. Keep right (north) of the shallow rapids. Cross Ingall to the next carry.

Waha Lake There are two campsites on the south shore of the narrows; the west site has room for three or four tents. Paddle northwest through Waha to the bridge at old Highway 11. Here, you must carry on the north side of the bridge into a shallow section of the creek. Cross the small beaver pond to its extremity, then carry over a good trail on the north side of the creek into Brophy Lake.

Brophy & Greenlaw Lake Proceed to the northwest bay for the next portage, located at a rough, grassy campsite clearing. The trail can be boggy in a couple of spots, so wear appropriate footwear. At the north end of Greenlaw there is a short portage west of the creek into a marsh filled with deadheads. After putting in, there may be some minor log obstructions. You now have to keep left (west), as the creek divides here and it's easy to get turned around. The depth of water is generally good for travel up as far as the short portage (north side of the creek) into Wasaksina Lake.

Wasaksina Lake Wasaksina refers to the white floating beaver sticks that wash up along the shore. This is a prime spot for a stay over; good fishing, spectacular campsites and generally beautiful landscape are all hallmarks of Wasaksina Lake. It's a one-day jaunt back to the town of Temagami via Route 4 through the Iceland Lake route, or you can return to Cross Lake again, or continue on this route.

Denedus & Olier Lake Paddle to the north end of Wasaksina and catch the trail to Denedus on the north side of the creek. There is an excellent campsite located on this easy trail. Denedus is striking, with its picturesque islands and high ridges. Paddle to the far west narrows and portage along a good trail to Olier Lake. On a point just before the final portage you can find solace at a small campsite, possibly your last night along the route. From the last portage into Shiningwood Bay it's a half-day paddle back to the central lake access point. You may have to buck the prevailing wind here.

Blue heron over Temagami. The Wakimika Triangle —
one of Canada's last remaining stands of old-growth red-and-white pine.

CANOEING, KAYAKING & HIKING TEMAGAMI

DIAMOND, WAKIMIKA *and* OBABIKA LAKE LOOP

This is one of the most popular loops, chiefly because of the many side routes, good fishing, superb camping and rugged landscape. The loop can be taken in any direction taking prevailing winds into consideration (traveling south on Obabika may be impeded by strong winds). Traffic flow is quite heavy in the summer, so for optimum success on this route I do recommend traveling in the buffer season (June or September).

CLASSIFICATION novice

DISTANCE variable with side routes. Basic loop (Sandy Inlet) 72 km

TIME 4–7 days

PORTAGES basic loop 6 (3.2 km)

MAP 41 P/1 (if starting from central Lake Temagami use 41 I/16)

FEATURES & ECOLOGY Old-growth forest, cultural importance, sand beaches, prominent rock shoreline, and clear water are all important facets of this classic Temagami loop. The geology of Sharp Rock Inlet and the clarity of water set this secluded bay apart from the rest of Lake Temagami. The primal forest of Diamond Lake, south to the sacred cliffs of Chee-skon Lake, is one of the largest contiguous pine forests in North America. Side routes offer a diversion from the main busy route and provide unique experiences in a variety of ways. Mixed with the grand escarpments and bold granite outcrops are confined fen communities (marsh marigold, pitcher plant), especially along the Wakimika River. Wakimika River passes through an old-growth eastern white cedar stand, while Small Lake is sheltered by an old-growth jack-pine forest (south ridge). Vegetation Site Code: UMF, UCF, C (North Lake Temagami), AC/MM and SM (Wakimika River).

Lake Temagami Sandy Inlet is subject to high winds; however, the beach provides ample tenting space in case of delay. The long portage into Whitefish Bay is strenuous, beginning with a steep climb, so if you have time, head south and take the shorter, easier carry. There are superb campsites in this quiet bay. The south

channel into Sharp Rock is too shallow for motorboats and is the preferred route for paddle craft. Head north to the end of the bay and keep left to enter the channel to the Sharp Rock portage. This was the site of the old jackladder used to haul logs up from Diamond Lake.

Diamond Lake Non-waw-kaming was once a busy crossroads for Native travel on several nastawgan routes that pass through here. Fishing for lake trout, northern pike and walleye is still fair, and blueberries can be found at campsites on the central islands. At the west end of Diamond there is an old 1940–50s logging-camp clearing, now used as a campsite. Several interesting artifacts can be found, including a rack of skidding sleighs, log booms and remnants of the small "village" that thrived here.

Two Routes to Bob Lake It's a straightforward carry along a good, level trail 1,175 m to Bob Lake from central Diamond Lake. The alternate route through Small is quite lovely but strenuous. If you are traveling north from Bob through Small, you have two choices of trails located on both sides of the creek, as indicated on the detail map.

Diamond to Wakimika Paddle west on Diamond along the south shore where you'll notice a unique faultline crevice in the rocks. There is a natural rock "umbrella" that makes a fine place to sit out a summer downpour. Continue to the end of the lake, winding through the jagged rocks as far as you can go, and pull up at a sloping rock landing (refer to sketch). The trail is over open bedrock, with several ledge steps to contend with before reaching Lain Lake. The next portage is located at a campsite across the far end of Lain, where the controversial Red Squirrel Road (abandoned) passes through. Follow the road to the trail cutoff on the left. Before entering Wakimika proper you may have to wade through a sandy spit that often clogs the channel. You may want to camp here, either to wait out the wind or simply because it's just a fine place to spend a bit of time.

Wakimika Lake There were over 120 people camped on the beach here in September 1989 during the Red Squirrel Road blockade. Remnants of the old trail can be found at the end of the beach. This leads to the road about 1 km away. The vistas to the north (as seen from central and southern positions) are spectacular.

Route # 6
Diamond, Wakimika and Obabika Lake Loop
(Includes Bob Lake crossover routes)

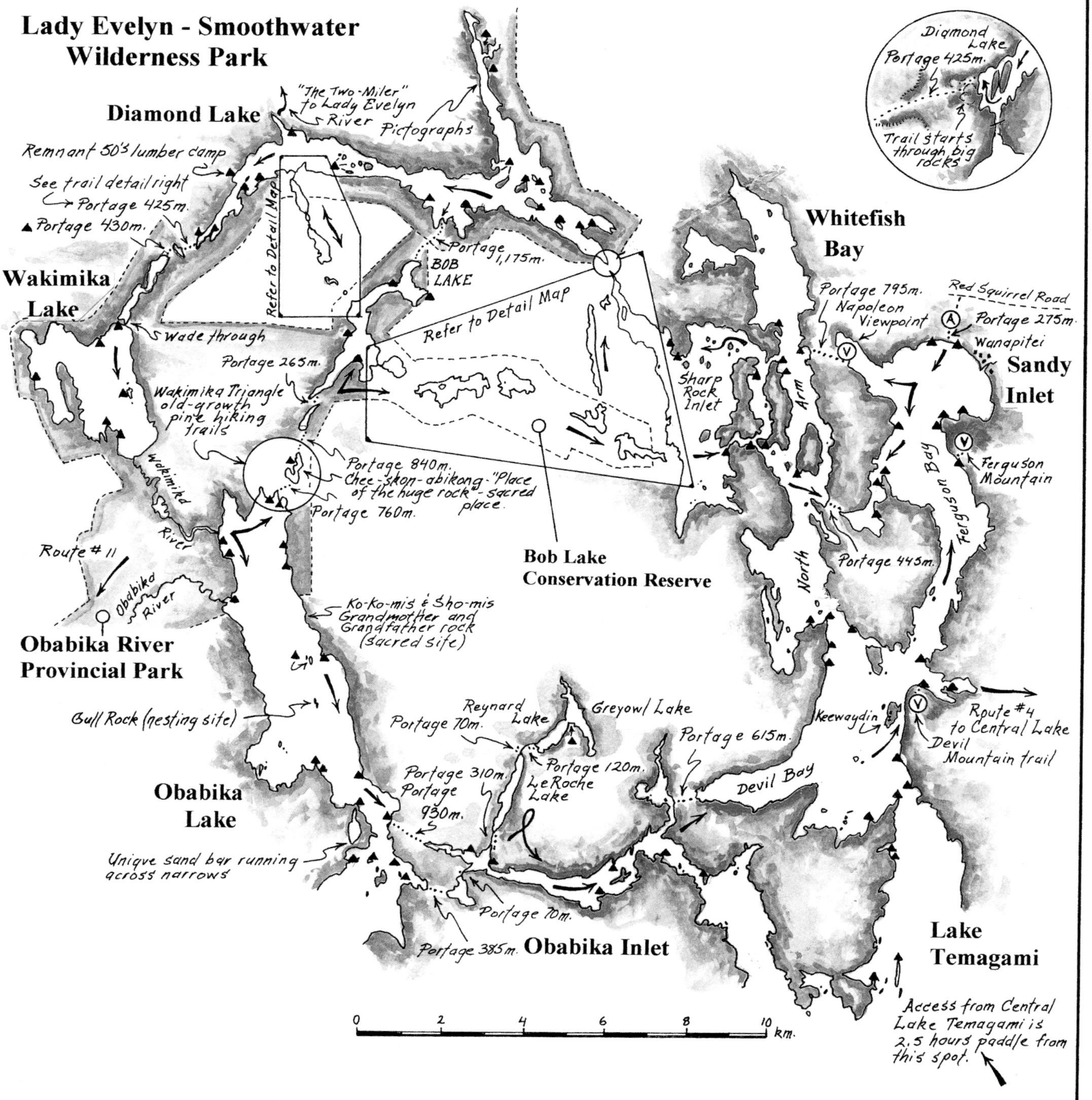

Lady Evelyn - Smoothwater Wilderness Park

Diamond Lake

"The Two-Miler" to Lady Evelyn River

Pictographs

Remnant 50's lumber camp

See trail detail right → Portage 425m.

▲ Portage 430m.

Diamond Lake Portage 425m.

Trail starts through big rocks

Whitefish Bay

Wakimika Lake

Refer to Detail Map

Portage 1,175m.
BOB LAKE

Refer to Detail Map

Wade through
Portage 265m.

Wakimika Triangle old-growth pine hiking trails

Portage 795m. Napoleon Viewpoint

Red Squirrel Road

Ⓐ Portage 275m.
Wanapitei

Ⓥ

Sandy Inlet

Sharp Rock Inlet

Ⓥ Ferguson Mountain

Wakimika River

Portage 840m.
Chee-skon-abikong "Place of the huge rock" - sacred place.

Portage 760m.

Bob Lake Conservation Reserve

North Arm

Portage 445m.

Route # 11

Obabika River

Obabika River Provincial Park

Ko-ko-mis & Sho-mis
Grandmother and Grandfather rock
(sacred site)

Reynard Lake
Portage 70m.

Greyowl Lake

Portage 615m.

Keewaydin

Ⓥ Route #4 to Central Lake Devil Mountain trail

Gull Rock (nesting site)

Portage 310m.
Portage 930m.

Portage 120m.
Le Roche Lake

Devil Bay

Obabika Lake

Unique sand bar running across narrows

Portage 70m.

Portage 385m. **Obabika Inlet**

Lake Temagami

Access from Central Lake Temagami is 2.5 hours paddle from this spot.

0 2 4 6 8 10 km.

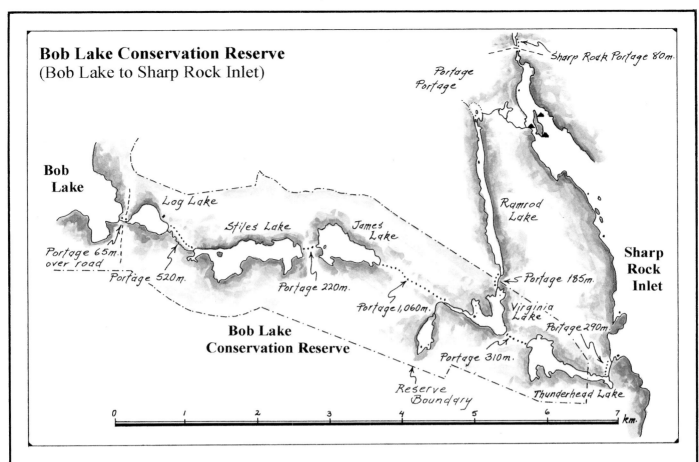

Bob Lake Conservation Reserve
(Bob Lake to Sharp Rock Inlet)

Bob Lake

Sharp Rock Portage 80m.

Portage Portage

Log Lake

Stiles Lake

James Lake

Ramrod Lake

Sharp Rock Inlet

Portage 65m. over road

Portage 520m.

Portage 220m.

Portage 1,060m.

Portage 185m.

Virginia Lake

Portage 290m.

Bob Lake Conservation Reserve

Portage 310m.

Reserve Boundary

Thunderhead Lake

0 1 2 3 4 5 6 7 km.

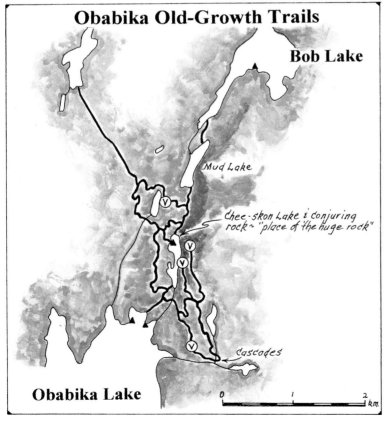

Obabika Old-Growth Trails

Bob Lake

Mud Lake

Chee-skon Lake & conjuring rock ~ "place of the huge rock"

Cascades

Obabika Lake

0 1 2 km.

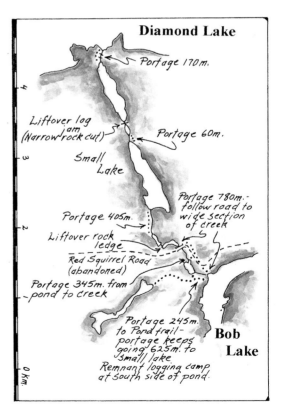

Diamond Lake

Portage 170m.

Liftover log jam (Narrow rock cut)

Portage 60m.

Small Lake

Portage 780m.- follow road to wide section of creek

Portage 405m.

Liftover rock ledge

Red Squirrel Road (abandoned)

Portage 345m. from pond to creek

Portage 245m. to Pond trail - portage keeps going 625m. to Small lake. Remnant logging camp at south side of pond.

Bob Lake

4 3 2 0 km.

Diamond Lake portrait.

Paddle to the south end of the lake and enter the river. You may have to wade through sand shallows during low water, but once in the creek you'll have little difficulty.

Wakimika River The river is easily navigated unless there are fresh downfalls or beaver dams to contend with. The flora and fauna is rich, with assured sightings of great blue heron, kingfisher, barred and horned owls, beaver and possibly moose. You'll pass under the shell of an unused logging bridge before reaching Obabika Lake.

Obabika Lake If the lake is rough when you first greet it, don't attempt to cross over to the hiking trails or head down the open stretch of lake to the south — it will get even more turbulent once you push farther out. There are a couple of good campsites down the shore on your right, so stay there until it's safe to venture out. Obabika has many features, starting with the Chee-skon (Wakimika Triangle) hiking trails. There is also the sand-spit campsite and spring, preceded by ko-ko-mis and sho-mis, "grandmother and grandfather rock," conjuring stones perched by the shore and highly visible. The gull rookery on Gull Island where hundreds of herring gulls nest may prompt a paddle by, but watch out for swooping adult birds in late spring.

Bob Lake Return Options There are three routes back to Sharp Rock on Lake Temagami, as indicated by the route map. These are not shorter routes, although traveling this way may be the logical choice if the wind is severe on Obabika.

Obabika Inlet The trail from Obabika to Lake Temagami is easily located. It's a slightly uphill climb, but the trail is quite easy and level (but could be boggy at the Obabika Inlet end).

Grey Owl Lake Route Whether or not Grey Owl (Archie Belaney) actually had something to do with the naming of the lake, no one seems to know; but if you want a quiet place to set up your camp away from the mainstream, this is the place to do it. It's a dead-end route, but that doesn't mean it doesn't go anywhere. You can even spend the day hiking on the old Eye Lake skid road, located along the east shore of Grey Owl Lake.

Lake Temagami The trail through to Devil Bay is easily spotted and the carry is not difficult. You may experience strong tail winds out on the bay as you head northeast towards Ferguson Bay. Two hikes are well worth the time — Devil Mountain and Ferguson Mountain — each with unique vantage points overlooking Lake Temagami.

Archie Belaney, better known as Grey Owl,
made the Temagami wilderness his temporary home in the early 1900s.

ROUTE 7

ANIMA NIPISSING *and* JACK PINE LAKE LOOP

This grouping of link routes fills the gaps connecting some of the major corridors. Some of the routes can be built into actual loops or added on as side trips. Over the years, Jack Pine Creek has become very difficult and unmaintained, so I have removed the detailed information from this write-up. Some logging has taken and still is taking place within portions of this region, although all portages are supposed to have sufficient protection from cutting practices.

CLASSIFICATION novice to experienced novice

DISTANCE longest loop (Anima Nipissing,
  Red Squirrel, Temagami and return) 115 km

TIME One week

PORTAGES 12

MAPS 31 M/4, 31 M/5, 41 P/1, 41 I/16, 31 L/13

FEATURES & ECOLOGY Hiking trails, viewpoints, creek environments, natural beauty . . . you can't go wrong. Anima Nipissing is one of the district gems, with several visible rock-painting (pictograph) sites found on prominent rock faces. The attractive nature of nature along these corridors is typical of creek and pond environments — intimate and visible. The Cliff Lake viewpoint is highly recommended. This was once second choice for the development of an international ski resort espoused by the Ontario Ministry of Tourism in 1972, after the ill-fated battle to keep developers out and off of Maple Mountain. Vegetation Site Code: UMF, TS and AC (Snare and Jack Pine creeks).

Route Notes There may be disruptions along some of these routes, but they would be of a localized nature. All portages indicated on the route map have been cleared at one time but may be impeded by recent windfalls. Please do your best to clear or mark the way for other canoe parties.

Porcupine — a common forest dweller, who's only predator other than humans is the fisher.

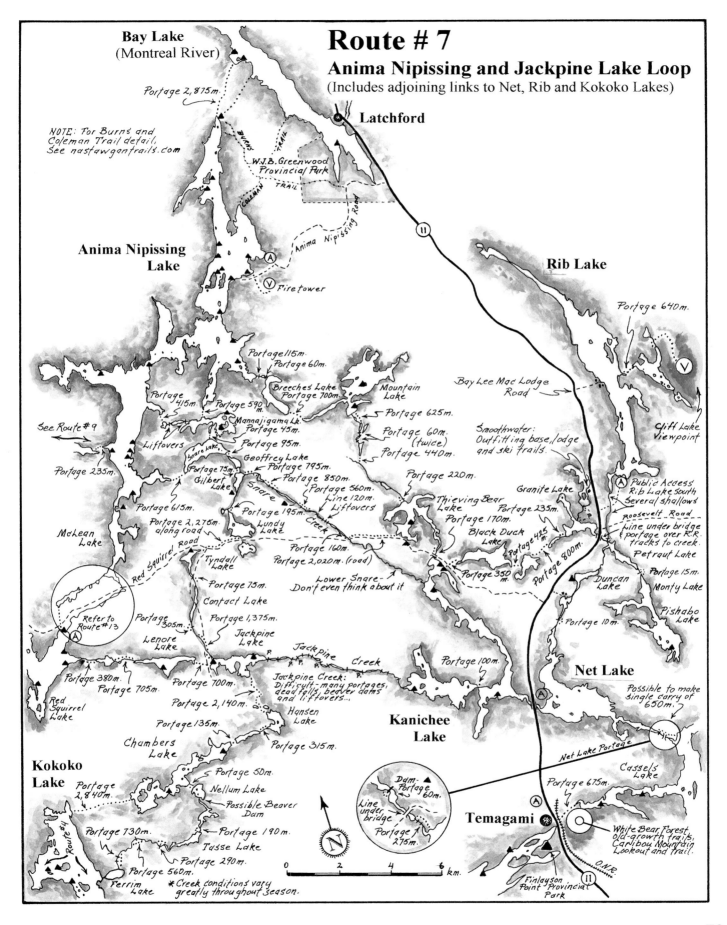

Route # 7
Anima Nipissing and Jackpine Lake Loop
(Includes adjoining links to Net, Rib and Kokoko Lakes)

Bay Lake
(Montreal River)

Portage 2,875m.

NOTE: For Burns and
Coleman Trail detail,
See nastawgantrails.com

Latchford

BURNS TRAIL

W.J.B. Greenwood
Provincial Park

COLEMAN TRAIL

Anima
Nipissing
Lake

Anima Nipissing Road

Ⓐ

Ⓥ Fire tower

11

Rib Lake

Portage 640m.

Portage 115m.
Portage 60m.

Breeches Lake
Portage 700m.

Mountain
Lake

Bay Lee Mac Lodge
Road

Ⓥ

Cliff Lake
Viewpoint

Portage
415m.

Portage 590
m.

Portage 625m.

See Route #9

Mannajigama Lk.
Portage 75m.
Liftovers

Snare Lake

Portage 95m.

Portage 60m.
(twice)
Portage 440m.

Smoothwater:
Outfitting base, lodge
and ski trails.

Granite Lake

Ⓐ Public Access
Rib Lake south
Several shallows

Portage 235m.

Geoffrey Lake
Portage 795m.

Portage 850m.

Portage 220m.

Portage 235m.

Roosevelt Road

Portage 75m.
Gilbert
Lake

Snare

Portage 560m.
Line 120m.
Liftovers

Thieving Bear
Lake
Portage 170m.

Line under bridge
portage over R.R.
tracks to creek

Portage 235m.

Portage 615m.

Portage 195m.

Lundy
Lake

Creek

Black Duck
Lake

Portage 425 m.

Petraut Lake

McLean
Lake

Portage 2,275m.
along road

Red Squirrel Road

Portage 350
m.

Portage 800m.

Duncan
Lake

Portage 15m.

Monty Lake

Tyndall
Lake

Portage 160m.

Portage 2,020m. (road)

Portage 10m.

Pishabo
Lake

Refer to
Route #13

Ⓐ

Portage 75m.

Contact Lake

Lower Snare—
Don't even think about it

Portage
305m.

Portage 1,375m.

Lenore
Lake

Jackpine
Lake

Jackpine

Creek

Portage 100m.

Net Lake

Possible to make
single carry of
650m.

Portage 380m.
Portage 705m.

Portage 700m.

P

Jackpine Creek:
Difficult—many portages,
dead falls, beaver dams
and liftovers...

Portage 2,140m.

Red
Squirrel
Lake

Kanichee
Lake

Ⓐ

Portage 135m.

Hansen
Lake

Net Lake Portage

Cassels
Lake

Chambers
Lake

Portage 315m.

Dam-
Portage
60m.

Portage 675m.

Kokoko
Lake

Portage
2,840m.

Portage 50m.

Nellum Lake

Line
under
bridge

Possible Beaver
Dam

Temagami

Ⓐ

Ⓒ

White Bear, Forest,
old-growth trails,
Caribou Mountain
Lookout and trail.

Portage 730m.

Portage 190m.

Portage
275m.

Tasse Lake

Route #4

Portage 290m.

N

Portage 560m.

Ferrim
Lake

*Creek conditions vary
greatly throughout season.

0   2   4   6 km.

Finlayson
Point Provincial
Park

O.N.R.

11

Route # 8
Rabbit and Twin Lakes Loop

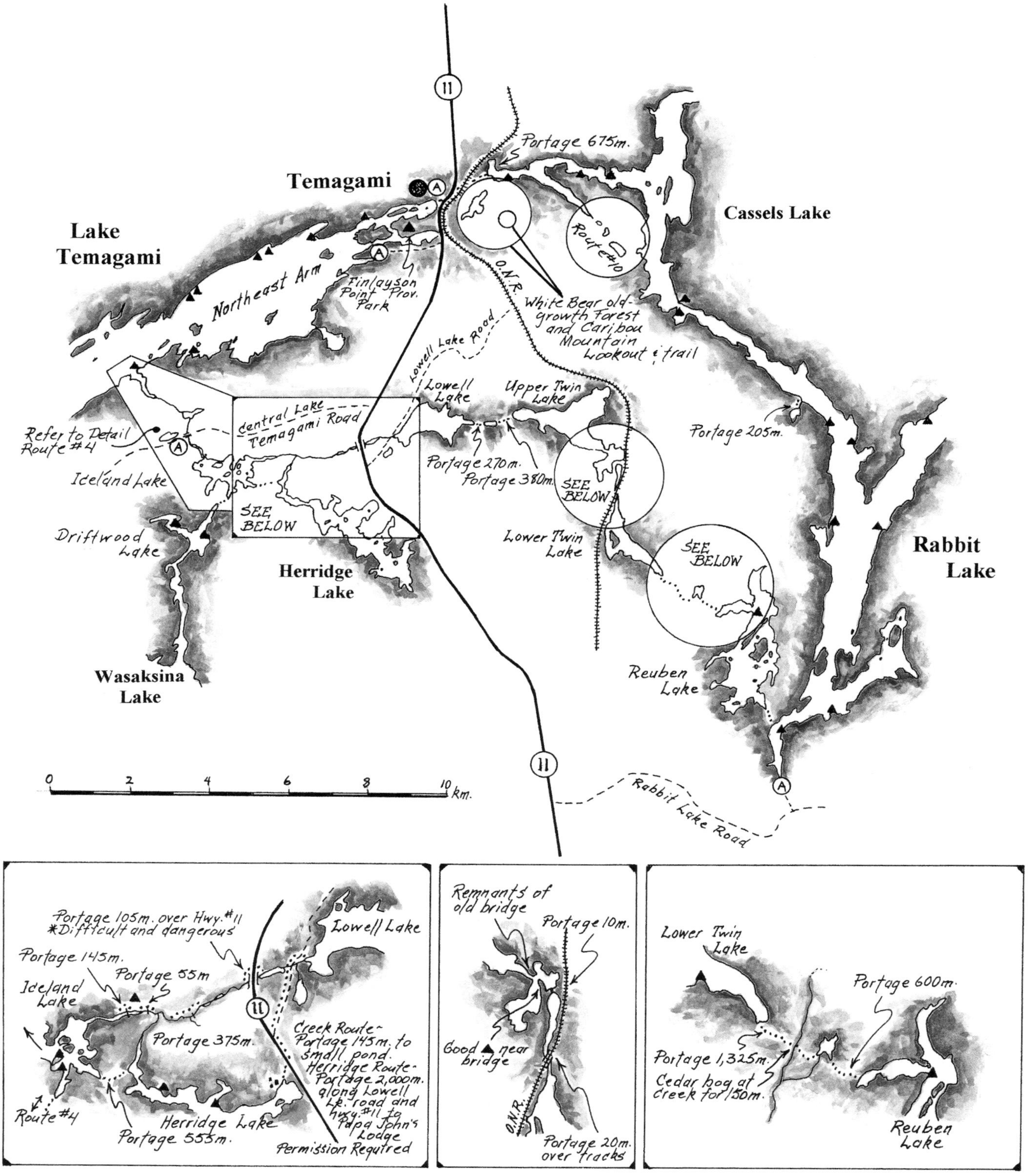

Temagami

Lake Temagami

Northeast Arm

Finlayson Point Prov. Park

Portage 675m.

Cassels Lake

Route #10

White Bear old-growth Forest and Caribou Mountain Lookout & trail

O.N.R.

Lowell Lake Road

central Lake Temagami Road

Lowell Lake

Upper Twin Lake

Portage 205m.

Refer to Detail Route #4

Iceland Lake

Portage 270m.
Portage 380m.

SEE BELOW

Lower Twin Lake

SEE BELOW

Rabbit Lake

SEE BELOW

Driftwood Lake

Herridge Lake

Reuben Lake

Wasaksina Lake

0   2   4   6   8   10 km.

Rabbit Lake Road

Portage 105m. over Hwy. #11
*Difficult and dangerous

Lowell Lake

Portage 145m.

Portage 55m.

Iceland Lake

Portage 375m.

Creek Route~ Portage 145m. to small pond. Herridge Route~ Portage 2,000m. along Lowell Lk. road and hwy. #11 to Papa John's Lodge.

Herridge Lake

Portage 555m.

Permission Required

Route #4

Remnants of old bridge

Portage 10m.

Good ▲ near bridge

O.N.R.

Portage 20m. over tracks

Lower Twin Lake

Portage 600m.

Portage 1,325m.

Cedar bog at creek for 150m.

Reuben Lake

CANOEING, KAYAKING & HIKING TEMAGAMI

RABBIT *and* TWIN LAKES LOOP

If you have a long weekend to devote to paddling, then this is one of the more interesting short trips in Temagami, and the good thing about it is that you can step off the train or bus with virtually the shirt on your back, get completely outfitted, and trek off without a worry. The fishing isn't too bad along this route, but there are a few portages to contend with, so don't expect an easy go of it. Because few people travel this route, you'll hit either welcome solitude or a bushpush through uncleared trails.

CLASSIFICATION experienced novice

  (some strenuous portages)

DISTANCE 62.5 km

TIME 3–4 days

PORTAGES 13 (total: 7 km)

MAPS 31 M/4, 31 L/13

FEATURES & ECOLOGY This route follows a typical Shield-bedrock shorescape with a generous growth of white and red pine along the back ridges. There are several small lakes with backshore fen environments; these are excellent places to fish or view wildlife. It is recommended that if you have an extra day, take in the White Bear Forest hiking trails. Vegetation Site Code: UMF, AC (Iceland and South Tetapaga rivers).

Temagami Begin at the town of Temagami. From the Ontario Natural Resources station follow the gravel road east and put in at the end of Snake Island Lake. There are several good campsites through Cassels and into Rabbit Lake.

Rabbit Lake Care must be employed while traveling south on Rabbit because of wind hazard. Keep to the west shore or hang tight until it is safe to go on. There is one large site located along the west shore opposite Rabbit Point. The Reuben portage can be found 250 m east of the picturesque creek flowing into Rabbit Lake. The first part of the trail climbs a steep slope, but soon levels out all the way to Reuben.

Side Trip to Lode Lake Just north of Rabbit Point, on the west shore you'll see a small campsite close to a small creek. There is a 205m trail into Lode Lake. Who knows, it could be the best fishing along this loop.

Reuben Lake Clear water makes swimming at the campsite indicated on the route map quite appealing.

The next portage is located on the north shore near the end of the northwest bay. The trail is moderately difficult and passes through a couple of wet spots before reaching the southeast bay of a small pond. At the small pond, keep to the south shore and around the point to the next portage. The next trail can be difficult if wet conditions precede your trip and impeded by deadfalls if it hasn't been cleared.

Lower Twin Lake There is only one, rough campsite located on a point on the south shore. Paddle north on Lower Twin to where the railroad crosses the north channel. Here, you have to portage over the tracks on loose gravel. Head north, where you will notice a shallow channel running through a rocky spit. Here, you have to lift over the rocks into the pond (old railroad bridge and concrete pillars on the west shore). There is a very good campsite located here, where wild strawberries are plentiful and pike fishing is excellent. The tracks carry on to an abandoned gravel pit. Depending on the water levels, you can either paddle or line under the old bridge through the shallows to Upper Twin Lake.

Upper Twin Lake Paddle to the extreme west end of the lake to the next portage. This is a good trail, slightly uphill at the onset, then leveling off through primrose and elderberry bushes and out to a small pond. Continue across the pond to the next portage located north of the small creek. This trail crosses the power-line clearing.

Lowell Lake There are two routes to Iceland from Lowell — following the creek, or keeping to Highway 11 to Herridge Lake. The former is dangerous and difficult while trying to gain access over the highway, so it is recommended that you use the road route (take care while portaging the canoe, as large trucks passing can cause the canoe to swing over the roadway. Use a spotter!).

Herridge Lake Although somewhat busy with cottages and small boats, Herridge remains quite pretty and quiet if you decide to camp near the north end of the lake. Paddle through the narrows in the extreme northwest bay and keep left for the trail into Iceland Lake. This is a well-used trail, and you'll probably see fishing boats at the far end of the portage.

Iceland Lake Refer to the description on Route 4. It's a full day's paddle back to the town of Temagami from Iceland.

TURNER LAKE LOOP

This is a popular loop through clear-water lakes and can be taken in either direction. The main loop route is described below. The Walsh Lake link will lengthen your trip by at least two days, while if you head north to Sugar Lake, the Isbister route may not be cleared.

CLASSIFICATION experienced novice

DISTANCE 54 km (Turner–Aston loop)

TIME 3–4 days

PORTAGES 16 (total: 9 km)

MAPS 41 P/1, 41 P/8, 31 M/4

FEATURES & ECOLOGY The most popular feature of this loop route is the small lakes, and that means easier travel, even during windy days. This is a bit of a work trip but well worth the slugging over the portages. You could easily spend a week exploring these lakes. Viewpoints at Eagle Lake and Sandy Inlet offer spectacular overviews of the route. Vegetation Site Code: UMF, MM (Eagle Lake and Creek and pond links).

ACCESS & EGRESS The route map illustrates three points of access, the most popular being Red Squirrel Lake, where parking is not a problem. From Red Squirrel Lake, enter the northwest bay where you will see the portage landing a short distance south of the river outlet. This is a good trail that will take you back to the river at a point where paddling is easy out to Camp Wanapitei and Sandy Inlet.

Lake Temagami There are two routes across Ferguson Bay, as indicated on the route map; the south trail is much easier but high winds may be a problem. Once in Whitefish Bay, head north and enter the mouth of the creek on the northeast shore behind the large island. The portage landing is obvious on the north side of the creek. The portage is well-used, rocky in sections and crosses Red Squirrel Road.

Aston Lake On a point just to the east of the portage you'll find a good campsite, with three other sites located farther down the lake. Paddle to the north end of the lake, where you will find a beaver dam at the grassy mouth of a small creek. Lift over the dam and paddle across the creek to the portage landing. This

trail is separated by a creek that bisects the trail. Paddle 50 m across this flooded section and continue about 275 m to Lynx Lake.

Lynx & Cole Lakes Continue north and stay right of the stream to catch the Cole Lake portage. This is a rocky trail and may be disturbed by a recent logging-road development. Cole Lake is very clear, but like Lynx it has no usable campsites. You'll find the next portage south of the extreme north end, on the east shore, with an easy carry into Turner Lake.

Turner Lake Entering Turner Lake, keep right of the large island and enter the small inlet. If you plan to camp here then the island site will accommodate several tents. The next portage actually begins on the east side of the inlet mouth, but this 300 m section is generally wet and unnecessary. Enter the inlet and proceed to the portage at the south end. The landing may be a bit boggy, but it's an easy 160m carry over rocky ground to a small pond. At the southeast end of this pond is the next portage. The trail is strenuous, passing over several small knolls, through minor wet spots and through an open marsh area. This brings you out to Eagle Lake.

Eagle Lake Kinay-oo-wab-koshing, known for its east-shore cliffs and eagle nests, is well worth the hard slogging to get there. There is an excellent viewpoint here but no established trail. Continue to the south end to a small outlet narrows and look for the portage on the east shore. About 100 m along the trail you may find some fresh beaver-dam activity; cross over it and continue on to an open part of the river. Travel south on the west arm of the small, shallow pond. Here you'll likely find more beaver dams to lift over and a gravel shallows to track the canoe through. The short carry into Little Eagle hops over a gravel esker where footing could be precarious.

Little Eagle Lake There is one large campsite located near the south end of the lake on the east shore. Near the campsite, you'll locate the next portage on the north side of the creek. One of the most difficult portage trails, you can expect some ups and downs and a bit of fancy footing over the rocks. This brings you out to a small pond. Go to the east end to catch the trail to the next pond. The end of this trail is quite bony at the end before the pond. The next trail varies in length depending on beaver activity that may result in

Route # 9
Turner Lake Loop

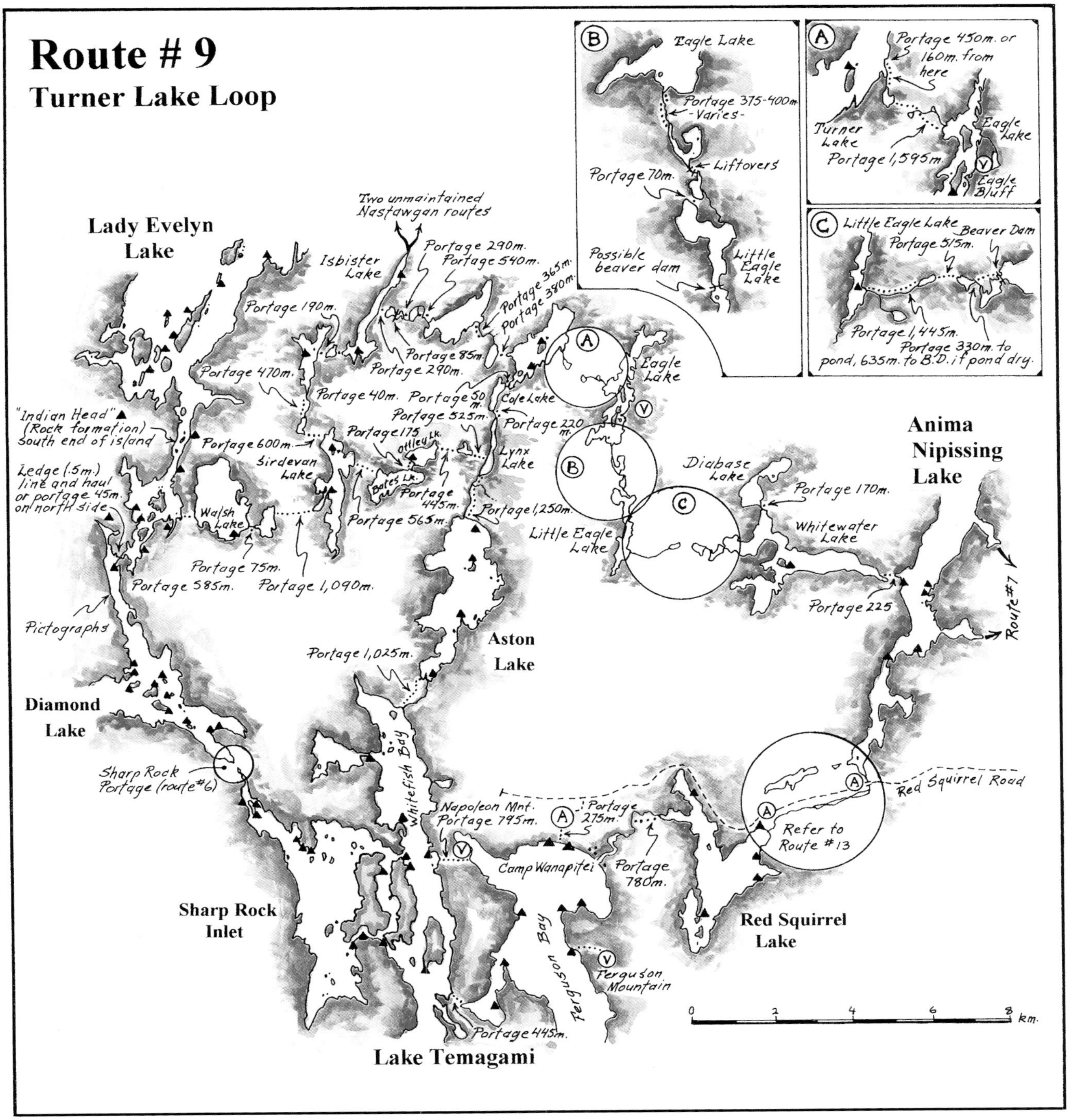

Lady Evelyn Lake
Anima Nipissing Lake
Aston Lake
Diamond Lake
Sharp Rock Inlet
Lake Temagami
Red Squirrel Lake
Two unmaintained Nastawgan routes
Isbister Lake
Portage 290m.
Portage 540m.
Portage 365m.
Portage 380m.
Portage 190m.
Portage 85m.
Portage 290m.
Portage 470m.
Portage 40m.
Portage 50 m.
Cole Lake
Eagle Lake
Portage 525m.
Portage 220 m.
"Indian Head" (Rock formation) south end of island
Portage 600m.
Portage 175
Ottley Lk.
Lynx Lake
Sirdevan Lake
Bates Lk.
Portage 445m.
Ledge (.5m.) line and haul or portage 45m. on north side
Walsh Lake
Portage 565m.
Portage 1,250m.
Little Eagle Lake
Diabase Lake
Portage 170m.
Whitewater Lake
Portage 75m.
Portage 585m.
Portage 1,090m.
Portage 225
Pictographs
Route #7
Portage 1,025m.
Sharp Rock Portage (route #6)
Whitefish Bay
Napoleon Mnt. Portage 795m.
Portage 275m.
Camp Wanapitei
Portage 780m.
Red Squirrel Road
Refer to Route #13
Ferguson Bay
Ferguson Mountain
Portage 445m.
0 2 4 6 8 km.
Eagle Lake
Portage 375-400m. -Varies-
Liftovers
Portage 70m.
Possible beaver dam
Little Eagle Lake
Portage 450m. or 160m. from here
Turner Lake
Eagle Lake
Portage 1,595m.
Eagle Bluff
Little Eagle Lake
Beaver Dam
Portage 515m.
Portage 1,445m.
Portage 330m. to pond, 635m. to B.D. if pond dry.

flooding. This may create a shorter than usual carry, but don't get your hopes up. This will eventually bring you out to Whitewater Lake.

Whitewater Lake This is an attractive lake with good fishing and a side-trip option to Diabase Lake. The one campsite is located on the northeast point of the large island atop a bedrock knoll. The downhill trail to Anima Nipissing is located slightly north of the creek outlet.

Anima Nipissing Lake Around the bend from the portage landing is a lovely, open, bedrock campsite. Please be mindful of the rock painting located along the shore below the site. One of the most scenic lakes in the district, Anima Nipissing offers fine camping and general touring for either canoe or kayak. Continue south to McLean Lake, but watch the rocks in the fast current in the narrows before the lake. Paddle to the southwest bay of McLean and line up the narrow channel, keeping to the right to catch the trail to Carrying Lake. Continue to the southwest end and portage south, crossing Red Squirrel Road to Red Squirrel Lake.

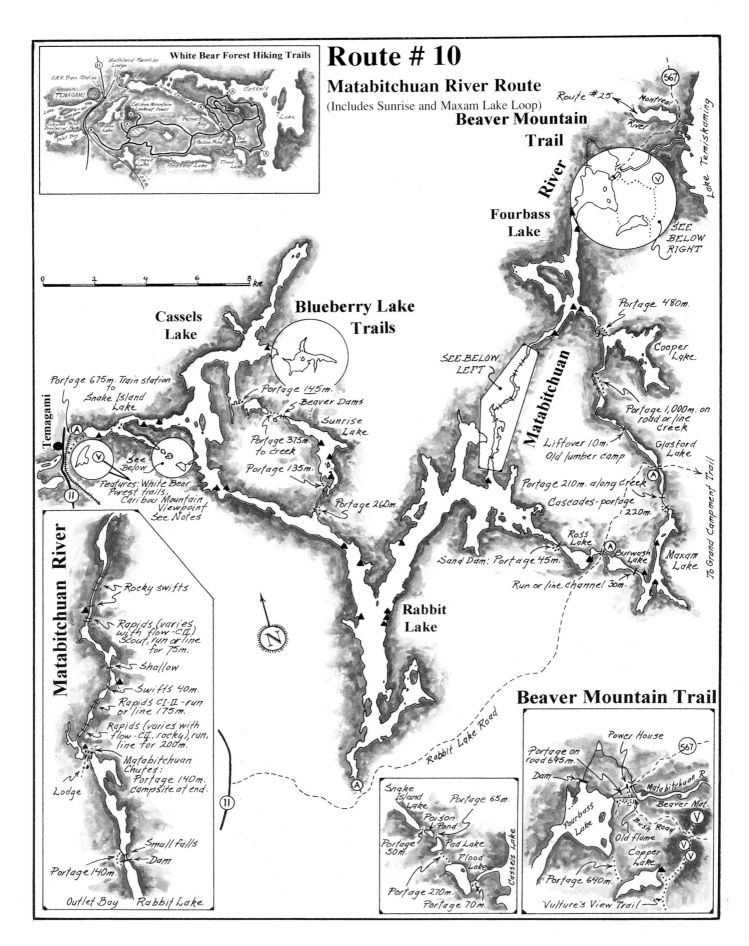

Route # 10

Matabitchuan River Route
(Includes Sunrise and Maxam Lake Loop)

White Bear Forest Hiking Trails

Northland Paradise Lodge

O.N.R. Train Station

TEMAGAMI

Caribou Mountain Lookout Tower

Snake Island Lake

Cassels Lake

Pecend Bay

Finlayson Point Provincial Park

Caribou Lake

Lake Temagami

Inlet Bay

Cinque Lake

Hessant Lake

Poison Pond

Pad Lake

Flood Lake

O.N.R.

Beaver Mountain Trail

Route #25

Montreal River

Lake Temiskaming

Fourbass Lake

SEE BELOW RIGHT

Portage 480m.

Cooper Lake

Cassels Lake

Blueberry Lake Trails

SEE BELOW LEFT

Portage 1,000m. on road or line creek

Portage 145m.

Beaver Dams

Sunrise Lake

Portage 375m. to creek

Portage 135m.

Matabitchuan

Glasford Lake

Liftover 10m. Old lumber camp

Portage 210m. along creek

Cascades - portage 220m.

To Grand Campment Trail

Portage 675m. Train station to Snake Island Lake

Temagami

See Below

Features: White Bear Forest trails, Caribou Mountain Viewpoint See Notes

Portage 260m.

Ross Lake

Burwash Lake

Maxam Lake

Sand Dam: Portage 45m.

Run or line channel 30m.

Matabitchuan River

Rocky swifts

Rapids, (varies with flow -CII) Scout, run or line for 75m.

Shallow

Swifts 40m.

Rapids CI-II - run or line 175m.

Rapids (varies with flow - CII, rocky), run, line for 200m.

Matabitchuan Chutes: Portage 140m. campsite at end.

Lodge

Small falls

Dam

Portage 140m.

Outlet Bay

Rabbit Lake

N

Rabbit Lake

Rabbit Lake Road

Beaver Mountain Trail

Power House

Portage on road 645m.

Dam

Fourbass Lake

Matabitchuan R.

Beaver Mat.

Bush Road

Old flume

Copper Lake

Portage 640m.

Vulture's View Trail

567

Snake Island Lake

Portage 65m.

Poison Pond

Pad Lake

Portage 50m.

Flood Lake

Cassels Lake

Portage 270m.

Portage 70m.

MATABITCHUAN RIVER ROUTE

Includes Sunrise and Maxam Loops

This is a multi-dimensional route with many options. Before the railroad was built to Temagami village, the only way to reach Lake Temagami was up the Ottawa and Matabitchuan rivers. This route, if not done as a loop circuit, could be a link to the Ottawa and points south. Canoe camps still run trips down here and head across the Ottawa and up the Indian portage to Lac Kipawa and the Dumoine River. This write-up includes the basic Maxam–Sunrise figure-eight loop, with notes on the river link to the Ottawa River. Other shorter weekend trips can be made from the town of Temagami (Blueberry or Sunrise loops), or the Maxam Lake loop accessed from the Rabbit Lake Road Bridge (two locations as indicated on the route map).

CLASSIFICATION   experienced novice

DISTANCE   90 km

TIME   4–6 days

   (one week including Blueberry Lake Trail hike)

PORTAGES   11 (total: 3.2 km)

MAPS   31 M/3, 31 M/4, 31 L/13

FEATURES & ECOLOGY   There are three major trail systems located on this route: White Bear and Blueberry old-growth pine trails and Beaver Mountain Lookout on the Ottawa River. Please refer to the detailed maps for location and make sure you pick up the handy booklets listed in the bibliography. Vegetation Site Code: UMF, RB, C (Ottawa River).

Snake Island & Rabbit Lake   Leave the town of Temagami and cruise down Snake Island to Cassells Lake and northeast up Rabbit to Outlet Bay; there are several good campsites along the way. Portage around the dam on the west side; avoid the road and take the trail to the right, downhill and past the rapids below the dam.

Matabitchuan River   Keep to the right before a log chute and falls (across from the lodge) and carry over the road and down to the pool below the chute. There is a rough campsite along the trail past the road. Past the small pool there are some rocks to watch out for in the narrow channel. Cross the next pond, where the river turns right into a set of rapids. Water levels play an important role here, but you must scout before running. The next rapids can be run in high water, or lined when low. Where the river widens out there is a set of swifts that can be run in the centre channel. Continue north to where the river narrows again to a rocky set of rapids. Line these for 75 m. To the left, just past the fast water, is a small campsite. Just ahead is a shallow, very rocky section that can be navigated through on the left side. Here, the river transforms into a canyon-like gorge with several swifts and some jagged rocks to watch before entering Fourbass Lake. From here the trip continues down to Cooper Lake and Maxam Lake and over to the Sunrise and Blueberry chain before returning back to the town.

River Continuation   Fourbass is a flooded lake but remains strikingly beautiful, set in a typical Ottawa, northern Laurentian landscape. Paddle to the dam site on northeast shore of Fourbass. Put in on the right side of the bridge and follow the roadway downhill to the power house and lower Matabitchuan River. There are remnants of the old log flume here — its length and vertical drop of 60 m make it one of the largest in the district. Access to the Beaver Mountain Trail can be found here (refer to Muir's book in the bibliography). There are several good campsites on the lower river and the point at the mouth of the Ottawa River.

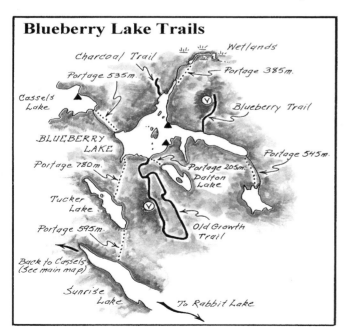

Blueberry Lake Trails

Charcoal Trail

Wetlands

Portage 535m.

Portage 385m.

Cassels Lake

Blueberry Trail

BLUEBERRY LAKE

Portage 545m.

Portage 780m.

Portage 205m.
Dalton Lake

Tucker Lake

Old Growth Trail

Portage 595m.

Back to Cassels (See main map)

Sunrise Lake

To Rabbit Lake

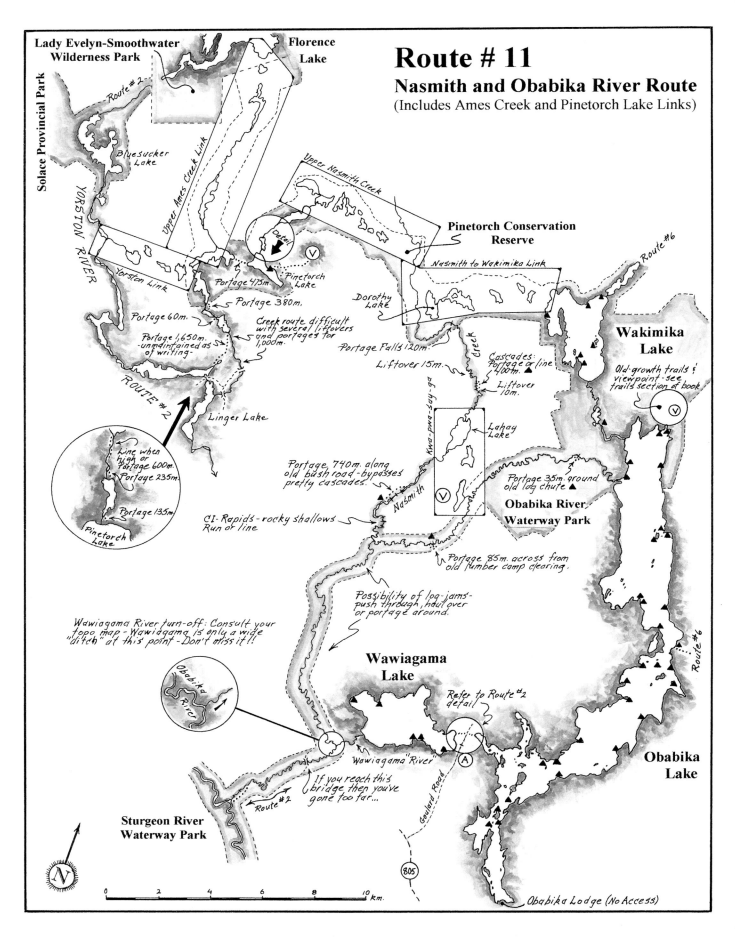

Route # 11
Nasmith and Obabika River Route
(Includes Ames Creek and Pinetorch Lake Links)

Lady Evelyn-Smoothwater
Wilderness Park

Florence
Lake

Solace Provincial Park

Route #2

YORSTON RIVER

Bluesucker
Lake

Upper Ames Creek Link

Upper Nasmith Creek

Pinetorch Conservation
Reserve

Route #6

Nasmith to Wakimika Link

Yorston Link

Portage 475m.

Pinetorch
Lake

Dorothy
Lake

Wakimika
Lake

Portage 380m.

Portage 60m.

Creek route difficult
with several liftovers
and portages for
1,000m.

Portage Falls 120m.

Liftover 15m.

Cascades:
Portage or line
100m.

Old-growth trails &
viewpoint - see
trails section of book

Portage 1,650m.
-unmaintained as
of writing-

ROUTE #2

Linger Lake

Liftover
10m.

Kwa-pwa-say-ga Creek

Lahay
Lake

Line when
high or
Portage 600m.

Portage 235m.

Portage 135m.

Pinetorch
Lake

Portage, 740m. along
old bush road-bypasses
pretty cascades.

Nasmith

Portage 35m. around
old log chute

Obabika River
Waterway Park

C1- Rapids - rocky shallows
Run or line

Portage 85m. across from
old lumber camp clearing.

Possibility of log-jams-
push through, haul over
or portage around.

Wawiagama River turn-off: Consult your
topo map - Wawiagama is only a wide
"ditch" at this point - Don't miss it!!

Obabika River

Wawiagama
Lake

Refer to Route #2
detail

A

Route #6

Obabika
Lake

Wawiagama "River"

If you reach this
bridge then you've
gone too far...

Route #2

Goulard Road

Sturgeon River
Waterway Park

N

805

Obabika Lodge (No Access)

0   2   4   6   8   10 km.

NASMITH AND OBABIKA RIVER ROUTE
FLORENCE TO WAKIMIKA ROUTE

These are two distinct routes, although connectable. They share much of the same localized natural diversity.

Nasmith and Obabika River Route

This route can be done as a loop from the 805 (Goulard Road) access at Wawiagama, or as an extension of Route 6.

CLASSIFICATION experienced novice

DISTANCE 38.5 km (river only),

add 11.2 km if doing the Nasmith option

TIME 2–4 days (excluding Obabika Lake)

PORTAGES 3 or 8

MAPS 441 P/1, 41 I/16

FEATURES & ECOLOGY You are entering a vast, impenetrable, spruce-bog lowlands, hemmed in by high ridges along the western fringe. Wildlife viewing is superb, especially for moose, as the corridor presents itself as an excellent nursing habitat and ample food source. I remember my first adventure down the Obabika while charting out the river for the initial inventory in 1977. My wife and I were confronted by a cow moose and newborn young only a paddle's length from the canoe as we rounded a tight meander. The mother had her hackles up and looked as if she would jump into the canoe; instead she turned abruptly and pissed in our general direction. The river runs fast in the spring, but by summer there may be several log liftovers, including actual logjams to contend with. The bugs may be a concern, but early June is the best time to see moose along this route. Summer trips may also prove fruitful, although considerably more effort is required to haul your boat over deadfalls. Some people find the meanders a bit monotonous, and they could be if you aren't there for the natural setting. The Wakimika Triangle and Obabika Trails are a must-see for everyone. Vegetation Site Code: SM, AC, UMF, B (Obabika River and Lahay Lake).

Coming of the Clouds Alex Mathias has been homesteading on his traditional land for some time, preferring the bounty of the land outside of the reserve life that he finds somewhat distasteful. He keeps an open door for visitors and, for a modest fee, will take you for a tour of the sacred Chee-skon Lake and the conjuring rock. His cabin is located at the mouth of the Obabika River.

Obabika River The first thing you'll notice is the clarity of the water and the current gently pulling on the maiden-hair weed coating the bottom of the river. About 2 km downstream you'll come to the old dam, which has pretty much fallen apart. You could run the sluiceway, but watch out for steel pegs and other remnants that may lay hidden under the water. It's an easy carry around on the left. If you plan on taking the Nasmith route, follow your route map carefully, or take a GPS coordinate on the small creek flowing into the Obabika from Kwa-pwa-say-ga, about 5 km past the dam. This is where you take out at an old log bridge crossing. Continue downstream (if not taking the Nasmith Route) for 3 km until you hear the sound of rapids. Take out on the south side and carry around a rocky chute. The old lumber camp clearing is a good place to camp, splitting the route nicely, and the adjoining skid roads make excellent hiking trails. Continue on through high sand banks, keeping a sharp eye out for swallows and kingfishers. You'll pass the Nasmith Creek mouth on your right. From here the river widens slightly, with several oxbow lakes where moose are often seen feeding. Logjams may present some minor problems; either push through, lift over or carry around if possible. Again, it's important that you follow your topo map, watching for a high ridge on your left marking the edge of Wawiagama Lake and the river mouth. It's easy to pass the mouth of the river because it resembles a small creek, not a river.

Wawiagama River When the water is high, the river is deep and clear with few liftovers. When it's dry, it's a slow process in and out of the canoe, humping over deadfalls. The weedy shallows below the cliff on Wawiagama Lake are prime pike habitat. The campsites on the south central shore point are excellent. When leaving the lake make sure you take the right trail at the north end of the east bay, not where you see some overturned boats at the foot of a trail that leads to the old Goulard lumber camp on the road. This trail passes through a large stand of old red pine trees and crosses the road about halfway along.

Nasmith Route Notes The trail to Kwa-pwa-say-ga is not well marked and grows over very quickly. It's a bit of a bushpush along the creek to an open bog that's usually dry enough to get close to the lake edge. There is an excellent campsite on the east shore and a spectacular vista from the ridge summit across the lake (no established trail at time of writing). The ridge rises almost 150 m above the vast lowlands of Obabika to the east. You may have to haul your canoe over the bog at the north end to gain access to the portage to the next lake. This trail follows an old skid road uphill and then levels off and drops slightly to the lake. At the very north end you'll find the Lahay portage. This trail is a bit rough, and ends at a good campsite once used as a prospectors' camp.

Lahay Lake A worthwhile side trip includes a walk through some gargantuan pine at the northeast end where *The Nature of Things* filmed old-growth for a Temagami feature that aired in 1990. The creek is quite interesting as it wends north, busy with beaver and black ducks, painted turtles and marsh birds, it is well worth the easy trek as far as the first rapid. When leaving the lake, paddle south to where a small falls occurs at a sharp bend in the river. Carry over 55 m to a small pool below the cascades. You may have to wade the canoe through some shallows here. The next portage bypasses several rapids and rocky ledges. You can wade through these with some difficulty or portage along the old road on the right side as far as an old bridge over the river. The tamarack trees are quite remarkable along this stretch of the river. The last two sets of shallow rapids can be run when high or lined when low. Continue down the Obabika as described earlier.

Florence to Wakimika Route

Want a challenging link route? You'll love this stretch of lake and creek. It may be wise to have a lightweight Kevlar if you plan to tackle this fine route.

CLASSIFICATION experienced novice to intermediate (difficult portages)

DISTANCE 30.4 km (excluding Ames Creek route)

TIME 3–4 days

PORTAGES 30 (total: 11 km), 35 percent walking, 65 percent paddling

MAPS 41 P/1, 41 P/2

FEATURES & ECOLOGY The Ames Creek route is known as the "Stein Valley of Temagami." The abrupt hills, cliff outcrops and deep pine forests are all hallmarks of the Ames link. The Pinetorch Conservation Reserve highlights a series of unnamed lakes of rugged prominence and a natural wildlife corridor from Florence–Yorston area, east to the Obabika watershed. There are several high-point lookouts and excellent wildlife viewing possibilities.

Bluesucker Lake Enter the Yorston River at the south end of the lake and follow the Route 2 description to Mudchannel Lake. Where the Yorston leaves Mudchannel you'll see a beaver dam on a creek flowing in from the east. Enter this creek and push your way up about 1 km to the first lake (follow numbers on the route map). The ease of paddling on this creek depends on height of water — any canoe over 16 ft in length may have difficulty navigating this narrow creek because of the tight turns and heavy sedge growth.

Lakes 1 to 5 Follow the route description carefully. One of the nicest campsites is located on Lake 2. At Lake 5, Ames Creek flows in from the north and leaves the lake close to the portage at the west end. There is a pretty route from here that will take you south to the Yorston River, but it is strenuous and not maintained. Paddle to the east end of Lake 5 and portage over a gently rolling trail to Pinetorch Lake.

Pinetorch Lake & Trail There used to be two trails here — one from the old rangers' cabin at the east end of the lake, and one that was cleared by our crew in 1979 from the campsite on the north shore. Neither trail was passable at the time of writing. Proceed to the northwest bay of Pinetorch and carry over an easy trail starting at a small beach landing and ending at a creek below a pond. Paddle north and keep right of the creek for the next portage. This trail will bring you back to Pinetorch Creek, where a short haul will bring you up to a channeled section of creek boulders over a distance of about 600 m. This section can be lined up or portaged along the rocks as far as Lake 6.

Lakes 6 to 14 Continue northeast on this lake to the low, marshy end where the portage begins east of the creek inlet and is poorly marked across the beaver meadow. The trail crosses the creek, enters the bush and pops out at Lake 7. There are two campsites in this vicinity — one on Lake 7 and one on Lake 8 (portage over the creek rocks). The next portage is steep, but footing is good. Lake 8 provides an excellent viewpoint with an unrestricted view at the 500-ft drop eastwards as the land slopes away from the plateau you are now standing on. Follow the route map to Lake 14, where you'll find an excellent campsite and a good place to rest up before the long carry to the Nasmith Creek. This is a

Yorston to Pinetorch Link

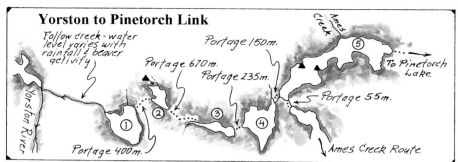

Follow creek - water level varies with rainfall & beaver activity

Yorston River

Portage 400m.

Portage 670m.

Portage 235m.

Portage 150m.

Portage 55m.

To Pinetorch Lake

Ames Creek

Ames Creek Route

① ② ③ ④ ⑤

Upper Nasmith Creek Link

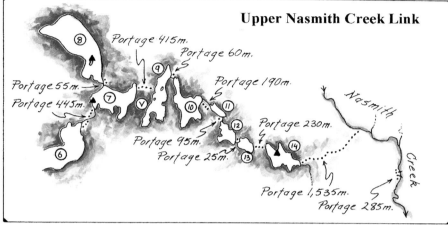

Portage 415m.

Portage 60m.

Portage 55m.

Portage 445m.

Portage 190m.

Portage 95m.

Portage 25m.

Portage 230m.

Nasmith

Creek

Portage 1,535m.

Portage 285m.

⑥ ⑦ V ⑧ ⑨ ⑩ ⑪ ⑫ ⑬ ⑭

Nasmith to Wakimika Link

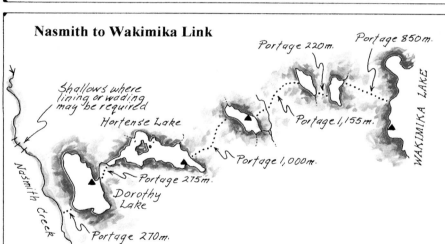

Portage 220m.

Portage 850m.

Shallows where lining or wading may be required

Hortense Lake

Portage 1,155m.

Portage 1,000m.

Portage 275m.

Dorothy Lake

Portage 270m.

Nasmith Creek

WAKIMIKA LAKE

Kwa-pwa-say-ga Lahay Link

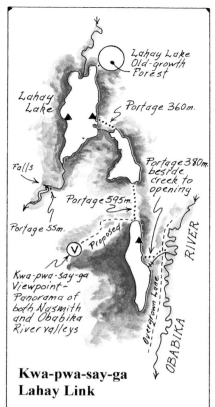

Lahay Lake Old-growth Forest

Lahay Lake

Portage 360m.

Falls

Portage 595m.

Portage 380m. beside creek to opening

Portage 55m.

Proposed

V

Kwa-pwa-say-ga Viewpoint - Panorama of both Nasmith and Obabika River valleys

Overgrown lane

OBABIKA RIVER

Upper Ames Creek Link

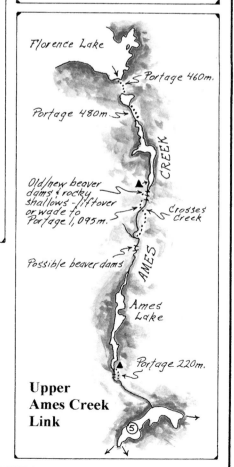

Florence Lake

Portage 460m.

Portage 480m.

Old/new beaver dams & rocky shallows - liftover or wade to Portage 1,095m.

Crosses Creek

AMES CREEK

Possible beaver dams

Ames Lake

Portage 220m.

⑤

Florence Lake Dolman.

challenging trail that drops over 120 vertical m to the creek below; footing is generally good over a dry trail.

Nasmith Creek Ease of paddling depends on time of year and water flow. There are gravel shallows that may be paddled over during high water but waded through when low. Watch the route and topo map carefully as far as the portage to Dorothy Lake (there may be a beaver dam right at the portage entrance. Carry through the jack pine stand to Dorothy. There are good campsites at Dorothy, Hortense and the next small lake.

Hortense Lake Directly north of the campsite on Hortense is the next trail. It's a tough carry rising 60 vertical metres at the start and leveling off to a sharp drop to the next small lake. The next portage begins right at the campsite or slightly down the lake. This portage has several minor wet spots. Paddle to the southeast end of the small pond and carry over a good trail to the next pond, as indicated on the route map. The final portage to Wakimika is located at the northeast end outlet creek. The portage entrance is rather obscure, but there are two trail beginnings, one below the creek outlet and another that can be found by entering the creek and keeping right. This trail is all downhill and smooth — a nice finale to this arduous but delightful canoe route.

Ames Creek Route Follow the route map carefully. Water levels certainly play a role in ease of paddling; however, it can be taken any time during the season. This may be considered the easier route from Florence to Pinetorch, although each route is exceptional in its own way.

LADY EVELYN, MAKOBE *and* MONTREAL RIVER LOOP

The Makobe and Grays watersheds are dependent on spring rainfall and winter melt for their ability to offer premium whitewater for adventure paddlers. As a spring trip you can't beat it, but by late June the Makobe route becomes a veritable walking trail. Although the Grays is passable throughout the season (I suggest you take the Makobe–Trethewey lake route in the summer), the Makobe would require long wades and has few running options in July and August. Optimum running time for the Makobe is right after break-up, usually after May 10, up until mid-June when moose viewing is best. Other running options for Makobe River are: fly-in start from Banks Lake (three days); fly-in start from Florence Lake (one week); drive-in shuttle to Lady Evelyn River (five days); and drive-in shuttle to Cooke Lake (one to two days, see map).

CLASSIFICATION intermediate

DISTANCE 160 km

TIME 10 days

PORTAGES 28 (TOTAL: 10.7 KM)

MAPS 41 P/8, 41 P/9, 31 M/5

FEATURES & ECOLOGY Paddlers can add two days to their trip and take in the Maple Mountain hike or one day for the Dry Lake Ridge climb. This is a classic Temagami adventure, offering just about everything you'd expect in a challenging and beautiful canoe route. The Makobe River has always been one of my favourite pre-bug trips. It's an awakening world; with little foliage you can see much more, and chance encounters with wildlife are guaranteed. The beauty of the Lady Evelyn "Golden Staircase" Falls, as winter run-off spills over granite ledges, is a sight to be witnessed. You can expect to see migrating birds (like old squaw ducks) taking a break from their northward trek, resident birds busy nesting, and moose moving out into the weedy shallows to escape the blackflies in June. Vegetation Site Code: UCF, UMF, RB, UDF (Montreal River), AC (Grays River).

Mowat Landing This popular public landing can get quite busy in the summer, but for spring trips you'll bump elbows with local lodge owners hustling in anglers for the opening of walleye season. Head for the Matawapika Dam and portage along the service road by Mitchell's Camp. Head south on the Lady Evelyn River to the main body of the lake. Because of the prevailing winds from the southwest, you may have to wait out the blow at any one of the fine campsites located at the narrows or nearby islands.

Lady Evelyn Lake Lost its Ojibwa title of mons-kaw-naw-ming or "haunt of the moose" to the wife of the Duke of Devonshire, probably because of the difficulty Whites had in pronouncing Native names. There are four fishing camps on Lady Evelyn, and about fifteen private cottages, thus the increased amount of boat traffic during peak periods. The lake is still large enough to allow seclusion, while the Sugar Lake cross-over route is often used to avoid headwinds and summer traffic. One of the features of the west body of the lake is the sand eskers. Continue through the Obisaga Narrows and head west, following the north shore of the lake to the top end of Sucker Gut Lake. The forestry depot can be seen on the island where the lake bends southward. This was once a busy ranger station, complete with overland telephone to the top of Maple Mountain. Stop along the shore and pick blueberries here in the summer. There are many choice campsites along Sucker Gut.

Lady Evelyn River, North Channel Men-jamma-ga-sibi or "trout streams" is a pool and drop river. That means upstream travel is not difficult, the fast water being restricted to each specific fall or rapid only. At Frank Falls, portage over open bedrock to the pool above. There is an optional route return from Maple Mountain via Chris Willis Lake — the portage coming out just above Frank's. Centre Falls, known locally as the "Golden Staircase," has always been a gathering spot for canoeists. The natural rock slide, located at the bend in the river below the falls, is a popular summer play spot. The entrance to the trail can be found left (south) of the final rapids. The trail itself passes through scattered jack pine over open bedrock terraces (watch carefully for rock cairns and tree blazes). There are two campsites here.

Upstream of the falls is a set of rocky rapids that is difficult to line or wade. You can run through these if you are going downstream and the water is high, but it

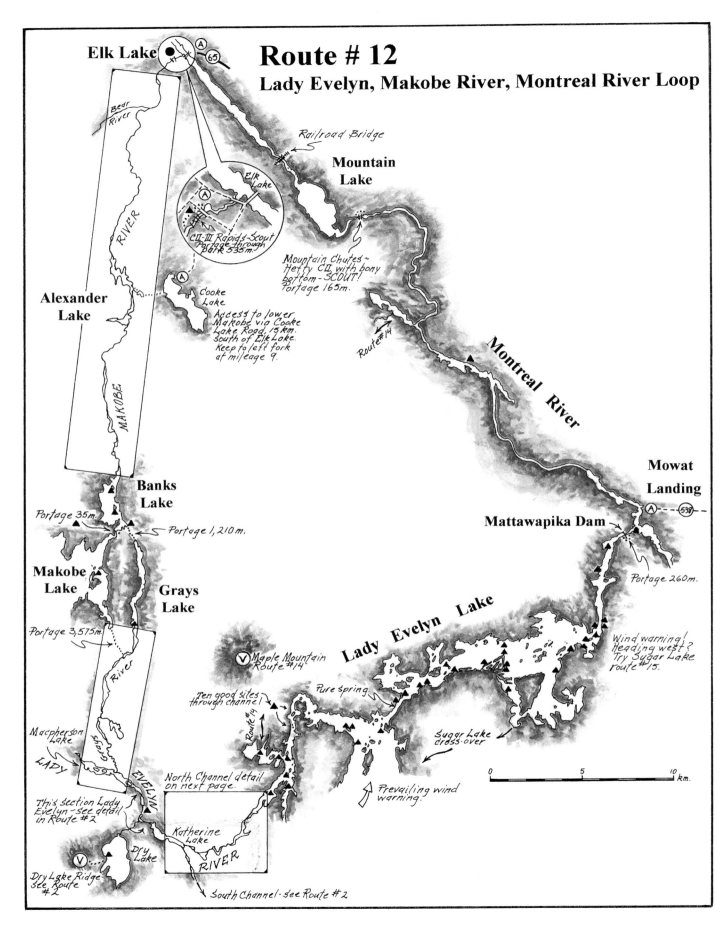

Route # 12
Lady Evelyn, Makobe River, Montreal River Loop

Elk Lake

Ⓐ 65

Bear River

Mountain Lake

Railroad Bridge

Elk Lake

Ⓐ

◣

CII-III Rapids-Scout
Portage through
park 535m.

Ⓐ

Cooke Lake

Route #14

*Mountain Chutes ~
Hefty CII with bony
bottom - SCOUT!
Portage 165m.*

Alexander Lake

Access to lower
Makobe via Cooke
Lake Road, 15 km.
south of Elk Lake.
Keep to left fork
at mileage 9.

Montreal River

Mowat Landing

Ⓐ 558

Banks Lake

Portage 35m.

◣

Portage 1,210m.

Mattawapika Dam

Portage 260m.

Makobe Lake

Grays Lake

Portage 3,575m.

Lady Evelyn Lake

*Wind warning!
Heading west?
Try Sugar Lake
route #15.*

Grays River

Ⓥ Maple Mountain
Route #14

Pure spring

*Sugar Lake
cross-over*

Macpherson Lake

LADY

Ten good sites
through channel

Route #14

0   5   10
|——————|——————| km.

EVELYN

North Channel detail
on next page.

*Prevailing wind
warning.*

This section Lady
Evelyn - see detail
in Route #2

Katherine Lake

Dry Lake

RIVER

Ⓥ

Dry Lake Ridge
See Route #2

South Channel - see Route #2

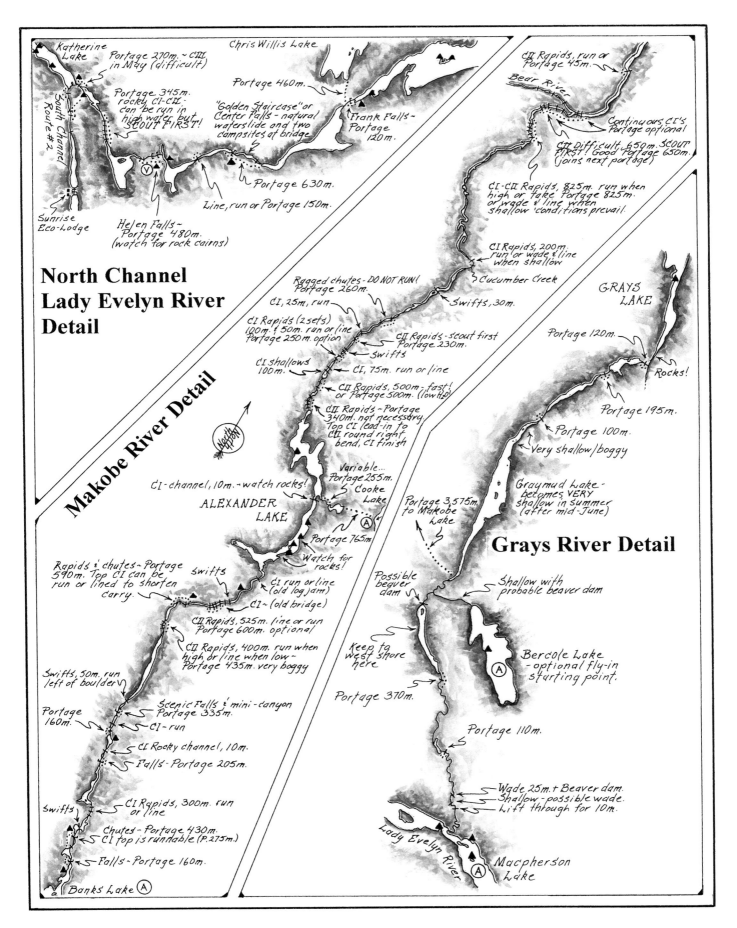

North Channel Lady Evelyn River Detail

Katherine Lake

Portage 270m. ~ CIII in May (difficult)

Chris Willis Lake

Portage 460m.

Portage 345m. rocky CI-CII - can be run in high water but SCOUT FIRST!

South Channel Route #2

"Golden Staircase" or Center Falls - natural waterslide and two campsites at bridge

Frank Falls ~ Portage 120m.

Sunrise Eco-Lodge

Portage 630m.

Line, run or Portage 150m.

Helen Falls ~ Portage 480m. (watch for rock cairns)

Ragged chutes - DO NOT RUN! Portage 260m.

CI, 25m, run

CI Rapids (2 sets) 100m. & 50m. run or line Portage 250m. option

CII Rapids - scout first Portage 230m.

CI shallows 100m.

Swifts

CI, 75m. run or line

Makobe River Detail

CII Rapids, 500m. - fast! or Portage 500m. (low H2O)

CII Rapids ~ Portage 340m. not necessary. Top CI lead-in to CII round right bend, CI finish

North

Variable... Portage 255m. Cooke Lake

CI - channel, 10m. - watch rocks!

ALEXANDER LAKE

Portage 765m.

Watch for rocks!

Portage 3,575m. to Makobe Lake

Rapids & chutes - Portage 590m. Top CI can be run or lined to shorten carry.

Swifts

CI run or line (old log jam)

CI ~ (old bridge)

CII Rapids, 525m. line or run Portage 600m. optional

CII Rapids, 400m. run when high or line when low - Portage 435m. very boggy

Swifts, 50m. run left of boulder

Portage 160m.

Scenic Falls & mini-canyon Portage 335m.

CI - run

CI Rocky channel, 10m.

Falls - Portage 205m.

CI Rapids, 300m. run or line

Swifts

Chutes - Portage 430m. CI top is runnable (P. 275m.)

Falls - Portage 160m.

Banks Lake Ⓐ

Bear River

CII Rapids, run or Portage 45m.

Continuous CI's Portage optional

CII Difficult, 650m. SCOUT FIRST! Good Portage 650m. (joins next portage)

CI-CII Rapids, 825m. run when high or take Portage 825m. or wade & line when shallow conditions prevail.

CI Rapids, 200m. run or wade & line when shallow

Cucumber Creek

Swifts, 30m.

GRAYS LAKE

Portage 120m.

Rocks!

Portage 195m.

Portage 100m.

Very shallow/boggy

Graymud Lake - becomes VERY shallow in summer (after mid-June)

Grays River Detail

Portage 3,575m. to Makobe Lake

Possible beaver dam

Shallow with probable beaver dam

Keep to west shore here

Portage 370m.

Bercole Lake - optional fly-in starting point. Ⓐ

Portage 110m.

Wade 25m. + Beaver dam. Shallow - possible wade. Lift through for 10m.

Lady Evelyn River

Macpherson Lake Ⓐ

The fragrant water lily is found throughout Temagami's many bogs, marshes and weedy bays.

may be best to carry over the rocks along the north side. Cross the next pond and do not pass through the narrow channel to the falls — the portage is located at the sloping bedrock before the channel. There is a good campsite below the falls, across from the portage, and one at the bluff on the side of the falls. The trail begins up a steep, course, gravel path; watch the tree blazes and rock cairns for guidance. Every year I've had to remove scads of fluorescent flagging tape from the trees along this trail. The portage levels out but is quite challenging from here. Spend a little time exploring the falls and bluff viewpoint; swimming and bathing is possible in the many pools in and about the series of rapids and falls here. Be mindful of the put-in at the top of the rapids, as the current is very strong in the early season and can easily draw your canoe and occupants into the maelstrom below. Enter a marshy pond and head north to the right bank portage across from a high bluff rising above a long set of rapids. The portage is mildly difficult but necessary. I've actually run and lined these rapids at various times when going downstream. Paddle up some current found just past the last portage at the bend in the river, and proceed to the rapids and keep right. The only difficult part of this carry is the bouldery landing. In the spring rush these rapids are a wily Class III, runnable by experts only.

Katherine Lake   I knew this lake as Divide Lake, years ago, and I have no idea who Katherine was (maybe Evelyn's sister?). From here up to Macpherson Lake refer to the detail found in Route 2. If you have the time, I highly recommend the climb up Dry Lake Ridge. Base camp at Shangri La and take the four-hour round-trip trek from there.

Grays River   Established in 1985 as a Waterway Provincial Park, along with the Makobe River, the Grays offers one of the best moose-viewing environments in Temagami. Although Graymud Lake becomes annoyingly shallow by summer, the river is generally navigable throughout the paddling season. Still, it is recommended as a spring route. The river starts off in a series of weedy meanders with minor gravel shallows to wade through as marked on the route map. The next two portages are straightforward, and you may want to pull your fly-cast rod out and try your luck for brookies. The river becomes obfuscated by back channels if the north end of the long pond is flooded. There will probably be a beaver dam to lift over and the creek from Bercole shortly after, followed closely by the long portage to Makobe Lake.

Graymud Lake It lives up to its name — at the best of times the channels are barely able to float a canoe. But it is a slow haul (just don't try and race a thunderstorm to the north end). This is an exceptional area in which to see moose that come out to feed on water lily tubers during bug season. The east side of the lake is slightly deeper, so keep right of the islands while heading north. At the north end you may have to pole and jerk the canoe over a section of muskeg. Keep to the far left channel until you come to a short, rock-infested rapid. The portages from here to Grays are well-used and easily located.

Grays Lake There is an excellent campsite on the left shore point, just north of the portage at the south end. The portage into Banks Lake is located at the extreme north end, starts off boggy but pans out into a smooth, dry trail, ending at a campsite.

Banks Lake There are several good places to camp, and the fishing is purported to be quite good. One of my favourite campsites is located at the portage into the Makobe River at the north end. Banks is a popular fly-in start point for three-day trips down the river.

Makobe River From here to Alexander Lake, the river is broken up into sections of easy paddling mixed with CI to CII water play. The river drops 85 m over its short length, offering thirty-four exciting rapids totaling more than 7 km of runnable whitewater. During high water flow, many of the rapids can be cleared easily, but once the levels drop, the amount of wading and lining increases. Portage where marked — there are no other options. One of the nicest campsites is located at the end of the long carry at the first large bend in the river. From here it's an easy paddle to Alexander. I usually pull in at the nice campsite at the northwest shore, make an early camp, and then play in the rapids at the north end. The landscape along the upper river is rugged, beautiful beyond description. The portage from Cooke Lake comes in at the mid-section of Alexander, a popular drive-in, one- or two-day trek down the river. From Alexander Lake it's a veritable roller-coaster ride. To Elk Lake it's an easy one-day paddle, chiefly because almost everything can be run. It is important to follow the route map closely and remember that conditions do vary. Watch carefully for sweepers (downed trees obstructing the navigable channel). Near Elk Lake, pull out on the left side of the rapids located across from the logging mill and portage through the municipal park. This is an excellent CIII play spot when the water is high.

Elk Lake As you enter the Montreal River the first thing you will notice is the murky or heavy turbidity of the water; this is due to the organic residue suspended over a clay river bottom. The Montreal River separates the Little Clay Belt, or farmland region of Lake Temiskamingue (the original spelling), from the typical northern transitional forest to the south.

Montreal River Head south, paying close attention to winds that may whip up while crossing Mountain Lake. There are two campsites located along the southeast shore. Then 2 km downriver from Mountain Lake is Mountain Chutes, a rather hefty CII–CIII rapids. The lodge owner here claims to have taken "many a canoe to the dump," so it is wise to scout before attempting to run this one. It's a volume flow at the top, steep pitch drop to an uncertain and very rocky bottom. Stay left at the top, side slipping to far left and either pull out and carry at the bottom, or be prepared to swing over to the far right at the bottom.

From here back to Mowat Landing it's clear sailing, rather monotonous with few camping possibilities. For a diversion, you may think about taking the Maple Mountain route (Route 14) back to the start point.

Route # 13
Anima Nipissing, Montreal River Loop

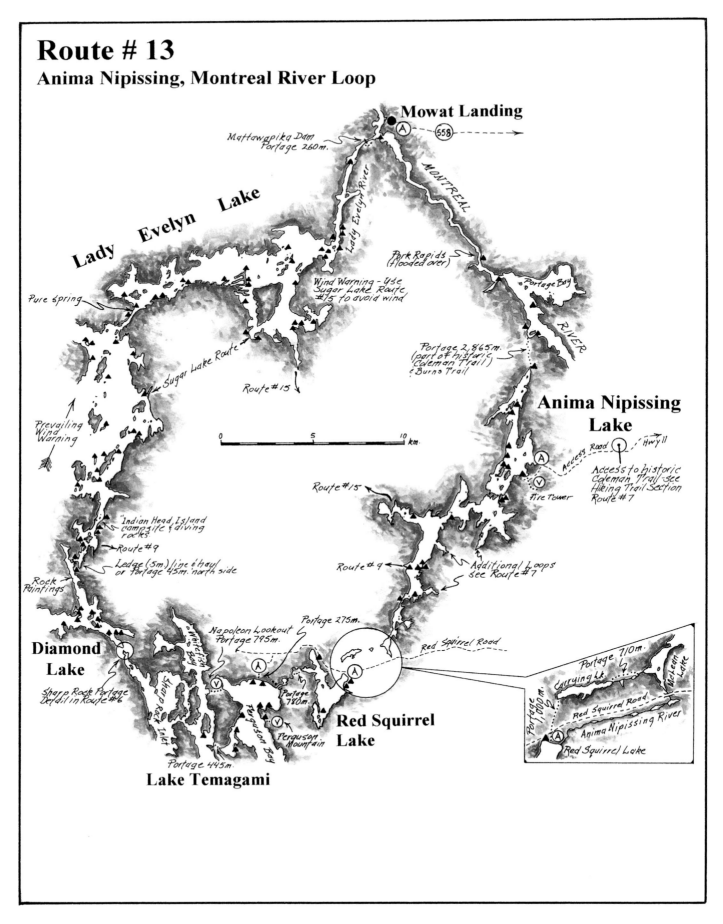

Mowat Landing

Mattawapika Dam
Portage 260m.

Lady Evelyn River

MONTREAL

Pork Rapids
(flooded over)

Lady   Evelyn   Lake

Pure spring

Wind Warning - Use
Sugar Lake Route,
#15 to avoid wind

Portage Bay

RIVER

Sugar Lake Route

Route #15

Portage 2,865m.
(part of historic
Coleman Trail)
& Burns Trail

Anima Nipissing Lake

Prevailing
Wind
Warning

Access Road

Hwy 11

Access to historic
Coleman Trail - see
Hiking Trail Section
Route #7

Fire Tower

Route #15

"Indian Head, Island
campsite & diving
rocks

Route #9

Ledge (.5m.) line & haul
or Portage 45m. north side

Route #9

Additional Loops
see Route #7

Rock
Paintings

Portage 275m.

Napoleon Lookout
Portage 795m.

Red Squirrel Road

Diamond Lake

Whitefish Bay

Portage
780m.

Red Squirrel Road

Red Squirrel Lake

Sharp Rock Portage
Detail in Route #6

Sharp Rock Inlet

Ferguson Bay

Ferguson
Mountain

Portage 445m.

Lake Temagami

Portage 710m.

Carrying Lk.

Mclean Lake

Portage 1,000m.

Red Squirrel Road

Anima Nipissing River

Red Squirrel Lake

0   5   10 km.

ANIMA NIPISSING, MONTREAL RIVER LOOP

This has been a long-time favourite route for first-time Temagami visitors, probably because of its simplicity, guarantee of good campsites, and relatively quiet persona. This route can be taken either way, although you may prefer to do it in a clockwise direction because of prevailing southwest-west winds in the summer, Lady Evelyn Lake being the prime suspect for delays.

CLASSIFICATION novice (one long but easy portage)

DISTANCE 118.5 km

TIME 6–7 days

PORTAGES 7 (total: 5.8 km)

MAPS 41 P/1, 41 P/8, 31 M/4, 31 M/5

FEATURES & ECOLOGY There is a lot of history along this route; the Montreal River makes up a major component of the Native nastawgan network of trails, with both the Lady Evelyn and Anima Nipissing link routes acting as travel corridors to the interior. In the 1830s, as timber supplies dried up along the Ottawa Valley, the company men moved their operations north and began cutting along the Lake Temiskaming shoreline. Forty years later, J. R. Booth purchased limits west of Latchford and used the Montreal River to float logs to the Ottawa. Logs were driven down the Lady Evelyn and Makobe rivers until the 1940s. The ecology adheres to large lake environments with bold, rock-exposed shorescapes. Large gatherings of loons have been seen on the major lakes after the nesting period, usually after July, and there have been frequent sightings of cormorants. The Burns-Coleman Historic Trail gives travelers an excuse to stretch their legs and explore the ecology off the main lake route. Vegetation Site Code: UMF, UDF (Montreal River).

Montreal River Mowat Landing is the staging point for this loop. Plan out your first-day camp so that you at least reach the entrance to the long portage into Anima Nipissing. These will be the only campsites along this stretch of river. Pork Rapids may exhibit a hint of swifts only. There are actually two historic trails, the north one being the most popular. The portage runs uphill at the start and then levels out over open bedrock and scattered jack pine. Hikers can catch the Coleman-Burns Trail at the campsite on the Anima Nipissing end.

Anima Nipissing Lake It was always odd to see an LCBO sign at the small cabin lodge just off the portage, and at such a remote location. Head south on the lake, where you have several side-trip options, including the old fire-tower trail and link routes as described in Route 7. There are many beautiful campsites on the lake and at least three rock-painting locations (pictographs). There is a set of rocky swifts separating Anima Nipissing from McLean Lake. Enter the southwesterly bay and follow a narrow channel up to the portage, lining where necessary. Follow the trail map as indicated to Red Squirrel Lake.

Red Squirrel Lake & Lake Temagami There are several good campsites on Red Squirrel, and you'll likely want to get away from the vicinity of the road. Portage into the Anima Nipissing River over a good trail and paddle out to Sandy Inlet. Camp Wanapitei started as a Jesuit mission and farm operated by Oblate priest Father Paradis in the 1800s. Today it functions as both an adult and youth camp.

Suggested hikes include Ferguson Mountain Trail and viewpoint, or Napoleon Mountain. The Ferguson Trail is accessed through Wanapitei property (please respect that this is private property), following the beach until it enters a winding trail in the bush just south of the old log cabin. Trail guides can be picked up at the lodge. The trail features old-growth pine, lake vistas, old mines and a side-route option. Take either portage out of Sandy Inlet, the south trail being easier but access more difficult if it is windy. Head west through Sharp Rock Inlet and into Diamond Lake to the north (see Route 6).

Diamond Lake Certainly one of my favourite lakes, Diamond has earned a stalwart reputation for surviving the onslaught of human error. Diamond is the site of the short-lived "Fort Destruction," a trading post set up by the Teme augama anishnabe to counter rival trade in the late 1800s. The lake was occupied by traditional families until the early 1940s, when A. J. Murphy, a local logging baron working under the J. R. Booth

Looking up the north arm on Diamond Lake.

licence, built a dam in 1942 in order to facilitate easy booming of logs. The dam flooded out the Native population; Murphy told them that "they had no right to occupy the land." The level has reverted back to normal now, with an easy line over the old falls into Lady Evelyn Lake.

Lady Evelyn Lake The south section of the lake is a veritable paradise, with secluded bays, Bahama-style beaches arcing out from bedrock points, and that desirable Temagami pine landscape. Take in the Maple Mountain hike, tour the north and south channel of the Lady Evelyn River, or take the Sugar Lake route; no matter what you decide to do, the wind will probably be in your favour. The portage around Matawapika Dam skirts Mitchell's Camp and drops you back into the Montreal.

MAPLE MOUNTAIN LOOP

A long-time favourite, this route tantalizes the adventure spirit with a congenial medley of lakes, creeks and river travel. The route may be taken in either direction; however, caution should be employed while traveling the open stretches of Lady Evelyn Lake, as the wind can toss up metre-high waves in a matter of a few minutes.

CLASSIFICATION   experienced novice
   (some difficult portages)

DISTANCE   93 km

TIME   6–7 days

PORTAGES   15 (total: 5.6 km)

MAPS   31 M/5, 41 P/8, 41 P/9

FEATURES & ECOLOGY   Without question, the main feature of this loop is Maple Mountain, and you'll see the crest of the ridge rising above the distant hills to the west as you strike out from Mowat Landing and hit the main body of Lady Evelyn Lake. Walleye fishing is fabulous, campsites are incredible and the variety of landscapes never-ending. Lady Evelyn Lake is a flooded environment, as seen in the deadwood still standing in the shallow bays. This in itself has created nesting sites for swallows and osprey. Moose are quite often seen once you pass through Betty's Hole — the entrance to the Maple Mountain trek northward out of Sucker Gut. Vegetation Site Code: UMF, RB, UDF (Montreal River), AC (creek links).

Lady Evelyn Lake   By now you probably get the idea that wind could be a problem on Lady Evelyn. You could lay up at the narrows and then paddle in the evening and early morning to avoid any delays. It's hard getting out of the wind here, and the shallow nature of this part of the lake can create rather large waves, even in the smaller bays. Once in Sucker Gut Lake, head west through Betty's Hole (known for its good bass fishing) and enter Willow Island Creek. The creek is deep and channeled in the appropriate places. Keep an eye out for kingfisher, golden eagle, merlin and osprey.

Hobart Lake   There are few views like the one from the campsite on the east shore of Hobart Lake, overlooking Maple Mountain rising over 350 m, its impressive stature embracing the sky with bold dignity. Other campsites are quite good, but remember that this particular area gets a lot of traffic in the summer, so pitch your tents early in the day and do the hike in the afternoon.

Tupper Lake   Tupper Lake is accessed via the creek north of Hobart, swinging west into Tupper Creek, and wending your way along to open water without too much difficulty. During periods of drought, Tupper Creek does become extremely shallow, necessitating several liftovers; the landing at the southwest end of Tupper also becomes a quagmire by late summer. The remains of the original rangers' cabin can be seen here. There is a pure spring located about 50 m due east of the cabin. The spring at the top of the mountain is seldom palatable, so you must either hike in your water or purify the water from the upper spring. Many paddlers opt to camp at the top, and I must admit, having camped out in the tower on two occasions (once during a rather nasty storm), I do recommend taking a tent instead. Follow the route as indicated on the map and expect to take at least three hours round trip to complete. The top was burned off many decades ago by the ranger's children playing with matches near a fuel barrel. Since then the blueberries have grown in unbelievable quantity and richness. Chee bay jing, or "Ghost Mountain," was an ancient burial ground for local Anishnabe. The mountain is a sacred place, so act accordingly. An offering of tobacco is suggested once you reach the top.

Route Continuation   Exit Willow Island Creek at the south end of Bill Lake and watch the rocks just below the surface there. Proceed to the northwest end and paddle up the creek for about 250 m through a marsh. The portage landing is on the left (west) bank. The trail is smooth and brings you out to Bessie Lake (Bill's mistress). Paddle to the north end and keep to the east side of the creek for the next portage. This rocky trail bypasses a rock-strewn rapid and brings you out to a small bay at Inez Lake (Bill's wife). Cross Inez (like Bill did), keeping west of the narrow bay, and find the portage into Anvil Lake (where it happened).

Route # 14
Maple Mountain Loop

Big Spring Lake

Montreal

Spray Creek: conditions vary with beaver activity - expect liftovers at beaver dams or flooded main channels.

Usual beaver dam locations

Portage 180m.

River

Mowat Landing

Lodge

Skull Lake
Portage 75m.
Little Skull Lake
Portage 775m.

Greenwater Lake

Mendelssohn Lake

Portage 85m.

Cooke Lake Road from Elk Lake

Portage 95m.

Portage 2,275m.

Portage 410m.

Holden Lake

Lockie Lake
Portage 230m.

Moccasin Lake

One of few wild rice beds in the Temagami area.

Mattawapika dam

Portage 260m.

Skull Lake

Willow Island

Niccolite Lake

Portage 90m.
Portage 80m.

Prospector's Cave

Bergeron Lake

Walleye off points

Pike fishing

N

Prospector's dave
Portage 805m.

Liftover rocks 30m.
Wade shallows 35m.
Liftover rapids 30m.
Portage 25m. over rocks
Portage 70m.

Beaver dam?

Creek

Wind Warning! Use Sugar Lake Route as option.

Trail to Argentium Silver Mine camp at Duncanson Lake

Hammer Lake

Anvil Lake

Esker formation

Portage 185m. Depression lake (brook trout)

Anvil Lake

Lady Sydney Lake

Portage 520m.

Lady Evelyn Lake

Walleye

Mountain

Portage 135m.

Inem Lake
Portage 385m.

Forestry Island -old Ranger base-

Pure Spring

Sugar Lake Route

Bessie Lake
Portage 400m.

Old Bill Lake

Beaver dam

Watch for moose here

0   2   4   6 km.

Tupper Lake

Hobart Lake

Maple

Hiking trail 1.5 hours 1 way.

Walleye

Ten camp sites through Sucker Gut narrows.

Wind Warning!

Rocky narrows -deep channel on west side

Sucker Gut Lake

Betty's Hole (Bass)

Alternate route to Lady Evelyn River via creek - paddle, haul by rope & liftover

Chris Willis's Lake

Side excursion to Center Falls via Route #12

Approaching Chee-bay-jing, (Maple Mountain). There are over 2 dozen ridge viewpoints in Temagami.

Anvil Lake   The rugged hills and Maple Mountain backdrop make Anvil a prime camping stopover. You also have the opportunity to hike along the old dirt track to the Argentium Silver Mine at Duncanson Lake. Campsites are superb, replete with sand beaches or rocky ledges, perfect for lounging or swimming. The creek and fen area, located over a beaver dam in the east central bay, is prime for wildlife viewing. Continue north and stay west of the island at the top of Anvil and enter a small channel to Hammer Lake (what Inez took to Bill's head). Slide by on the east side of Hammer, not even entering the lake, and follow the creek upstream until you hit a series of log liftovers and gravel shallows, where wading is required. You will eventually come to a jammed part of the creek where you'll locate a short trail along the east bank that brings you out to an old bridge crossing. Just upstream there is a gravel shallows and then rocky rapids, which can be bypassed by carrying over the river rocks. A short paddle then brings you to other rocky rapids and a possible beaver dam. Lift over these obstructions. There are two more minor obstructions before entering an L-shaped pond. Follow the creek upstream past a

small creek coming in from Bergeron Lake to the next portage (north bank). This trail is smooth, and when you reach the end, look for the old mine shaft just off the trail end.

Bergeron Lake   Pine-clad, rock-rimmed and postcard perfect, Bergeron epitomizes Temagami, and that's probably why there are so many campsites here. Proceed north to the narrows, where you will come to the remains of an old log dam with just enough room to squeeze a canoe through (watch the rocks here). Shortly past here, on the east shore below the creek, is a good trail to a small lily pond. On the east bank you'll find another prospecting cave filled with water. The old route used to follow the creek north into Niccolite, but now crosses over to the lake from the north end of the lily pond, just up the creek.

Niccolite Lake   Niccolite, like Bergeron, boasts of fine campsites and secluded magic. The nicest site is located on the island, and the other two are on the west shore across from the island. The next easy portage is located west of the creek (left side) at the north end of Niccolite. Keep to the east shore of Lockie Lake and skirt a floating pitcher-plant bog. Go to the north end, and if the water levels allow, there is a channel you can push up to get into the portage at the far east bank. This trail begins at the boggy end of Lockie and traces a mostly smooth path to the marshy south shore of Holden Lake. At the north end of Holden, east of the creek, you'll see the next portage into Greenwater Lake.

Greenwater Lake There are two good campsites here: the south point site is somewhat exposed to the elements and the east shore site sits in a very nice stand of pine. Proceed to the northwest end of the lake to the portage into Little Skull Lake. This trail is quite bony and owns three minor wet spots along the way. The Willow Island Creek (spring route) begins in Little Skull, as indicated on the map. Head to the north end of Little Skull and find the next portage, located above the creek. This will take you out to Skull Lake.

"Maple Murphy,"
caretaker of the Argentium Silver Mine
located near Anvil Lake.

may pose a problem getting out to deep water. Canoeists generally lay logs out across the muck to make things a bit easier.

Mendelssohn Lake Surrounded by high hills, this pretty lake demands some attention. There are two excellent campsites on the west shore peninsula and an old prospecting cave behind the north site. Fishing for bass and lake trout is still reasonably good. Paddle to the north end of the lake and enter Spray Creek.

Spray Creek About 500 m along the creek you'll stop at a logjam and shallow rapids. Carry over on the east side of the creek. Downstream you will come to several beaver dams that may vary in location and cause the creek to flood, making it a bit confusing as to where the main channel is located.

Skull Lake There is an alternate access to this route via the Cooke Lake Road from Elk Lake, located at the campsite at the north end. The portage to Mendelssohn Lake is easily located on the east central shore. The start of the trail heads uphill and is quite bouldery; from here it levels out over gently rolling terrain then drops suddenly to a small spring about halfway along. The creek water is cool and refreshing — a good place to stop and rest. There is a boggy stretch for 100 m past the spring. The trail descends abruptly in sections and is very strenuous if you are traveling west. About 200 m near the east end of the portage, you must cross a small stream before coming to a marshy bay at Mendelssohn Lake. If water levels are low, this landing

Beyond here the creek is deep and easily navigated. The creek widens out to a large marsh and small pond; stay east of the pond and lift over one or two more beaver dams before reaching Big Spring Lake. This is a wonderful marsh environment, where moose sightings are frequent.

Big Spring Lake Paddle into the Montreal River and head southeast, back towards Mowat Landing. Gauge your campsites according to distance, as there is only one rather poor site located on the north shore of the narrows at Indian Lake.

Maple Mountain
Chee-bay-jing "Ghost Mountain"

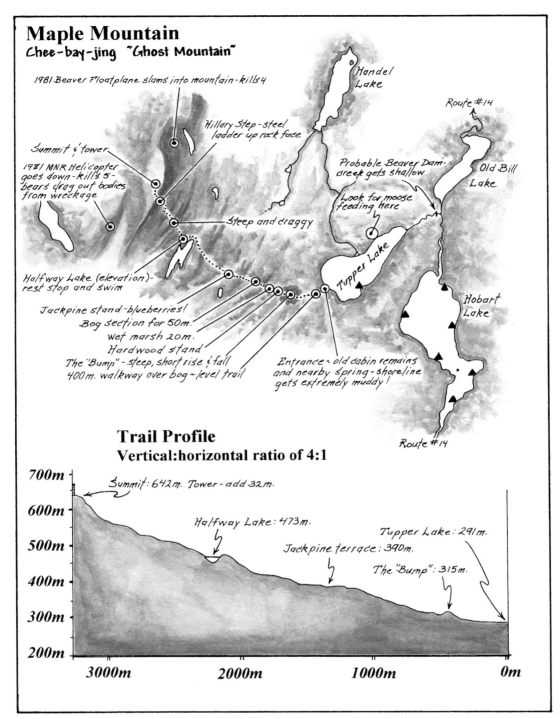

1981 Beaver Floatplane slams into mountain-kills 4

Hillary Step - steel ladder up rock face

Summit & tower

1981 MNR Helicopter goes down - kills 5 - bears drag out bodies from wreckage

Steep and craggy

Halfway Lake (elevation) - rest stop and swim

Jackpine stand - blueberries!

Bog section for 50m.

Wet marsh 20m.

Hardwood stand

The "Bump" - steep, short rise & fall

400m. walkway over bog ~ level trail

Entrance ~ old cabin remains and nearby spring - shoreline gets extremely muddy!

Handel Lake

Route #14

Probable Beaver Dam - creek gets shallow

Old Bill Lake

Look for moose feeding here

Tupper Lake

Hobart Lake

Route #14

Trail Profile
Vertical:horizontal ratio of 4:1

Summit: 642m. Tower - add 32m.

Halfway Lake: 473m.

Tupper Lake: 291m.

Jackpine terrace: 390m.

The "Bump": 315m.

700m · 600m · 500m · 400m · 300m · 200m

3000m · 2000m · 1000m · 0m

Note: distance from Tupper to summit calculated by straight-line configuration – not actual ground measurement. True walking distance is 4.3 kilometers, one way.

ROUTE 15

SUGAR LAKE *and* MUSKEGO RIVER LINK

This pocket of link routes is quite exceptional. Isolated, yet easy to get to, and you have that feeling of solitude without really working that hard to get there. The Sugar Lake route is used frequently by canoeists who want a diversion from the immensity of Lady Evelyn Lake. Whether you're ducking high winds or peak motorboat season, Sugar is well worth the portaging, and the fishing is great. This route can be taken either way, but the write-up follows a west-to-east direction. The following information pertains to the Sugar Loop link only.

CLASSIFICATION experienced novice
   (one long portage)
DISTANCE 12.8 km
TIME 1–2 days
PORTAGES 7 (total: 3 km)
MAPS 41 P/8 (Sugar Lake), 31 M/5 (Muskego)
FEATURES & ECOLOGY Primarily, this grouping of four lakes is typical of the rock and pine setting that is the hallmark of the Temagami experience. Deep, clear water, large bedrock-based campsites and transitional boreal forest are featured here. Vegetation Site Code: UMF, AC, MM (Muskego River).

Lady Evelyn Lake The south section of Lady Evelyn is a camper's paradise. If you have a couple of extra days then I'd definitely put them to optimum use. Depart from Lady Evelyn just north of Snake Point and enter the narrow channel into a marsh filled with cattails. Where the channel narrows, just before it bends to the left, there is a shallow, rocky section before the portage. This trail bypasses the log-filled stream on the left bank and comes out to a long, narrow pond. There is an alternate trail (1,295 m) to Goodfish Lake. The pond you are now in is quite picturesque, surrounded by low hills clad in a lush covering of red and white pine. At the end of the pond, on the left side of the creek, is a good trail to the next small lake. This is a lovely little spot with a campsite to match. The Sugar Lake portage is located at the extreme north end along a rocky shoreline. The trail is also filled with boulders. As you

continue on the creek, just after the portage, you will probably have to wade or line the canoe through a cut channel in order to gain access to the pond. Cross the pond to a narrows and navigate through the next rocky section of creek. During low-water periods you'll have to get out and wade.

Sugar Lake There are two campsites in the west bay and two large, excellent sites at the central narrows. There is also one small campsite located before the long portage in the northeast bay on the north shore. From the west end of Sugar, you can paddle directly across and portage into Lady Evelyn Lake and on to Mowat Landing, or take in some fine fishing and swimming on Goodfish and Angler. At the extreme northeast end of Sugar, you'll locate the Angler portage found on the right side of the creek. This will bring you out to a small bay, usually flooded by beaver.

Angler Lake From here you have to manoeuvre through a narrow channel of rocks and deadfalls before reaching the main body of the lake. There are several nice campsites on the lake; my favourite is located in the west bay. The Ontario government had this lake posted as a "dead" lake, in light of the lack of fish due to acidification in the late 1970s. However, the Angler has always been one of the better smallmouth bass lakes in the district, contrary to Ontario Ministry of Natural Resources' findings. Paddle to the far end of Angler for the next portage. In the narrows you'll likely have to lift over a beaver dam into a small pond. The trail is located at the south end of this pond.

Goodfish Lake This is a pretty lake and demands at least a bit of your time (a swim off the campsite before the portage). At the end of the southeast bay you'll see the easy trail back to Sugar.

Lady Evelyn Portage The trail leaving Sugar is located at the northeast end of the lake through a rocky inlet. The beginning of the trail (500 m) travels over open bedrock covered in sedge and blueberry bushes. It then drops down a steep bank, levels off over a few rocky sections and minor wet spots, and ends in a bay beside an old lumber camp. From here it is a half-day paddle back to Mowat Landing.

Route # 15
Sugar Lake, Muskego River Links

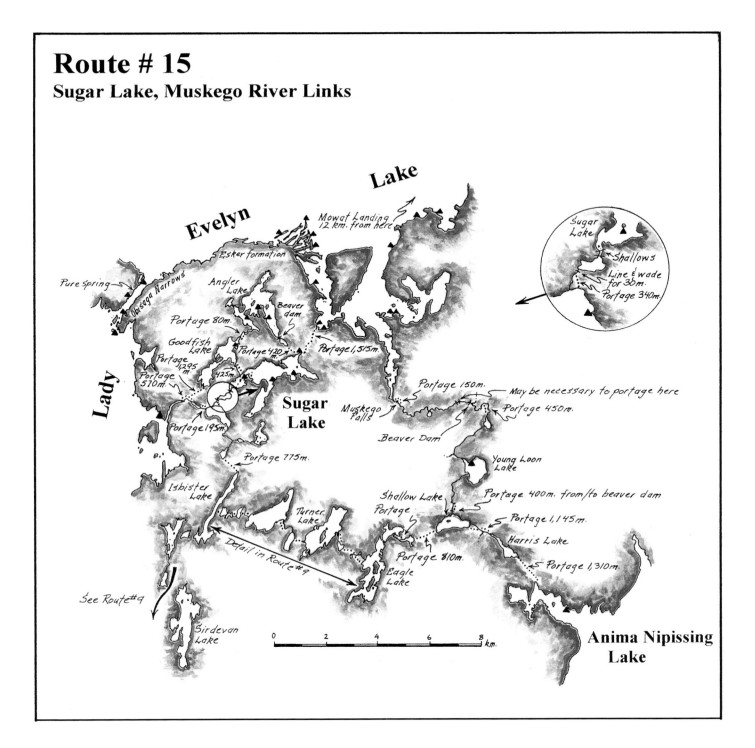

Muskego River Route This 17km diversion is a two-day trek and link to Anima Nipissing Lake. The route follows an old nastawgan route. There is a pretty waterfall as you first enter the river. Beyond the falls, the level of the river depends upon and fluctuates with beaver activity. That means relatively good travel for most of the season, because wildlife abounds along this route. The trails are marked and cleared, with one good campsite located on the north point of Young Loon Lake.

Isbister Route Link These are old nastawgan routes that have not been cleared recently but offer new challenges to those who want to get off the prescribed mainstream routes. Creek travel is best done in the early season when water levels allow. This applies to the creeks adjoining the route to the north end of Isbister. Once in Isbister, there are no seasonal variations — just hoofing over portage links. Good luck!

ROUTE 16

GOWGANDA to ELK LAKE ROUTE

Within the Kirkland Lake District, or northern region of the Temagami backcountry, there are routes contiguous with the original nastawgan Native system of trails, namely the Montreal River Route. Because of the length of the Montreal River, it is broken up into five sections (from its source waters at Smoothwater Lake, the routes are 18, 16, 14, 13 and 25). As an independent route not adjoined to another route as a link, Route 16 remains the most popular section of the river. Adding Route 17 to this route is an excellent option. An alternate start point could also be Route 18 near the source, or add Route 14 to the end of the trip. Shuttles can be arranged with local outfitters.

CLASSIFICATION experienced novice

DISTANCE 87.6 km

TIME 4–5 days

PORTAGES 11 (total 4 km)

MAPS 41 P/9, 41 P/10, 41 P/15, 41 P/16

FEATURES & ECOLOGY Although you may find moderate motorboat traffic on a few of the route lakes, it does not detract from the pristine nature of the experience. The Montreal River corridor exhibits a fairly recent forest of jack pine over predominant rock-terrace geology. There is some easy whitewater to deal with and good trails around all sets for those who want to avoid them entirely. Fishing is good and campsites are plentiful throughout the route. Under the Living Legacy Program, this portion of the Montreal River has been introduced into the Waterway Park system. Vegetation Site Code: UCF (Upper Montreal River), UDF (Lower Montreal River).

Continuation of Route 18 from Gowganda Lake Proceed past Outlook Point to Highway 560 where it skirts Outlet Bay. Do not try and take the river through the dam route, as there are continuous rapids to Burk Lake. Portage along the highway to the Edith Lake Access Road and take the first bush road left to Burk Lake. Option: If you are starting your trip here, then take the Edith Lake Access Road off Highway 560, 2 km to Edith Lake public access. This avoids the 165 m

carry between Burk and Edith. Paddle to the northwest outlet of Edith Lake and portage 155 m around a small falls into Obushkong Lake.

Obushkong Lake A rugged and ragged topography of low hills crested with wind-moulded jack pine and deep marshy bays. The north end of the lake can become very shallow, requiring deft manoeuvring through areas of muskeg. Heading north on the Montreal River you'll notice a campsite just past a group of islands; 1 km farther on there is an obstructed narrows where another very good campsite is located. Portage just west of the river outlet to Crotch Lake.

Crotch Lake There are two good campsites on Crotch, one at the portage on the north extremity, the other located about 500 m from the south end on the east shore. Before attempting to run the rapids at the north end, check the status of the log dam, otherwise take the portage to the narrows. Following the portage, about 100 m of swifts that pose no problem for navigation. On the far side of the small pond, the river can be partly run or portaged, depending on water flow. The first rapids may have to be lined at the end, but the final two sets can be run. The portage on the east bank follows a good trail. Shortly past the portage you'll see a campsite on a small jut of land. Paddle about 1 km but be cautious; there is a small falls coming up. Take the rocky trail (right of the outlet) into Tommy Lake.

Tommy Lake The best two campsites are located on the north end, one on an island, the other at the start of the next portage trail. The campsite at the portage sits left of a picturesque falls and chute. The actual trail skirts the campsite and takes you to a narrow channel of the river. Shortly past the portage is a short rapid that can be run keeping left, taking you into a pond. In the narrows at the north end you'll spin down 100 m of swifts (stay centre).

Sisseny Lake Past the rugged beauty of the narrows you'll notice a slight change in scenery. Gravel beaches, birch and scattered pine have replaced the granite shorescapes and back cover of jack pine. There are two excellent campsites here, one at the north end of the large island replete with level, stony beach, while the other site is nestled in the jack pines at the narrows on the north end of the lake. Continuing on to the far north

Route # 16
Gowganda to Elk Lake Route (Montreal River)

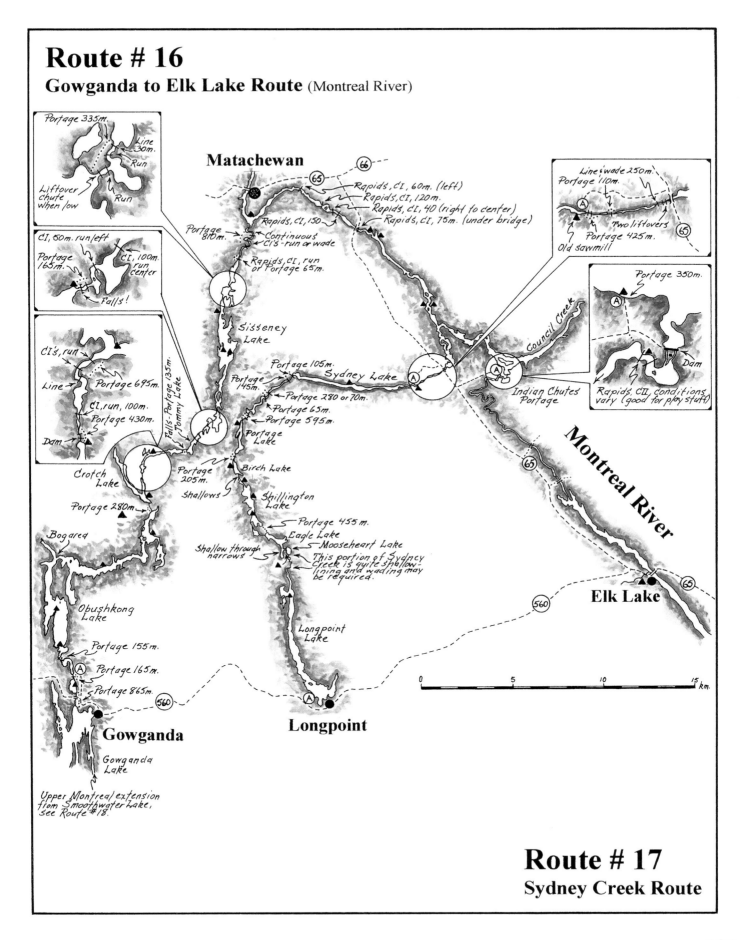

Matachewan

Portage 335m.
Line 30m.
Run
Liftover chute when low
Run

CI, 50m. run left
Portage 165m.
CI, 100m. run center
Falls!

CI's, run
Line
Portage 695m.
CI, run, 100m.
Portage 430m.
Dam

Crotch Lake

Portage 280m.

Bog area

Obushkong Lake

Portage 155m.
Ⓐ Portage 165m.
Portage 865m.
560

Gowganda

Gowganda Lake

Upper Montreal extension from Smoothwater Lake, see Route #18.

66
65
Rapids, CI, 60m. (left)
Rapids, CI, 120m.
Rapids, CI, 40 (right to center)
Rapids, CI, 150
Rapids, CI, 75m. (under bridge)
Portage 810m.
Continuous CI's - run or wade
Rapids, CI, run or Portage 65m.

Sisseney Lake

Falls - Portage 135m.
Tommy Lake

Portage 105m.
Portage 145m.
Sydney Lake
Portage 280 or 70m.
Portage 65m.
Portage 595m.
Portage Lake
Portage 205m.
Shallows
Birch Lake
Shillington Lake

Portage 455m.
Eagle Lake
Mooseheart Lake
Shallow through narrows
This portion of Sydney Creek is quite shallow-lining and wading may be required.

Longpoint Lake

Ⓐ
Longpoint

Council Creek

Montreal River

Ⓐ
Indian Chutes Portage
Ⓐ

65
560

▲●
Elk Lake
65

Line & wade 250m.
Portage 110m.
Ⓐ
▲
Two liftovers
65
Portage 425m.
Old sawmill

Portage 350m.
Ⓐ
▲
Dam
Rapids, CII, conditions vary (good for play stuff)

0   5   10   15 km.

Route # 17
Sydney Creek Route

end, take the portage (left of the outlet) out of Sisseny Lake. The rapids here can be run when the water levels allow. Scout first, as there used to be a log chute here with protruding iron stakes. There is a short rapid at the north end of the small lake. This can be run if you keep to the right near the end; if you have doubts then take the left-bank portage. The next narrows is very shallow up to the portage, just before the river bends eastward. It's a good trail, long but avoids about ten sets of very shallow rapids. These can be run during high water without any trouble, but in the summer you may have to walk the canoe through. The river is shallow out to the forks of the Montreal. If supplies are needed, Matachewan is only a short distance up the West Montreal. There is a good campsite on the north shore of the forks and a road into town.

Montreal River Continue southeastward to the first set of rapids; these are easily run if you stay on the left. The rapids following are shallow but can also be run without trouble. Shortly after, you will come to the next shallow rapids, which can be run keeping slightly right of centre. The next set is technical, running to the left (east) side of a small island. There is a sharp swing right at the bottom. A scenic bluff runs along the left side of the river here. The next set of rapids, under the Highway 65 bridge, is easily run. Two campsites are located on the north bank, about 1 km past the bridge. About 5 km past these sites you'll find two more grassy camping areas, about 1 km south of the junction of the Sydney Creek route.

Indian Chutes Continue southeast, about 5 km to the dam and power house. Here you can portage along the west side of the dam to the narrow section of the Montreal River. Elk Lake village is an easy cruise, with strong current to assist. If you paddle up the Makobe River for about 1 km, you will find the only camping available, at the municipal park.

ROUTE 17

SYDNEY CREEK ROUTE

This route can be taken in either direction. Shuttles can be arranged locally if you parked your vehicle in Gowganda or the Montreal River access (Beauty Lake Road). As a weekend jaunt, this route is perfect; it's just a matter of leaving one vehicle at the Sydney Lake public access point or at Longpoint Lodge and a relatively short drive back to retrieve the second vehicle. Or arrange a shuttle drop at Longpoint.

CLASSIFICATION Experienced novice

DISTANCE 39.2 km

TIME 2–3 days

PORTAGES 9 (total 2.2 km)

MAPS 41 P/9, 41 P/10, 41 P/15, 41 P/16

FEATURES & ECOLOGY Think of this route as a jeweled necklace — sparkling clear lakes joined together by one common riverlet. Be prepared to be confronted by curious otters, circled overhead by osprey, dive-bombed by herring gulls guarding their nests, or serenaded, as you sit by your campfire, by an ensemble of howling wolves. The only negative feature is that it only lasts for two days. Vegetation Site Code: UDF.

Starting at Longpoint Lake (downstream) You can put in at the public access and parking area located west of the lodge at Longpoint. Camping is limited to one site only, and that's tucked away at the north end on the west shore. Paddle north into the narrows. If the water is low, there is a section that may require wading or lining for about 1 km (off and on) before entering Mooseheart Lake. There is one small campsite on the east shore of the peninsula in the centre of the lake. Through the peninsula is a gravel shallows that may require some wading. Continue north through a tight, very shallow, sand-bottomed channel to Eagle Lake.

Eagle Lake Eagle acquired its name from the eagle nests perched high on the northeast shore bluffs. Do not attempt to take the creek at the northwest end of Eagle, as there are too many obstructions to make it worthwhile. The trail is steep at both ends but levels out between the grunts.

Shillington Lake Paddle through the north end narrows to two short, easily run or lined rapids. This will bring you out to Birch Lake, where there is an excellent campsite located at the northwest end. Paddle through the small north bay of Birch to a good trail located along the west bank of the creek. This brings you to Portage Lake.

Portage Lake Proceed north about 1.5 km and you will notice a rough campsite on the west bank before the next portage. The trail is relatively easy and comes out to a wide section of the creek. From here on, keep a look out for river otters. About 1 km farther on is a short section of fast water that can be run when water levels allow; otherwise, take the portage along the west bank. Soon enough you'll come to another section of rapids and swifts. The portage is located on the west bank. If the water is high, you can portage 70 m then run the last section of swifts. The total portage length going in the upstream direction is 280 m. Continuing on, after the swifts is a marsh area. Watch for heron, bittern, goldeneye duck and moose. Where the creek narrows, there is a small falls and a good portage skirting it. Shortly after the falls is a short, rock-strewn rapid. This should not be run. Portage on the west bank over a rocky trail to the west end of Sydney Lake.

Sydney Lake Halfway across Sydney Lake on the north shore is a quaint little campsite, large enough for one or two tents. Sydney Lake is quite picturesque with its cedar-lined shores and intimate nature, more typical of a river environment and landscape. Proceed east until you come to an old sawmill site on the south shore. There is unlimited camping here. Across the creek is the public access point where you may decide to leave your vehicle. At this point you cannot take the creek. Portage over the rocks along the south bank and cross over a grassy clearing. You will see an old bridge and logjam over the creek. The trail from here follows rocky terrain 425 m, bypassing several shallow rapids and log obstructions. Paddle a short distance to the next portage that skirts a rock-infested rapids. Carry on the north side over good ground as far as an exposed bedrock beach. From here it is good paddling for over 1 km. Thick cedar lines the shores — a good place for a barred owl to peer out from as you paddle by. Before reaching Highway 65, there are steep-pitched, rocky rapids for about 250 m. These must be lined or tracked and waded through, a rather tedious set as there is no clear channel and it's difficult in high water when the shoreline is flooded. Shortly past the rapids there are two liftovers before paddling under the bridge at the highway. Heading out to connect to Route 16 to Elk Lake is an easy paddle.

Route # 18
Smoothwater Lake to Gowganda Route (Montreal River)

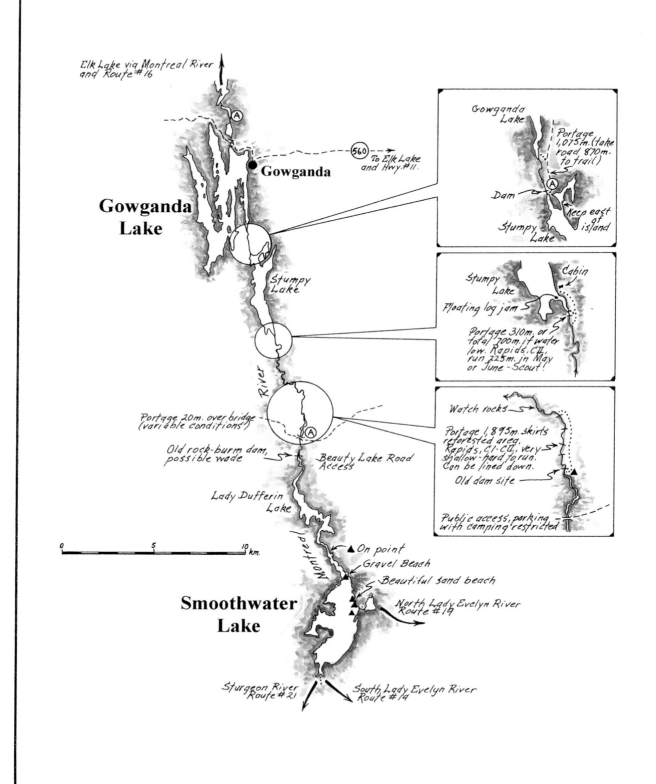

Elk Lake via Montreal River and Route #16

Gowganda

560 → To Elk Lake and Hwy. #11.

Gowganda Lake

Stumpy Lake

River

Portage 20m. over bridge (variable conditions)

Old rock-burm dam, possible wade

Beauty Lake Road Access

Lady Dufferin Lake

Montreal

On point

Gravel Beach

Beautiful sand beach

North Lady Evelyn River Route #19

Smoothwater Lake

0   5   10 km.

Sturgeon River Route #21

South Lady Evelyn River Route #14

Gowganda Lake

Portage 1,075m. (take road 870m. to trail)

Dam

Keep east of island

Stumpy Lake

Stumpy Lake

Cabin

Floating log jam

Portage 310m, or total 700m. if water low. Rapids, CII, run 225m. in May or June - Scout!

Watch rocks

Portage 1,895m. skirts reforested area. Rapids, CI-CII, very shallow - hard to run. Can be lined down.

Old dam site

Public access, parking with camping restricted

Smoothwater Lake to Gowganda (Montreal River)

This is used primarily as a link route for other routes. This write-up follows the river north, downstream on the Montreal River. Access to this route can be made from the town of Gowganda, the bush road to the dam at the north end of Stumpy, or the Montreal River access on the Beauty Lake Road.

CLASSIFICATION experienced novice (2 long portages)

DISTANCE 32 km

TIME 2 days

PORTAGES 3 (total 3 km)

MAPS 41 P/7, 41 P/10

FEATURES & ECOLOGY The upper Montreal from Lady Dufferin to Gowganda passes through a huge boreal swamp. Moose can frequently be seen feeding offshore during the late spring and early summer in an attempt to rid themselves of pesky biting insects. At this point, the river resembles a large creek, meandering through thickets of alder, tamarack and cedar. Vegetation Site Code: SM, AC, TS, UMF.

Smoothwater Lake Assuming that you may be accessing the Montreal from points south (Lady Evelyn River), the route starts at the north end of Smoothwater Lake. There are two campsites at the north end of the lake; however, you've probably just come from the fabulous beach sites near Marina Lake portage. Entering Lady Dufferin Lake, you will find it quite weedy through the shallow narrows. The private cabin on the lake was built in the early 1900s during the height of the logging era and used as a corporate getaway and, as rumour goes, it was somewhat of a bordello for the pleasure of entertaining clients. The only campsite is located 1.5 km downstream at a grassy clearing on the east bank. An old camboose camp (logging camp) was perched here (look for the old barge pulled up from the river edge).

Montreal River This portion of river can get shallow, and moose seem to congregate here throughout the summer. You may have to hump over an old rock and crib dam as you near the public access point. Depending on the state of the bridge and height of water, you may have to make a short lift to get around it. About 1.5 km downstream, where the river narrows, you will come to the site of another decrepit dam. There is a portage starting here on the right bank. The trail has a couple of steep sections, minor wet spots and occasional blow-downs. The shallow rapids can be carefully navigated by creative play, careful wading and lining — a fair bit of work but pleasurable on a hot day. Passing the portage there are some submerged rocks to watch in low water. From here, the paddling is unrestricted as far as the portage into Stumpy Lake. The rapids running into the south end of Stumpy can be run when water levels permit. There is a good trail here and an excellent campsite. At one time, floating logs hindered access at the end of the trail; if this is the case then you may have to carry around them.

Stumpy Lake Paddling to the north end of Stumpy you will come to a public access point. The road is your portage for 870 m until you see a trail off to the left that takes you down to Gowganda Lake. Head north about 3.5 km to the town site or continue on to Route 16. There is access to Hangingstone Lake over a good portage around the dam. This lake derives its name from a huge boulder that hangs precariously on its edge.

SMOOTHWATER LAKE, LADY EVELYN RIVER LOOP

There are two sections that are navigable in the early spring only: from Isabel (Beauty) Lake south to Gamble, following the connecting creeks (upper Lady Evelyn River), where portages are generally in poor shape; and the South Lady Evelyn River from Whitemud Lake to Florence River.

All other sections are navigable throughout the paddling season. There are several ways to build onto this route by adding the Makobe Lake loop, or parking or shuttling vehicles at the prescribed access points and doing a straight run back to your selected end point. The most popular choice of route would be to loop from the Montreal River access point, north of Lady Dufferin Lake (Smoothwater to Lady Evelyn River to Sunnywater and return).

CLASSIFICATION   experienced novice to intermediate

DISTANCE   87.2 km (Isabel as start and end point)

TIME   7–9 days

PORTAGES   20

(you don't want to know the total distance)

MAPS   41 P/7, 41 P/8, 41 P/10

FEATURES & ECOLOGY   I can't say enough about this region of Temagami. If you want challenge, grit and sweat and get-down honest canoe tripping, then this route is exactly what you are looking for. Spring is prime time, and you won't be disappointed. Just make sure you've brought along extra film for your camera. The beach on Smoothwater rivals any you might find in the West Indies; you can see to a depth of 30 m in Sunnywater Lake, or tour back to the original Aurora trout lakes — the only species of its kind in the world. Smoothwater Lake was the place of world rebirth in Anishnabe legend, and artifacts found in the area date back at least 5,000 years. It's an ancient land that best typifies the magic and spirit of the Temagami backcountry. Vegetation Site Code: UMF, SM, AC.

Isabel (Beauty) Lake   For those adventuresome souls with a death wish, I've included the write-up from Isabel Lake. There is an access launch 1 km south of

the road junction, located in the northeast bay of Beauty. At the south end of the lake, take the easy trail into a small lake. If water levels allow, take the river outlet and lift over where necessary. There is a fair trail that skirts the river along the east side and brings you to Paddle Lake.

Paddle Lake   The best route out of Paddle is the river. The river is very shallow but passable using a variety of techniques to get through.

Carmen Lake   There is no portage from Carmen to Gooseneck. Enter a small bay at the southwest end of Carmen and follow the river for about 1.5 km into Gooseneck Lake. After break-up the river is easily navigated but quickly becomes shallow as the season progresses. Beaver dams, fallen timber and rocky shallows can impede your way. Persevere. Follow Gooseneck to the south-end outlet and paddle about 350 m along the river into Kaa Lake. There is a portage at the south end of Gooseneck to Kaa, but it is generally unmaintained.

Kaa Lake   On the east central shore, camping is possible on a point or on the roadside. The river south of Kaa is broken several times by the road. The first bridge is about 500 m downriver, where you'll have to make a short liftover. The second low bridge is right after the first. Portage from here up the road and you'll see a good campsite by a pretty chute on the right side. Because of the many obstructions in the river, it is best to continue on the road as far as the last meander, just before a small pond. Paddle across the pond, watching out for rocks in the narrows, to the next pond. There is a rough campsite on the east side of the narrows. Enter the river at the south end of the pond but watch carefully for the portage landing along the west bank (may be overgrown). The landing passes over shore boulders to a trail that can be found directly across the road. If you've hit the next bridge then you've gone about 100 m too far. Back up. The trail is strenuous but not difficult to follow. This brings you out to a small, narrow pond.

Kaa Lake option   As a diversion, you can enter the southwest bay of Kaa and take the scenic route south to Wabun Lake. The portages are easily located but moderately difficult.

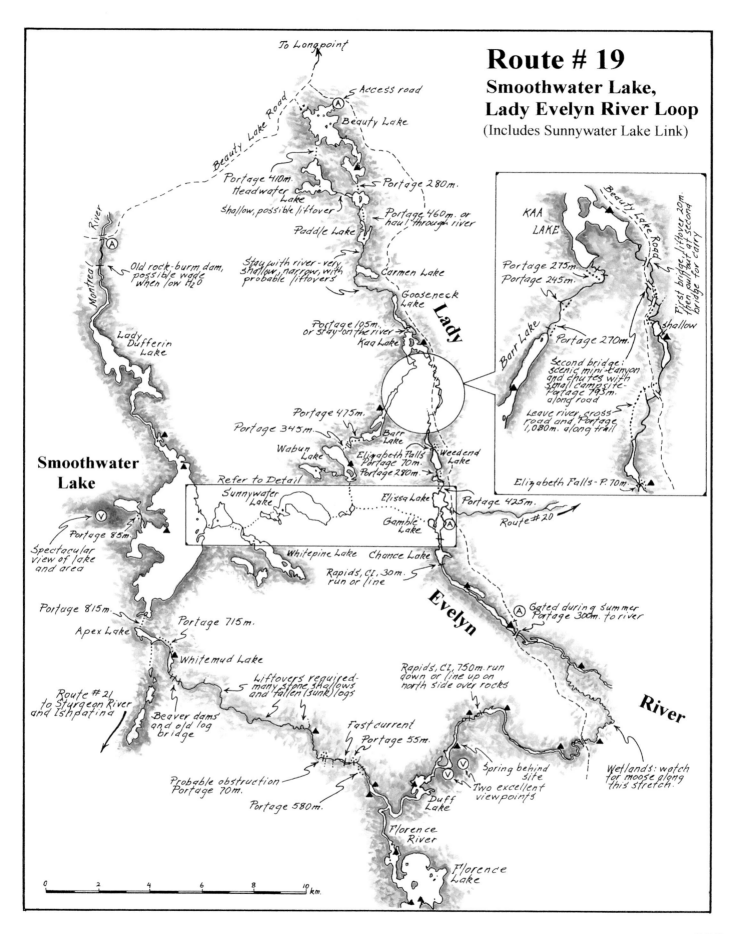

Route # 19
Smoothwater Lake, Lady Evelyn River Loop
(Includes Sunnywater Lake Link)

To Longpoint

Access road

Beauty Lake

Beauty Lake Road

Portage 410m.
Headwater Lake
Shallow, possible liftover

Portage 280m.

Portage 460m. or haul through river

Paddle Lake

Stay with river - very shallow, narrow, with probable liftovers

Carmen Lake

Montreal River

Old rock-burm dam, possible wade when low H₂O

Gooseneck Lake

Lady Dufferin Lake

Portage 195m. or stay on the river

Kaa Lake

Lady

Portage 475m.

Portage 345m.

Barr Lake

Wabun Lake

Elizabeth Falls Portage 70m.
Portage 280m.

Weedend Lake

Smoothwater Lake

Refer to Detail

Sunnywater Lake

Elissa Lake

Portage 425m.

Portage 85m.

Spectacular view of lake and area

Gamble Lake

Route #20

Whitepine Lake

Chance Lake

Rapids, Cl. 30m. run or line

Evelyn

Portage 815m.

Portage 715m.

Apex Lake

Whitemud Lake

Gated during summer
Portage 300m. to river

Route # 21 to Sturgeon River and Ishpatina

Liftovers required - many stone shallows and fallen (sunk) logs

Beaver dams and old log bridge

Rapids, Cl. 750m. run down or line up on north side over rocks

Fast current
Portage 55m.

River

Probable obstruction Portage 70m.

Portage 580m.

Spring behind site

Two excellent viewpoints

Wetlands: watch for moose along this stretch.

Duff Lake

Florence River

Florence Lake

Detail (inset)

KAA LAKE

Beauty Lake Road

First bridge, liftover 20m. then pull out at second bridge for carry

Portage 275m.
Portage 245m.

Barr Lake

Portage 270m.

shallow

Second bridge: scenic mini-canyon and chutes with small campsite - Portage 793m. along road

Leave river, cross road and Portage 1,080m. along trail

Elizabeth Falls - P. 70m.

0 2 4 6 8 10 km.

Elizabeth Falls At the south end of the pond, keep to the east side of the outlet and do not continue. There is a very pretty falls here — the first on the Lady Evelyn. Take the portage over the rocky terrain around the falls. There is an excellent but small campsite here. At the south end of Weedend Lake there is a good trail around some shallow rapids. From this pond, look for the next trail at the south end. The portage is generally boggy. Continue south on Elissa Lake to Gamble. There is a public drop-off location at a campsite on the east shore of Gamble; another large campsite can be found nestled in the thick cedars across the lake on the peninsula.

Portages to Smoothwater Lake (total 7.2 km)

This is a difficult route but well used by youth camps. In the small bay on the west shore of Gamble Lake is the portage landing. After about 400 m you will come to a shallow pond; this is a great spot to view moose feeding in the marsh in the early morning or evening. The portage then skirts the pond along the north (right) shore, along the edge of the tree line. There may be sections of wet bog here in the spring. From the marsh, the trail enters the bush and travels over gently rolling terrain through a spruce forest for about 2,000 m. There are a couple of minor wet spots near the end of this section, but canoeists generally keep logs thrown over the worst spots. The trail now rises sharply alongside a small stream. This is where it gets hard. For about 600 metres you will climb over 90 vertical metres, crossing the creek at one point, leveling off at the top to a small pond. Across the pond is a good trail that takes you to a second pond. Continue over this pond to the portage to Sunnywater Lake.

Sunnywater Lake Sunnywater Lake is considered the clearest lake in the district, allowing you to see bright objects at the bottom to a depth of over 25 m. To the south of the trail landing is a small campsite, and another located at the west end above the next portage. This trail slips abruptly downhill over rocky ground to a small pond. Cross the pond and catch the next portage. This trail is quite strenuous near the bottom, where it passes through a small gorge and around large, broken boulders. This brings you to the northern tip of Whitepine Lake. It's a stone's throw to the next portage. You also have the opportunity to explore the Aurora trout lakes, a unique collection of beautiful lakes that still have remnant populations of this species of fish. The trout were threatened with extinction from a combination of acid fallout from the superstack in Sudbury and from illegal dynamiting of the fish by a local trapper. Continue downhill along a

good trail (crossing a spring) to Marina Lake. The short trail to Smoothwater can be found a short distance above the creek outlet at the southwest end of the lake.

Smoothwater Lake Once you step onto the white sands of Smoothwater beach, the sweat and toil it commanded to get there makes it well worth it. You'll think you've made it to paradise. There is unlimited camping on the beach and one large site on the offshore island close by. I've seen this lake as smooth as glass, or whipped into a frenzy by rogue winds. There is a commemorative marker on the shore down the lake dedicated to four men who drowned during one such wind storm. The water is clear and cold — excellent for swimming and snorkeling. There is also a superb afternoon trek to the small lake west of Smoothwater where you can bushwhack to the summit of a high ridge that rises 200 m above the surrounding area.

Paddle to the south end, entering a bay to the southwest until you come to a grassy clearing and the remains of an old dock. The portage from here to Apex is not difficult.

Apex Lake Paddle to the extreme west end, beyond the bay where the portage to the Sturgeon begins, and look for the next portage to Whitemud Lake. This trail is uneven and rocky.

Whitemud Lake It wasn't long ago when brook trout were so plentiful here that they blackened the bottom of this shallow lake. Enter the river at the end of the lake, where you'll likely have to lift over a couple of beaver dams followed by the remains of a log bridge. Ease of paddling from here depends on water levels and beaver activity. After late May, you will be dragging over stumps and logs littering the channel. After break-up, for about three weeks, the water level will allow you to easily pass over these obstructions. About 1 km past the first log bridge is another. Lift over if necessary and continue to a rocky shallows, where you may have to get out and wade or portage for about 75 m. For the next 3 km, shortly past an open marsh, there are several deadfalls over the river and probable beaver dams to lift over before entering a wide section of the Lady Evelyn. There is an excellent campsite located about 500 m past a small stream entering the Lady Evelyn on the north bank. The site is located on top of a large bedrock knoll and is large enough to house three to four tents. It has an excellent view of both the river you just paddled over and the scenic ridge to the north. At the far end of the open marsh you will immediately hit shallow rapids. These can be run a short distance, but watch carefully for sweepers

Gamble to Smoothwater
Cross-over Route

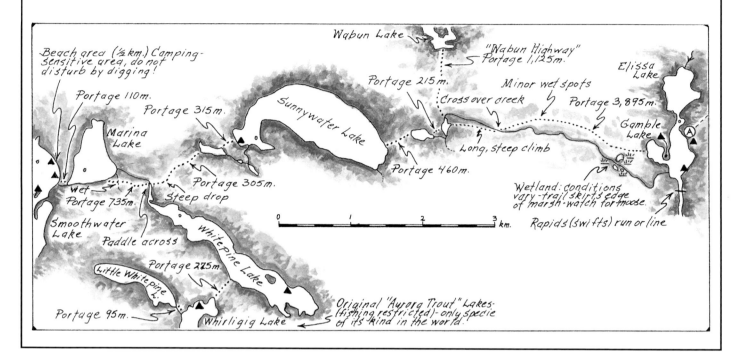

Beach area (½ km.) Camping- sensitive area, do not disturb by digging!

Portage 110m.

Portage 315m.

Marina Lake

Wabun Lake

Sunnywater Lake

"Wabun Highway" Portage 1,125m.

Portage 215m.

Minor wet spots

Cross over creek

Portage 3,895m.

Elissa Lake

Long, steep climb

Gamble Lake

Portage 460m.

Wet

Portage 735m.

Portage 305m.

Steep drop

Smoothwater Lake

Paddle across

Whitepine Lake

Little Whitepine L.

Portage 275m.

Portage 95m.

Whirligig Lake

Wetland: conditions vary - trail skirts edge of marsh - watch for moose.

Rapids (swifts) run or line

0   1   2   3 km.

Original "Aurora Trout" Lakes - (fishing restricted) - only specie of its kind in the world!

(fallen logs). Across another open marsh, where the river widens, you will come to some fast water that can be run in the centre channel. North of the narrows you'll have to portage a short distance around some obstructions, and again along a rocky trail that brings you to the wide section of the river above the Florence turnoff. Fishing is quite good here, with two campsites nearby. Continue on to Duff Lake, watching for moose along the way.

Duff Lake   Cross Duff Lake or camp at the good site located on the west shore. This has to be one of the most picturesque lakes in the district, perched neatly between high, pine-topped ridges. Shortly past Duff are two excellent viewpoints (no trails). The campsite up on the high bedrock perch, past the canyon, has a pure spring that runs throughout most of the summer months. Where the river constricts you'll hit a long set of easily run CI rapids. These can also be lined from the bouldery shore. There is a tight left turn at the very bottom of the run where it empties into a wide section of the river. From here, the river meanders for several kilometres through tag alder and tamarack — a good place to bump into a moose. Time your travel here according to campsite destination; after the junction of

the two rivers, there is a large campsite a short ways downriver and one beyond, a short distance before the first rapids. If you get stuck for a site, head upstream and camp at the bridge crossing. About 4 km north of the bridge you will have to line up a short rapid to Chance Lake. This can be run down during high water, but watch the sharp left turn at the bottom. At the north end of Chance you'll find a very shallow section of river with barely room to clear the canoe, followed by shallow swifts up to Gamble. From here, if you started at Beauty Lake, continue back through the same route as previously described.

MAKOBE LAKE, TRETHEWEY LAKE LINKS

This 42 km loop can be done as an addition to Route 19, or added as a link to Route 12 down the Makobe River. The loop can be made using the campsite at Gamble Lake as the staging point.

CLASSIFICATION experienced novice to intermediate
DISTANCE 42 km
TIME 3–4 days
PORTAGES 23
MAPS 41 P/7, 41 P/8

FEATURES & ECOLOGY This combines small-creek travel with picturesque lake travel. Although both Makobe and Trethewey may become quite rough, there are ample campsites to use during inclement weather. Aside from the odd motorboat on Trethewey, this route is quite isolated, with good opportunity to view moose in the small connecting creeks and ponds. Portage maintenance is sporadic, and I do recommend that only those used to such conditions take this route. Vegetation Site Code: UMF, MM (creek routes).

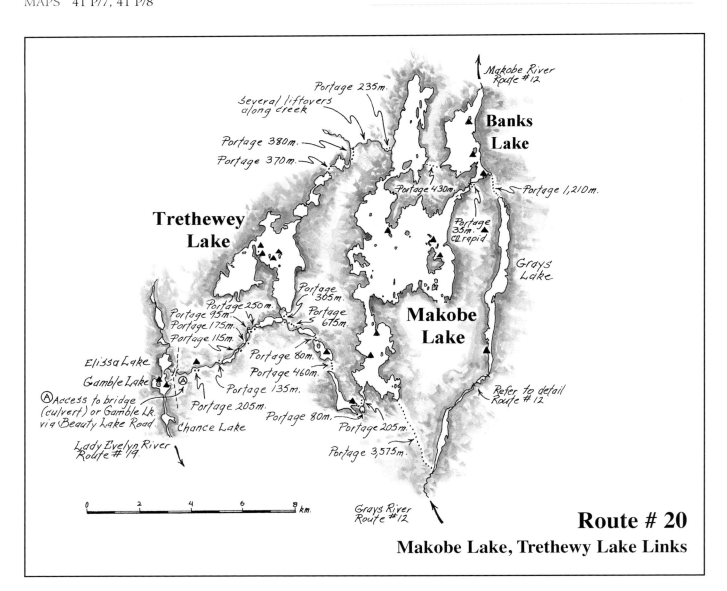

Route # 20
Makobe Lake, Trethewy Lake Links

SMOOTHWATER LAKE *to* STURGEON RIVER

This route could begin at the Montreal River access via the Beauty Lake Road, or by float-plane drop at Smoothwater, Scarecrow or Paul lakes. For those with a lot of time on their hands, the Sturgeon could bolster a long loop route staged from the Lake Temagami area. The description in this write-up begins at Smoothwater Lake and ends at the Chiniguchi River junction. The description from there down to River Valley is covered in Route 1. The best time to run the Sturgeon, especially for the whitewater, is late May through June. In the summer, many rapids will have to be lined, and the chance of broaching rocks is much greater. Regardless, the Sturgeon is a fine trip at any time during the season.

CLASSIFICATION   intermediate

DISTANCE   150 km

TIME   8–10 days

PORTAGES   28 (total 7.4 km)

MAPS   41 P/2, 41 P/7, 41 I/9, 41 I/15E, 41 I/16

FEATURES & ECOLOGY   For whitewater lovers, the Sturgeon offers excellent CI to CIII rapids through an incredible scenic corridor. The scenery constantly changes, and the river responds to those terrestrial shifts. One minute you are drifting through quiet meanders, the next moment you're plunging through tight canyons. One of the key features here is the hike up Ishpatina Ridge — the highest point of land in Ontario. Other excellent ascents can be made at the Gate, some distance down the Sturgeon River. The Sturgeon is unique in that it gathers its water from the highland plateau surrounding Ishpatina Ridge, exemplified by bold escarpments typical of the Canadian Shield. Then lower down, past the Gate and easily marked by Upper Goose Falls, the river tries to straighten itself out as it coils endlessly through a sand plain. Vegetation Site Code: RB, C, UMF (Ishpatina Ridge area), UMF (Upper Sturgeon River), UDF and AC (Lower Sturgeon River).

Smoothwater Lake   Portage along a good trail into Apex Lake (as described in Route 19).

Apex Lake   Apex denotes the height of land where water to the north and east follows the Montreal River drainage system and those waters to the south flow into the Sturgeon River drainage area. Paddle to the south bay. Do not take the Route 19 portage at the east-end bay. The portage south follows an old bush skid road to a small lake. Head to the south end of this lake and portage 65 m to the next unnamed lake. At the head of this trail is an alternate portage that connects to Route 19 below Whitemud Lake. Continue on south, across the small lake, and portage into the third lake. At the outlet, keep to the west side for the portage into McCullock Lake. There is one good campsite located at the beginning of the trail to Mihell Lake. This trail also stays west of the outlet and comes out to a narrow, shallow pond. On the west shore of Mihell there is one campsite of questionable use. Here you have a choice of taking the portage route at the south end of the lake, or sticking with the creek.

Scarecrow Creek   Paddling is good during high flow but declines in the summer season. Again, as with most creeks, ease of navigation is based upon the amount of beaver activity. At the start the creek meanders constantly, and there will, no doubt, be two to three beaver dams to lift over. Heading south through a wide marsh you will come out to a small pond. Where the creek continues south, there is the likelihood of hitting one more beaver dam and a rocky shallows. The final leg of the creek, before getting to Scarecrow, is very shallow with many partially submerged fallen logs.

Scarecrow Lake & Ishpatina Ridge Hike   As you enter Scarecrow Lake, directly to the right is a small clearing where the fire rangers' cabin stood. Camping is possible here, at the start of the Ishpatina hike. The trail to the tower runs north for about 4.5 km. You can either pack water with you or refill your Nalgene bottles at Dick Lake, the site of another older cabin near the summit. As on the Maple Mountain trek, you have the option of camping at the top; expect blackflies late into the season here among the scrub oak and blueberry bushes. This is considered an easier trail than Maple Mountain because of its more relaxed pitch, and with only one minor wet section (at the second lake along a marsh), it should only take you about three hours round trip. The view is unprecedented. To the north you'll see a steep drop off to one of Ontario's deepest

Route # 21
Smoothwater Lake to Sturgeon River Route

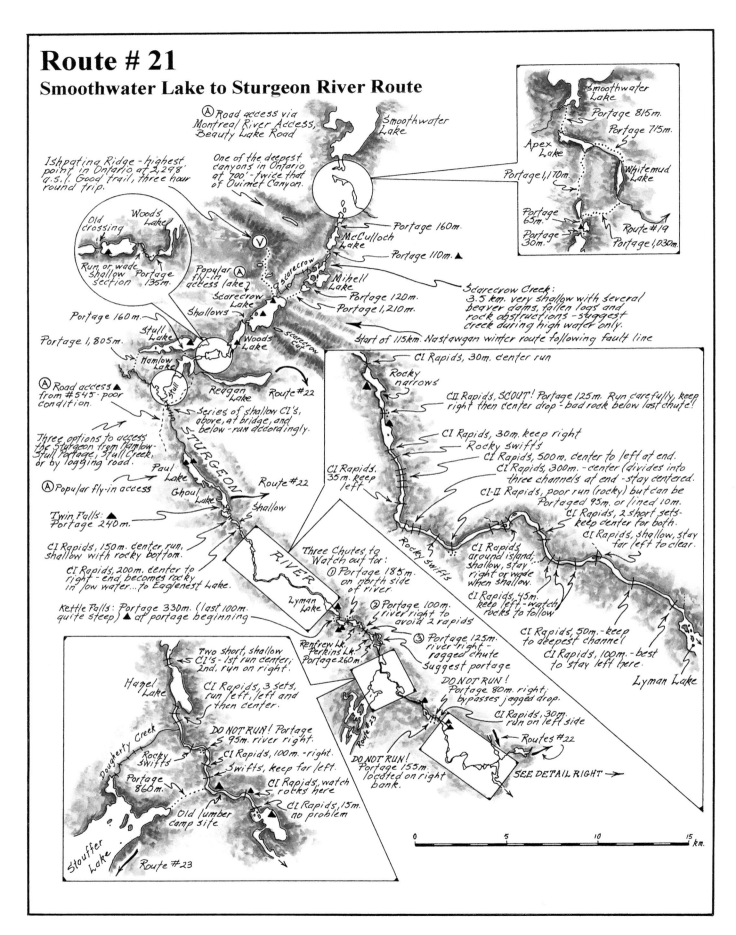

CANOEING, KAYAKING & HIKING TEMAGAMI

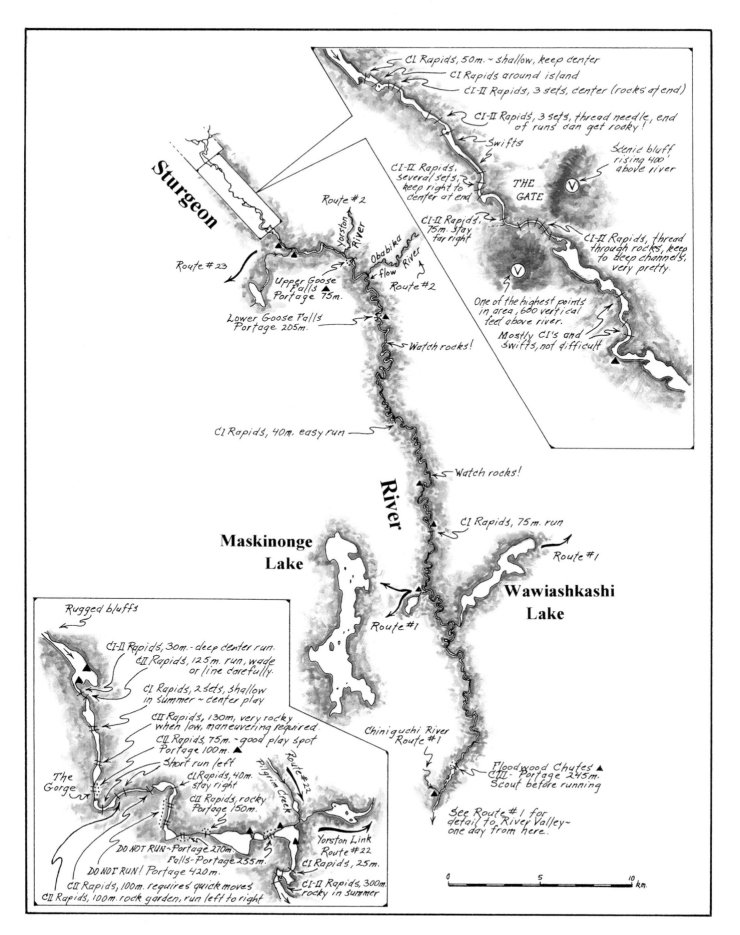

CI Rapids, 50m. ~ shallow, keep center

CI Rapids around island

CI-II Rapids, 3 sets, center (rocks at end)

CI-II Rapids, 3 sets, thread needle, end of run's can get rocky!

Swifts

Scenic bluff rising 400' above river

CI-II Rapids, several sets, keep right to center at end

THE GATE

Ⓥ

CI-II Rapids, 75m. Stay far right

CI-II Rapids, thread through rocks, keep to deep channels, very pretty.

Ⓥ

One of the highest points in area, 600 vertical feet above river.

Mostly CI's and Swifts, not difficult

Sturgeon

Route #2

Yorston River

Obabika flow River

Route #2

Route #23

Upper Goose Falls Portage 75m. ▲

Lower Goose Falls Portage 205m.

Watch rocks!

CI Rapids, 40m, easy run

Watch rocks!

River

CI Rapids, 75m. run

Route #1

Maskinonge Lake

Wawiashkashi Lake

Route #1

Route #1

Chiniguchi River Route #1

Floodwood Chutes ▲
CIII- Portage 245m.
Scout before running

See Route #1 for detail to River Valley~ one day from here.

Rugged bluffs

CI-II Rapids, 30m.- deep center run.

CII Rapids, 125m. run, wade or line carefully.

CI Rapids, 2 sets, shallow in summer ~ center play

CII Rapids, 130m, very rocky when low, maneuvering required.

CII Rapids, 75m. ~ good play spot Portage 100m. ▲

Short run left

CI Rapids, 40m. stay right

The Gorge

CII Rapids, rocky Portage 150m.

Route #22

Pilgrim Creek

DO NOT RUN~ Portage 270m.
Falls-Portage 255m.

DO NOT RUN! Portage 420m.

CII Rapids, 100m. requires quick moves

CII Rapids, 100m. rock garden, run left to right

Yorston Link Route #22

CI Rapids, 25m.

CI-II Rapids, 300m. rocky in summer

0   5   10
|___|___|___|___| km.

canyons (over 200 m), and as you look to the east, you'll see two more deep cuts, the northernmost rift valley forming the beginning of the 115 km long nastawgan winter trail that ends at the Ottawa River.

Route Continuation   The nicest, bug-free campsite is on the island on Scarecrow. Paddle to the southwest end of the lake and pass through a narrow channel of swifts. Pike fishing is quite good below the rapids. Continue southwest on Woods Lake to a short portage around creek obstructions. This brings you to a small pond. At the far end, you will come to three sets of shallow, gravel-bottomed rapids, runnable in the spring but usually requiring lining in the summer. Enter another pond, then another gravel rapids, which can be run in the spring but lined in the summer when low. In the next small lake there is a rough, grassy campsite on the southwest shore. At the west end of this lake there is a low bridge over the creek. You may have to portage on the south side if the bridge is jammed with logs.

Three Routes to the Sturgeon from Hamlow Lake

Route One   There is an old sawmill site in the southwest bay of Hamlow. It also serves as an all-terrain vehicle access. The portage follows the road for 3.5 km and crosses the Sturgeon River.

Route Two   Portage 160 m into Stull Lake at the northwest end of Hamlow. The portage begins about 50 m past a winter skid road, just before a dried-up river bed. Paddle to the extreme west end of Stull. The trail to the Sturgeon is located opposite a winter skid road leading to McKee Falls. This portage is quite strenuous, passing through old burns and over rough terrain, and comes out at the mouth of a creek that drains into the Sturgeon.

Route Three   This is a pretty, natural route that should not be taken during high water. As a summer route, Stull Creek is preferable, however, there are several short portages and liftovers to confront, the longest carry being only 75 m in length. Allow at least three to four hours for this option.

Sturgeon River   On entering the Sturgeon, from whichever route you decide upon, the first thing you'll notice is the marked contrast in the turbidity (clarity) of the water. The rust-brown colour of the Sturgeon water comes from the density of organic matter collected from the massive headwaters fenland to the north. From Stull Creek, the river runs through a channel by high bluffs. The first rapids can be run by keeping right.

Where the road and bridge once crossed the river, you can run the rapids on the right side then swing left at the shallow end. Around the next bend are several sets of shallow CIs, which can all be run easily. The river above Paul Lake passes through a marsh with several side ponds. If you approach these ponds carefully and quietly, you may be able to glimpse a moose or two wading through the shallows.

Paul Lake   There are a couple of fair campsites on Paul, with good pike fishing along the northeast shore bluffs. In the narrows below the lake you have to watch the rocks as you pass through the channel. The landscape along here is indicative of the beautiful scenery along the upper Sturgeon. Continue into Ghoul Lake, where you will pass the portage route east (Route 22) and head for the southwest end portage across Twin Falls.

Twin Falls   There is an excellent campsite at the portage landing. Ghoul seems a fitting name for the lake — I remember well the huge number of giant leeches that honed in on the landing as we tried to swim off the campsite. The trail rises slightly uphill over bedrock then drops down to a pool below the falls. Fishing is good here, and an evening paddle around the black pools usually conjures up a few discussions with local beaver.

Twin Falls to Kettle Falls   Along this stretch the river has numerous shallow rapids with a gravel to rocky bottom. Most can be run in the early season, but lining and wading may be necessary in late summer. If you are heavily loaded, you may bottom out at the end of these rapids, so be prepared to hop out on the upstream side of your canoe and keep your track line at the ready. Continue downstream from Twin Falls. On re-entering the river channel there are shallow rapids; these can be run by keeping centre, but watch the rocks at the bottom before entering a narrow pond. This pond is shallow near the far end where you also have to watch for rocks while entering another 200 m stretch of rapids. These are easily navigated during high water. Keep centre at the start, then sideslip over to the right channel near the finish to avoid some well-placed rocks.

Eaglenest Lake   Paddle just over 1 km to the end of the lake where you can run a short rapid (centre channel) to a pond. Be careful of the rocks in the narrows two-thirds of the way across the pond before the next rapids. Scout these rapids! Not a difficult run in high water, but there is a precarious boulder at the end. Start off in the right channel then slip to the centre to clear the bottom rocks. The portage should be taken if in doubt; this is located on the left bank. From here to Kettle, follow the notations on the map carefully.

Kettle Falls Keep to the right (west) of the river outlet to access the portage around the falls. The trail is a bit confusing because it travels over open bedrock, so follow the rock cairns carefully. There is a campsite at the beginning of the trail with an offshoot pathway to the edge of the falls. The end of the portage is very dicey, as it drops suddenly over loose gravel to the pool below the falls. The falls acquires its name from the kettle, or bowl-shaped depressions made in the rock caused by the swirling motion of the water carrying small stones. On the pond below the falls are two excellent campsites with great views of the falls. Do not run the next rapids; instead, portage along the north bank on a good trail to Renfrew Lake.

Renfrew Lake Do not run either of the next two rapids between Renfrew Lake and Perkins Lake. The first portage is on the right bank and avoids two sharp-turning rapids; the next portage is also located on the right bank and avoids a pretty chute.

Perkins Lake Midway along Perkins are two good campsites on either shore. This is a very pretty lake with scenic jack-pine stands graduating back to high ridges. Do not follow the river from here. Take the portage at the south bay over a good trail around some rock-infested rapids. Paddle on a short piece to the end of the pond and run two short rapids, keeping centre at the initial run then river right on the second. From here you will see a momentary change in forest cover, from jack pine to low fen and marsh.

Hazel Lake Paddle south to the end of Hazel and enter the river where there are three sets of shallow rapids. Keep right for the first set and then left for the last two; you may have to line these in low water. Watch the rocks just around the bend to the left before the next set of rapids. Do not run these rapids; portage along the right bank over an easy trail. The next shallow section can be navigated by taking the far left channel. Unlimited camping is possible at an old lumber camp and bridge clearing (no bridge). Paddle 500 m to a short rapid, but watch the rocks carefully on this one. There is a sandy campsite along the left bank. Just past the island where the river narrows, do not run the next two sets of rapids. These are steep-pitched and ragged. Portages are located on the right bank for both sets. Shortly after the last portage is a 30 m stretch of shallow rapids; keep left here before entering a small lake. There are two campsites here on the east shore.

Continue downriver, where you'll come upon deep, centre-run rapids. The set after this may have to be lined or run in high water flow only. Cross a small pond to the next rapids. There are two small sets that can be run in the centre channel. About 500 m downriver is another shallow set that requires some quick and precise moves in order to clear several main channel rocks. Cross the next pool, keeping left of the next rapids that run through a narrow gorge. Scout first! There is a good trail along the left side and a superb campsite midway along the trail. During high water this is a very good run and a fine place for free floating or play boating. From here the route is quite picturesque and the rapids shallow and fast. Continue downriver, passing a small creek on the right bank. Round the bend to a short rapids and run these on the left side. The following set requires a shift from left channel at the start over to the right side near the end of the run. Watch the rocks on this one. The following set has a deep left channel. Before entering a pond, the next 100 m of rapids can be run carefully, avoiding the rocks at the bottom. Rounding the bend past the pond is a section of fast water; it is shallow but navigable along the right bank channel. Do not run the next rapids — there are several steep ledges. Carry around over a strenuous trail 420 m. Paddle across a pond and do not run the rapids; portage on the right over rocks and exposed cedar roots. The next rapids should be checked before running because of the exposed boulders at the end of the run. This is predominantly a right-side run, but if unsure, take the portage along the left bank over a fairly tough trail. Paddle to the far east end of a small lake and pass through a narrow channel. There is a campsite located on a peninsula here. The next portage can be found to the left of the river outlet. Do not run these rapids. This rocky portage crosses an old bush road and bypasses the remains of a log bridge and chutes. There is a campsite at the gravel beach at the far end of the carry and another nice site down the river on the left shore with room enough for three tents. Pilgrim Creek flows into this pool at the northeast end, as well as the link route to Yorston Lake.

There is obviously more flow here, as the current picks up. Class I rapids easily become volume CIIs in the spring, or bump-and-grind boulder riffles in late summer. Follow the small lake to the south end, where you can run the rapids down the middle. Cross the next pond and run three sets of shallow, rock-garden rapids totaling about 300 m. Follow the next wide section to the end narrows, where you can run a 50 m section of rapids, keeping to the centre channel. Just after that you'll find an easy run around the small island in the river. Three sets of rapids follow; these can be run or lined. The last set is quite rocky. Continue about 500 m to three more consecutive sets that can be run. Swifts will carry you along for almost 1 km until you reach four sets of CI–CII rapids; these can be run without difficulty. From here you'll be passing through the Gate — magnificent hills rising 200 m above the river. There are two ridges here that can be climbed (no trails), both with a commanding view of the river. As you pass through the high ridges, the river carries you along quickly through several sets of shallow, rocky rapids. At the far end of the wide section of river, you will encounter three more sets of runnable rapids. The river widens and slows down as the landscape levels out. You'll see an abundance of clams on the sandy bottom of the river. The Yorston River enters the Sturgeon at this point. Take caution, as Upper Goose Falls comes up quickly.

Upper Goose Falls Portage on the right bank past a campsite overlooking the falls and down a steep trail to the rapids below the falls. The landing is set among a scrabble of large boulders that make entry to the river difficult. The rapids here can be run easily during high water but may require some wading in the summer. You will notice huge chunks of bank collapsing; trees attached still present a slight problem with sweepers when the river runs high. Shortly past Upper Goose you will see the crystal waters of the Obabika flowing in from your left. Watch the approach to Lower Goose, as the channel has changed over the years with spring washouts. Portage on the left side and down to a large beach camping area. You'll notice that ATV campers use this site.

From here the scenery is quite unique. The eroded sand banks are very prominent, while the river meanders constantly. Each year, the spring rush of water claims more of the bank vegetation in an effort to straighten itself out. Follow the map write-up for the occasional rapids below Lower Goose Falls. The two main campsites are located at Kelly's farm and at the junction of the Chiniguchi River. For information on the route from here to River Valley, see Route 1.

SOLACE LAKE *and* PILGRIM CREEK ROUTES

The Solace Waterway Provincial Park was established in 1989, and for good reason. This grouping of lakes forms the final frontier of the Temagami backcountry. As an important link, the Bluesucker to Sturgeon route gives paddlers the option to bypass the Yorston River if the water flow is minimal, adding several days to the loop, or to use an alternate crossover from Ishpatina to Florence if the Sturgeon River is low. One other little-utilized route is the Solace–Pilgrim Creek route. As a spring trip, this has to be one of the finest in Temagami. These two routes are highlighted in the write-up. Two additional links, the Sturgeon to Yorston and the Solace to Hamlow routes, are also illustrated as alternative diversions from the more heavily used corridors.

Bluesucker Lake to Twin Falls (Sturgeon River) Route

CLASSIFICATION experienced novice

DISTANCE 19.2 km

TIME 2 days

PORTAGES 13 (total 4.2 km)

MAP 41 P/2

FEATURES & ECOLOGY Regional archeologist Thor Conway, in the early 1980s, claimed that the "Pinetorch Corridor" had never been fully surveyed for artifacts or Native cultural sites. He was implying that this area may be virtually littered with important historical data regarding pre-White Native use. This seems to be the case. In 1977 while surveying this area, I located a pictograph site that had not been identified. The wealth in nastawgan history alone is incredible — the very trails you will travel over are thousands of years old. Rugged topography, jack-pine forests and rocky bluffs dominate the landscape. Vegetation Site Code: UMF (Solace-Pilgrim Lake route), AC/SM and TS (Solace and Pilgrim Creek route).

Bluesucker Lake Once on Bluesucker, head for the southwest shore where there is an almost enclosed bay. Enter the bay and portage to Benner Lake over a good trail. There is an excellent campsite on Benner, and the swimming is wonderful in the clear water. The north-

shore backdrop of jack pine adds to the general beauty of this lake. The next portage out of Benner is located in a shallow bay at the west end. For the first 150 m the trail runs uphill gradually over and around several boulders, levels out and then drops slightly to the southeast end of Rodd Lake. Paddle north on Rodd to the creek at the northwest end. Portage 10 m over the shore rocks (south side of the creek) and catch the trail through cedar and spruce bush the rest of the distance to Pilgrim Lake.

Pilgrim Lake On Pilgrim there is one campsite located on the east shore point, after the first narrows. This site, although nicely situated, is not level, and too rocky, with few tent sites available. Another site can be found on a point west of the last site, about 500 m away. Pilgrim is a beautiful lake, especially looking north and northeast from the campsites. Jack pine predominates along the shoreline with a scattering of birch groves, mostly along the west side of the lake. Paddle to the west bay, beyond the campsite, and portage into Maggie Lake. The landing of sloped bedrock makes unloading the canoe difficult, especially if it has been raining. This is a tough trail, starting off in mud and slop (35 m), with several wet spots as you go. This is followed by 450 m of steep, rocky ascents and descents until you reach the bottom end of Maggie.

Maggie Lake This is a pretty lake with jack pine covering its continuous sand and gravel banks. The Pilgrim River flows out of the bottom of Maggie and connects with the Solace (main route) to the south. This portion of creek has not been examined, and although it could be used as an early spring route, the creek is quite small where it joins the Solace and may be seriously impeded by fallen timber. You can also add an extra day to your trip by heading north and looping back around to Solace, as indicated on the map.

Continue north a couple of hundred metres, where the next portage is easily found on a good gravel beach landing. Not quite as difficult as the last carry, this portage rises 700 m in "steps," and then levels out and drops suddenly to Bill Lake.

Bill Lake Head northwest to the creek outlet. Take the portage, located just south of the jammed stream, to

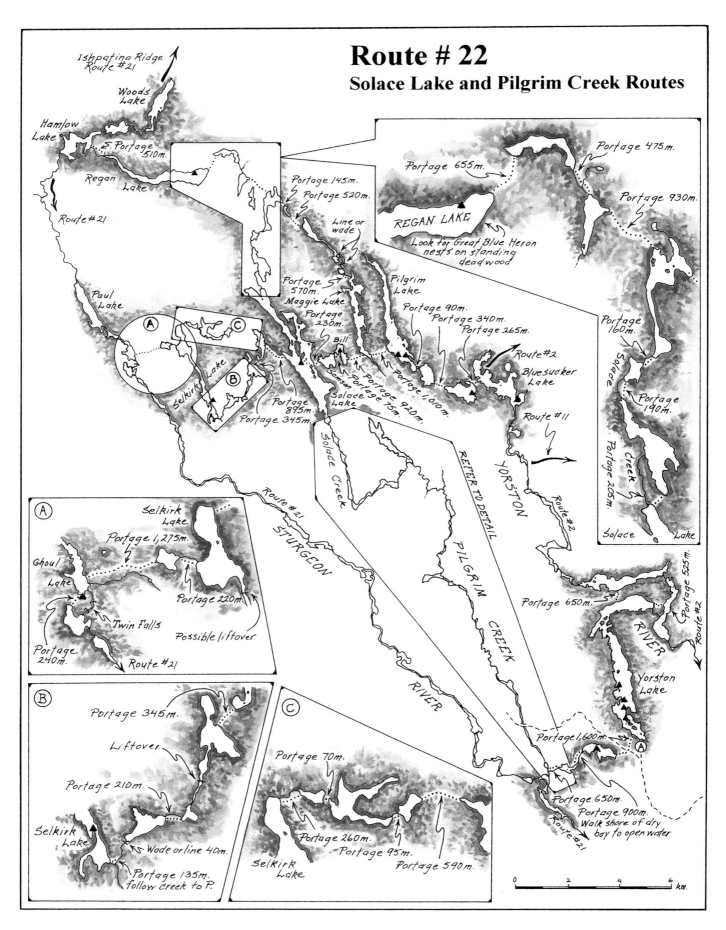

Route # 22
Solace Lake and Pilgrim Creek Routes

Ishpatina Ridge
Route #21

Woods Lake

Hamlow Lake

Portage 510m.

Regan Lake

Route #21

Paul Lake

Portage 145m.
Portage 520m.

Line or wade

Portage 570m.

Maggie Lake

Portage 230m.

Bill

Portage 895m.
Portage 345m.

Samson
Solace Lake

Portage 75m.

Portage 920m.

Portage 1,010m.

Pilgrim Lake

Portage 90m.
Portage 340m.
Portage 265m.

Route #2

Bluesucker Lake

Route #11

Portage 655m.

Portage 475m.

REGAN LAKE

Portage 930m.

Look for Great Blue Heron nests on standing deadwood

Portage 160m.

Solace Creek

Portage 190m.

Portage 205m.

Solace Lake

REFER TO DETAIL

YORSTON

PILGRIM CREEK

STURGEON

Solace Creek

Route #21

RIVER

Portage 650m.

Portage 525m.

Route #2

RIVER

Yorston Lake

Portage 1,600m.

Portage 650m.
Portage 900m.
Walk shore of dry bay to open water

Route #21

A
Selkirk Lake
Portage 1,275m.
Ghoul Lake
Portage 220m.
Twin Falls
Possible liftover
Portage 240m.
Route #21

B
Portage 345m.
Liftover
Portage 210m.
Selkirk Lake
Wade or line 40m.
Portage 135m. follow creek to P.

C
Portage 70m.
Portage 260m.
Portage 95m.
Selkirk Lake
Portage 590m.

0   2   4   6 km

Samson Lake. There are several offshore rocks to watch as you approach the next portage. This trail is often flooded in sections but easily skirted, is very rocky but mostly downhill to a good landing at Solace Lake.

Solace Lake   The large rock outcrops create a rugged visage: a beautiful lake with many outstanding features. You may want to base camp here for a couple of extra days. There is one good campsite located on the south point of the large central island. The surface is rocky, with room for two or three tents, with additional room farther back. From here you can continue west to the Sturgeon or head south on the Solace and Pilgrim creeks (see write-up to follow). Paddle to the west bay and look carefully for the next portage, located south of the creek. The portage entrance is quite boggy, and it gets worse. For the first 200 m the trail follows to the left of the cascading creek. The portage seems to track over an old rocky riverbed and is strenuous right to the end. Paddle south on a small, low-profile lake lined with spruce and pine, and continue to the far end of the bay. This trail landing can be muddy, but the rest of the portage is quite easy, and brings you out to a large pond. Continue south along the west shore. Note: There are no rapids here as marked on the topographic maps, just a shallow section around a mid-channel island (stay west, or right, of the island for deep water). Paddle a short distance and then lift over a beaver dam. Proceed through the grassy narrows to a large pond, keeping to the west bay. Paddle into a creek mouth and put in to the left beside a large rock face. The landing may be rough if the pond is flooded. Portage mostly downhill over a good trail and out to a small lake. Go to the southwest end of this lake and enter the small creek. Be mindful of the rocks guarding the narrows. Depending on water levels, you will have to wade with the canoe for about 40 m to where the creek flows out through a marsh. Follow the creek as far as the next beaver dam (where the other creek comes in to the left), and keep directly right for the next portage. This is an easy trail to Selkirk Lake. The landing at the end is boggy, but logs have been tossed down to make loading and departure easier.

Selkirk Lake   Just north of the portage, on the west point, you will notice a nice campsite. The beaver actually build dams across the narrows of Selkirk Lake, which is more like a river. Keep to the northwest end of the bay for the next portage, located to the left of the creek outlet. The portage is smooth, slightly downhill to the rocky shores of a pond. The next portage begins over 30 m of shore boulders before entering the bush. The jack pine-lined path is good, up until a 120 m stretch of bog about 400 m in, and then winds gradually downhill. The trail then skirts a swamp at one point, where you will have to cross a small stream. There is one short, steep climb and then a drop down to a bedrock outcrop on Ghoul Lake.

Solace and Pilgrim Creek Route

Special Note   In the mid 1980s I outfitted a couple of guys who flew in to Paul Lake to run the Sturgeon. It was early summer, and the bugs were still in full force. They accidentally missed the Twin Falls portage and carried over the long trail that heads east towards Solace Lake. They were poor map readers and thought they were still on the right track, at least for a short while until things just didn't seem to fit. Realizing how far they had gone and not wanting to return to the Sturgeon River over the long portage, they kept going, headed for the Solace–Pilgrim creek. There was no write-up for the route, and they blazed their own way down, finally reaching the Sturgeon a few days later. Although extremely difficult, they claimed the route was "one of the best," having seen more moose than they could count along the way. So finally in 2002 I flew in with Ted Krofchak from Temagami Outfitting and did the creek route for myself. Unfortunately, I have misplaced my detailed field notes (some might think that was karma), but luck had it that Ted kept some rough notes, which I borrowed to draw up the maps. Hopefully, my memory served me correctly and I've made an accurate assessment of the route. If not, please let me know.

CLASSIFICATION intermediate

DISTANCE 24 km

TIME 2 days

PORTAGES 7

MAP 41 P/2

FEATURES & ECOLOGY   This route is an absolute treasure, best run before mid-June, where you'll be assured of some good CI and CII action. Beyond the thrill of whitewater, it's a photographer's paradise. You can be sure of numerous moose sightings throughout the entire route. Conditions are variable. We did manage to mark and cut some trails around chutes (except one), and travel is relatively good, at least in the sense that there are no unmanageable hurdles to get over aside from a bit of bush pushing around one waterfall. The Pilgrim is very pretty, with several outstanding chutes and waterfalls and several camping areas available along the route. You'll just have to try this one for yourself.

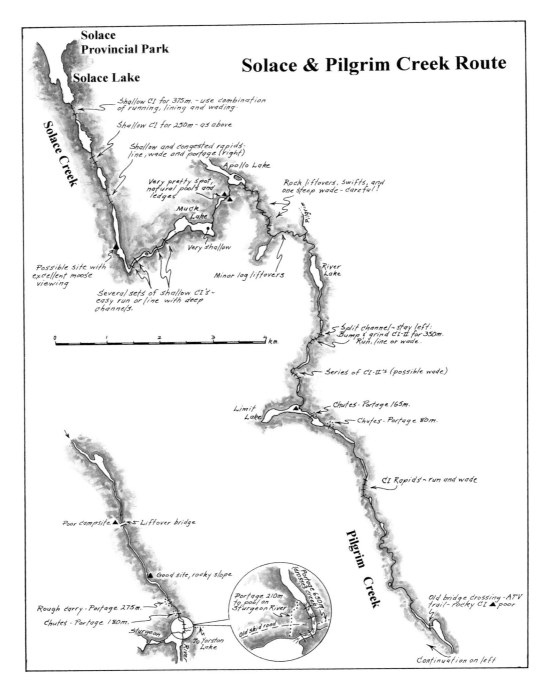

The following text appears within the map:

Solace Provincial Park

Solace Lake

Solace Creek

Solace & Pilgrim Creek Route

Shallow CI for 375m. - use combination of running, lining and wading.

Shallow CI for 250m - as above

Shallow and congested rapids - line, wade and portage (right)

Apollo Lake

Very pretty spot, natural pools and ledges

Rock liftovers, swifts, and one steep wade - careful!

Muck Lake

Very shallow

Minor log liftovers

River Lake

Possible site with excellent moose viewing

Several sets of shallow CI's - easy run or line with deep channels.

Split channel - stay left: Bump & grind CI-II for 350m. Run, line or wade.

Series of CI-II's (possible wade)

Limit Lake

Chutes - Portage 165m.

Chutes - Portage 80m.

CI Rapids - run and wade

Pilgrim Creek

Poor campsite   Liftover bridge

Good site, rocky slope

Portage 210m. to pool on Sturgeon River

Portage 650m (crosses creek)

Old skid road

Rough carry - Portage 275m.

Chutes - Portage 180m.

Sturgeon River

To Yorston Lake

Old bridge crossing - ATV trail - rocky CI   poor

Continuation on left

0 1 2 3 4 km.

Link Routes

Sturgeon to Yorston Link Straightforward, but you have to cross Pilgrim Creek to gain access to the portage, and you may not be able to cross here in the early season.

Selkirk to Solace Link An old nastawgan route that is well worth the time to explore; just follow the map for details.

Hamlow to Solace Link This an optional route whichever way you are heading. This may be an interesting diversion from the usual trek to the Sturgeon from Smoothwater Lake.

Note: Trails were not cleared at the time of writing, although plans were underway to do so during the summer of 2003. Check with local outfitters for current conditions and to find out which routes have been maintained.

WOLF LAKE and LAURA LAKE ROUTE

ROUTE

23

This attractive route can be taken in either direction or added on as a loop or connecting link. Loop route: This seven-to-eight-day trip would commence at the public access point at the bottom end of Matagamasi Lake. Follow this route north to the Sturgeon River, downstream to the Chiniguchi River (Route 1), and upstream back to the start point. The loop is 170 km in length and can be shortened somewhat by using the Ozhway Lake–Maskinonge Lake portage route. The write-up for Route 23 begins at the Sturgeon River and heads south. If the Sturgeon is extremely low, this is the best route to take, continuing on via the Chiniguchi River to the lower Sturgeon, where water levels are not such a factor.

CLASSIFICATION novice (experienced novice for loop)

DISTANCE 42 km

TIME 2–3 days

PORTAGES 12 (total 3.5 km)

MAPS 41 P/2, 41 I/15

FEATURES & ECOLOGY Wolf Lake is considered one of the most beautiful lakes within the Temagami paddling area. There are three excellent viewpoint hikes (no trails), as indicated on the route map. Although there has been some development, chiefly mining activity with some logging and prospecting, and you will see the occasional motorboat on some of the larger lakes, this route remains exceptional in its pristine beauty. Vegetation Site Code: UMF, RB.

Stouffer Lake Follow the gently rolling trail 860 m from the Sturgeon River to the north end of Stouffer. This is a very pretty lake, dotted with pine-covered islands and deep, secret bays. The large campsite at the north end can accommodate several tents.

Frederick Lake The easy portage brings you into the lake (the beginning of the trail may be very shallow in summer). Head south and portage a short distance around a low bridge and site of a large camping area. You can still pick up logging artifacts, and the swimming is excellent here.

Dougherty Lake This portage trail is moderately difficult as it manoeuvres over precarious rocks, ending at a swampy outlet into the lake. The water clarity is much like that of Smoothwater Lake, and with the spruce and pine shoreline, you won't want to go any farther. There is a large campsite on the central island that will accommodate four or five tents. The next portage (560 m) is the most difficult carry along the route. A steep, rocky trail at both ends and a small marsh at the mid-section make footing rather tedious at times. Cross Button Lake and take a short portage over an old road. The creek may be navigable here depending on the height of water. The next portage will take you to Sawhorse Lake. The first 60 m follows an old logging road and then cuts off at the junction of two roads, then follows a level trail and down to the lake. A pure spring is located just to the right, off the end of the trail. Evidence of fire can be noted around the shores of the shallow lake. Continue to a short portage over an old road that leads to Chiniguchi Lake.

Chiniguchi Lake You will notice a few buildings at the entrance of the lake, but the beauty of the setting is unmarred. Bypass the main body of the lake by canoeing south along the east side of Caribou Island; you can then portage back to the east side of the lake over a 205 m trail. There is also a slight diversion via Musko Bay in the east. The rocky shores, pine hills and clear crystalline waters present a scenic panorama, especially seen from the summit of White Mountain.

Old logging camps are scattered throughout the canoeing district.

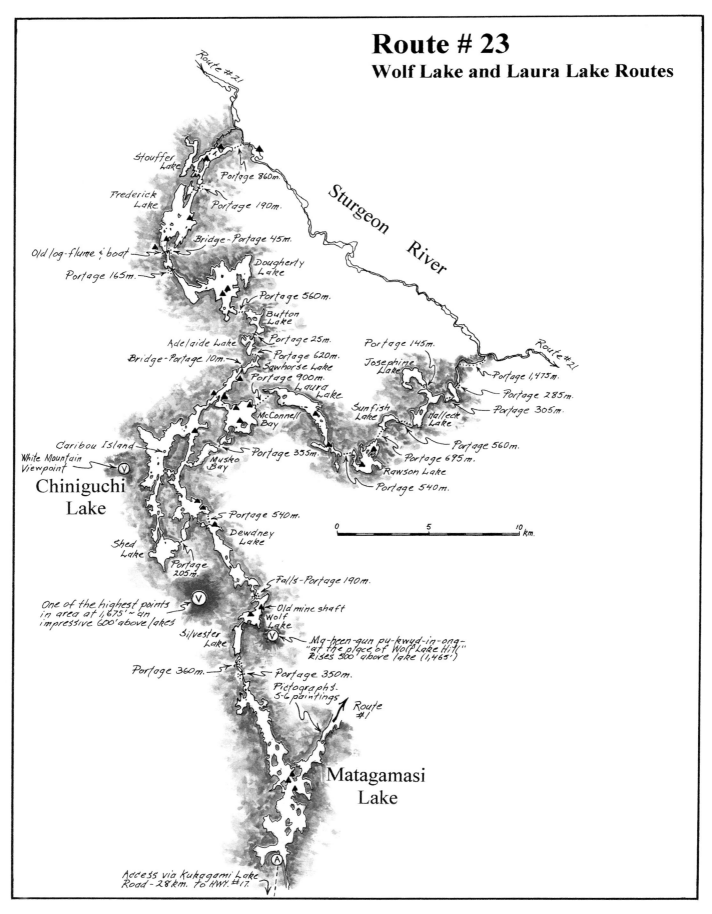

Route # 23
Wolf Lake and Laura Lake Routes

Route #21

Stouffer Lake

Portage 860m.

Frederick Lake

Portage 190m.

Bridge-Portage 45m.

Old log-flume & boat

Dougherty Lake

Portage 165m.

Portage 560m.

Button Lake

Sturgeon River

Adelaide Lake

Portage 25m.

Portage 620m.

Bridge-Portage 10m.

Sawhorse Lake

Portage 900m.

Laura Lake

Portage 145m.

Josephine Lake

Route #21

Portage 1,475m.

Portage 285m.

Portage 305m.

McConnell Bay

Sunfish Lake

Halleck Lake

Caribou Island

Portage 355m.

Portage 560m.

White Mountain Viewpoint

Musko Bay

Portage 695m.

Rawson Lake

Chiniguchi Lake

Portage 540m.

Portage 540m.

Dewdney Lake

Shed Lake

Portage 205m.

0   5   10 km.

Falls-Portage 190m.

One of the highest points in area at 1,675' ~ an impressive 600' above lakes

Old mine shaft

Wolf Lake

Silvester Lake

Mg-heen-gun pu-kwyd-in-ong ~ "at the place of Wolf Lake Hill" Rises 500' above lake (1,465')

Portage 360m.

Portage 350m.

Pictographs- 5-6 paintings

Route #1

Matagamasi Lake

Access via Kukagami Lake Road - 28 km. to HWY. #17.

Dewdney Lake The 540 m trail brings you to Dewdney Lake, named after the famous Ontario archaeologist. The high, rolling topography and white, exposed rocks make this a particularly enchanting setting.

Wolf Lake Bypass two cascading falls tumbling through thick, white birch over a good trail. This brings you to Wolf Lake. Why is this such an attractive place? The high rock bluffs, aquamarine water, red-pine forest and scenic vistas, all enjoyed from several perfect campsites. One of the nicest is located on a rocky, pine-covered point that juts out on the east central shore and is large enough to house several tents. The site is adjacent to an old mine shaft and offers excellent cliff diving (5 m) above the water. Continue south into Sylvester Lake to the next portage. This trail skirts a 30 m cascading waterfall and winds along a cavern overlooking the rushing water. Follow the Chiniguchi River a short distance to the next portage. Landing may be difficult through large boulders and rocks if the water levels create heavy current. This trail leads to the north arm of Matagamasi Lake.

Matamagasi Lake The north end of the lake is quite shallow, and winds could pose a problem if they blow in from the south. Take your time! Continue your route as planned.

Laura Lake Route This little-used route could be included as an addition to the Wolf–Sturgeon Route. Head south down the Sturgeon, and re-enter the Chiniguchi–Wolf route via the Laura Lake route. You will only have to retrace the route through Wolf, and that's worth it.

ROUTE
24

WANAPITEI RIVER ROUTE

There are several ways to approach this route; starting as a two-week (200 km) venture, you could put in at Lower Onaping Lake, off Highway 144, 80 km north of Sudbury; or fly in with Sudbury Aviation out of Azilda to Scotia Lake for a ten-day trip; or fly in to Welcome Lake as a one-week adventure. From points east you could even hike across from the Sturgeon River through beautiful Haentschel Lake. This route has been included in the Temagami book because of its cultural history and connection through the nastawgan travel routes. I've run this river from Scotia Lake and can attest to the wonderful drama that unfolds through that particular environment along the upper river. This write-up is brief and lacks the usual detail, primarily because I would prefer this river to continue being a challenge, albeit better documented and safe, yet mysterious. Discover for yourself.

CLASSIFICATION intermediate (CII to CIII rapids)

DISTANCE 64 km (welcome to Wanapitei Lake)

TIME 4–6 days

PORTAGES 19 (many can be eliminated through creative play)

VERTICAL DROP 110 m

MAPS 41 P/2, 41 P/3, 41 I/15

FEATURES & ECOLOGY The first section of the Wanapitei River, through Onaping and Scotia lakes, is typical Precambrian Shield country with a mix of granite outcrops and low-lying spruce bog and fen. The upper river, below Scotia Lake to Welcome Lake, is a slow-moving, meandering river broken occasionally by rocky outcrops, chutes and rapids. Moose sightings are guaranteed, as are sightings of osprey, heron, black ducks, mergansers and kingfisher. The lower Wanapitei, unlike the Sturgeon, does not meander, and follows a rift line through steep hills all the way to the meteor crater-formed Wanapitei Lake. The sand dunes at the mouth of the river are unique. Vegetation Site Code: UMF.

General Information For current trip reports, go to www.canadiancanoeroutes.com.

Whitewater Characteristics The Wanapitei River is best run in the early part of the season, through late May up to early July. Rapids become very bouldery by late June, necessitating more portaging and lining. Long sets of Class II rapids, littered with "pillow" rocks (rock gardens) exposed as water flow diminishes, make this river either very interesting and challenging, or very dangerous for those without the required skills.

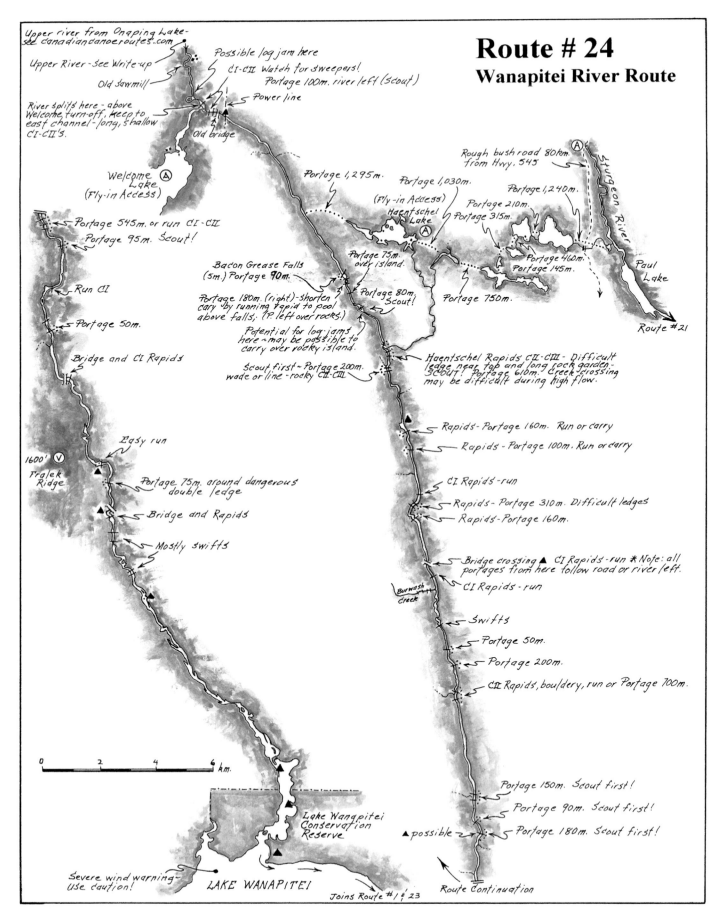

Route # 24
Wanapitei River Route

Upper river from Onaping Lake—see canadiandanoeroutes.com

Upper River—See Write-up

Old sawmill

River splits here - above Welcome, turn-off. Keep to east channel-long, shallow CI-CII's.

Possible log jam here
CI-CII Watch for sweepers!
Portage 100m. river left (Scout)
Power line

Old bridge

Welcome Lake (Fly-in Access)

Portage 545m. or run CI-CII
Portage 95m. Scout!

Run CI

Portage 50m.

Bridge and CI Rapids

Portage 1,295m.

Portage 1,030m. (Fly-in Access)

Rough bush road 80km. from Hwy. 545

Portage 1,240m.

Portage 210m.
Portage 315m.

Sturgeon River

Haentschel Lake

Paul Lake

Portage 460m.
Portage 145m.

Portage 750m.

Route #21

Bacon Grease Falls (5m.) Portage 90m.

Portage 75m. over island.

Portage 80m. Scout!

Portage 180m. (right)—shorten carry by running rapid to pool above falls; (P. left over rocks.)

Potential for log-jams here ~ may be possible to carry over rocky island.

Scout first ~ Portage 200m. wade or line - rocky CII-CIII

Haentschel Rapids CII-CIII - Difficult ledge near top and long rock garden-SCOUT! Portage 610m. Creek crossing may be difficult during high flow.

Easy run

1600'
Frajek Ridge

Portage 75m. around dangerous double ledge

Bridge and Rapids

Mostly swifts

Rapids- Portage 160m. Run or carry

Rapids - Portage 100m. Run or carry

CI Rapids - run

Rapids - Portage 310m. Difficult ledges
Rapids- Portage 160m.

Bridge crossing ▲ CI Rapids - run ✱ Note: all portages from here follow road or river left.

Burwash Creek

CI Rapids - run

Swifts

Portage 50m.

Portage 200m.

CII Rapids, bouldery, run or Portage 700m.

0 2 4 6 km.

Lake Wanapitei Conservation Reserve

Portage 150m. Scout first!

Portage 90m. Scout first!

▲ possible

Portage 180m. Scout first!

Severe wind warning- Use caution!

LAKE WANAPITEI

Joins Route #1 & 23

Route Continuation

Route # 25
Lower Montreal River Route

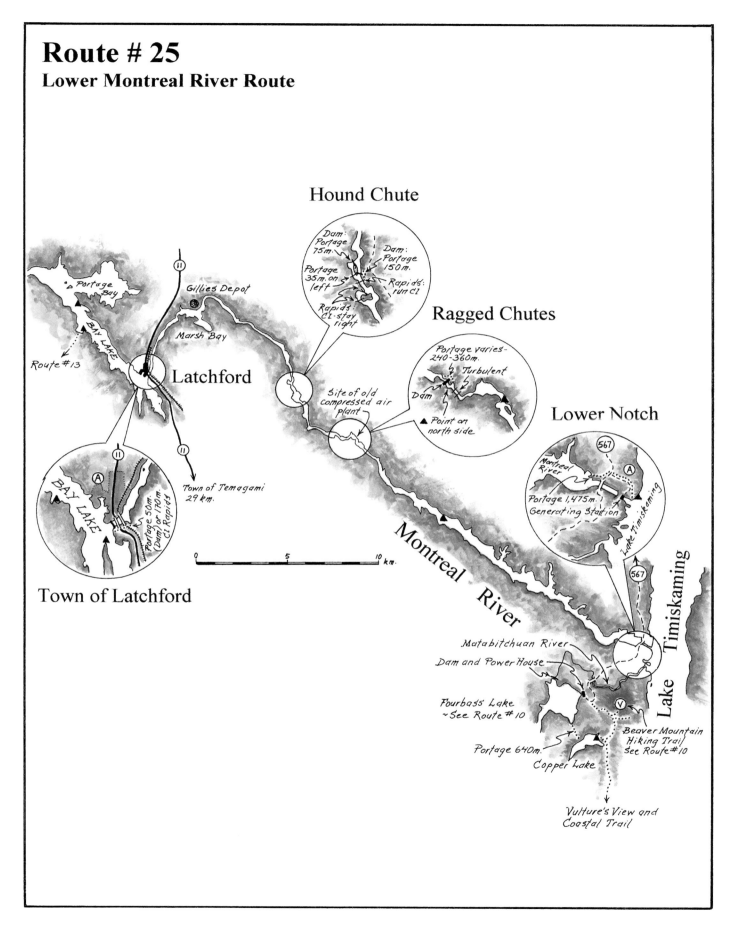

Hound Chute

Dam:
Portage
75m.

Dam:
Portage
150m.

Portage
35m. on
left

Rapids:
run C1

Rapids
C1-stay
right

Ragged Chutes

Portage varies—
240-360m.

Turbulent

Dam

Point on
north side

Lower Notch

Montreal
River

567

Portage 1,475m.
Generating Station

Lake Timiskaming

567

Portage
Bay

Route #13

BAY LAKE

11

Gillies Depot

Marsh Bay

Latchford

Site of old
compressed air
plant

11

A

BAY LAKE

Portage 50m.
(Dam) or 110m.
C1 Rapids

11

Town of Temagami
29 km.

0   5   10 km

Town of Latchford

Montreal River

Matabitchuan River

Dam and Power House

Fourbass Lake
~ See Route #10

Portage 640m.

Copper Lake

V

Beaver Mountain
Hiking Trail
See Route #10

Vulture's View and
Coastal Trail

Lake Timiskaming

ROUTE 25

LOWER MONTREAL RIVER ROUTE

I remember my first trip down the lower Montreal River in 1970, the year it was denuded of trees and flooded by the Lower Notch Dam. Once a beautiful, meandering river with several rapids, it is now a placid lake with eroded sand banks and limited camping. This route can be joined with other routes and can be traveled in either direction. It is recommended as a kayak touring route.

CLASSIFICATION experienced novice

DISTANCE 46 km

TIME 2 days

PORTAGES 2

MAPS 31 M/3, 31 M/4, 31 M/5

FEATURES & ECOLOGY The Montreal River forms the natural division between the transitional forest and Shield country to the south, with the "Little Clay Belt" to the northeast. Low-lying, rather nondescript in nature except where it flows through Ragged and Hound chutes, the poplar-and-birch forest contrasts with the ruggedness that defines Temagami elsewhere. The Native and White use of the river is interesting, and there are several locally written books about the area available at the famous Cobalt Bookstore (Highway 11 north of Latchford). Vegetation Site Code: UMF, SM.

Latchford Begin this route at the village of Latchford on Highway 11. If you are continuing down the Montreal River from Bay Lake, you will find two good campsites near the town site: one on the south point and one before the dam on the north shore. Portage to the right of the dam, and watch the traffic on the highway and the trains on the ONR Line. If you want to run the Class I rapids after the dam, you can put in before the highway bridge. This run becomes quite rocky when low (keep to the right channel).

Montreal River Proceed northeast past Gillies Depot, then head southeast about 2 km and you'll notice a rough, grassy campsite on the northeast bank. There is another site 3 km downriver.

Hound Chute At Hound Chute power house and rapids you have two choices. (1) Proceed past the first holding dam on the west shore and go on to the power house. Portage east of the dam to a trail and continue down a steep bank to the mid-section of the rapids. Take this route if traveling upstream, tracking the rapids to get to the portage. (2) To shoot the rapids in their entirety, portage at the first holding dam on the south side over bare rock to the river below. Paddle a short distance to a shallow rapids and portage on the left, directly below the power house. Go to the top of the rapids and put in. These rapids vary greatly with water flow. Proceed a short distance and keep right (west) of the island through a section of swifts.

Ragged Chutes Paddle about 4 km to Ragged Chutes. There is a rough, grassy campsite on the northeast bank, just before the dam, and another good site overlooking the chutes. Previously, there were rapids running below the dam and around the bend below. Now, because of the raising of water levels above the Lower Notch Dam at the Ottawa River, there are turbulent swifts below the old compressed-air plant. The portage begins up and across a grassy opening, then continues down a gravel bank to the river. When the water is low, portage via the same route but continue along the shore rocks to the open section of the river. The river flows through a rocky gorge, where you may encounter some turbulence.

Compressed-Air Plant This abandoned and unique plant, believed to be the last of its kind in the world, began serving Cobalt area mines around 1910. It used water falling down a shaft (110 m), forcing compressed air through a network of pipes that covered the entire Cobalt mining district. The blow-off of mixed air and water shot 30 m into the air over the Montreal River. Continue downriver across a large pool and around a bend by an old dam, where there is a good camping site on the northeast bank by a gravel road. From here to the hydro dam is easy cruising. Campsites may have been established along the way since I last traveled this route.

Lower Notch Dam Paddle to the north side of the dyked channel before the warning signs at the dam and start your portage here. Follow the gravel road uphill, then left and downhill to a fenced-off road to the right that continues below the dam to the Ottawa River. If the gate is closed, carry around and put in below. Camping is possible in the large opening. If you are heading downstream on the Ottawa River, refer to Route 26 for detailed information.

ROUTE
26

OTTAWA RIVER KAYAK TOUR

There are few undeveloped coastlines within the Canadian interior, aside from Hudson Bay and sections of Lake Superior or Georgian Bay. The Ottawa River is an anomaly, having been one of the busiest historic travelways used to open up the Canadian interior, yet remaining virtually undeveloped. One of the reasons is its magnificent, rugged personality. As a kayak tour it ranks very high, and for many reasons, including the scenic landscape; the variety of activities (including ridge hiking and nature interpretation); history (human and geological); and the number of excellent camping areas along the way. The route can be divided into three equal sections: New Liskeard to Lower Notch (Montreal River) 48 km, Lower Notch to Temiskaming 56 km and Temiskaming to Mattawa 58 km.

CLASSIFICATION   experienced novice

DISTANCE   162 km (total)

TIME   8–10 days total

PORTAGES   2 (under 500 m)

MAPS   1:250,000, Ville Marie 31M, North Bay 31L

FEATURES & ECOLOGY   The Native and White European history alone should entice the adventuring kayaker. The bold cliffs rising 100 m at Devil Rock, site of Ojibwa legends of the May-may-gwi-shi-wok (Stone People), now used as a climbing wall, typify a landscape that follows through all the way to Mattawa. There is virtually no development except at the community sites, and the camping is superb. The Ottawa River can be traveled throughout the season, although it can get rough, especially at the northern end where it is much shallower. Some sections of the river near Grand Campment Bay are over 225 m deep. The Ottawa River is on several migratory pathways, so don't forget to bring along your binoculars and bird guide. For more detailed information see the bibliography. Vegetation Site Code: C (upper to middle river), UMF (mid to lower river).

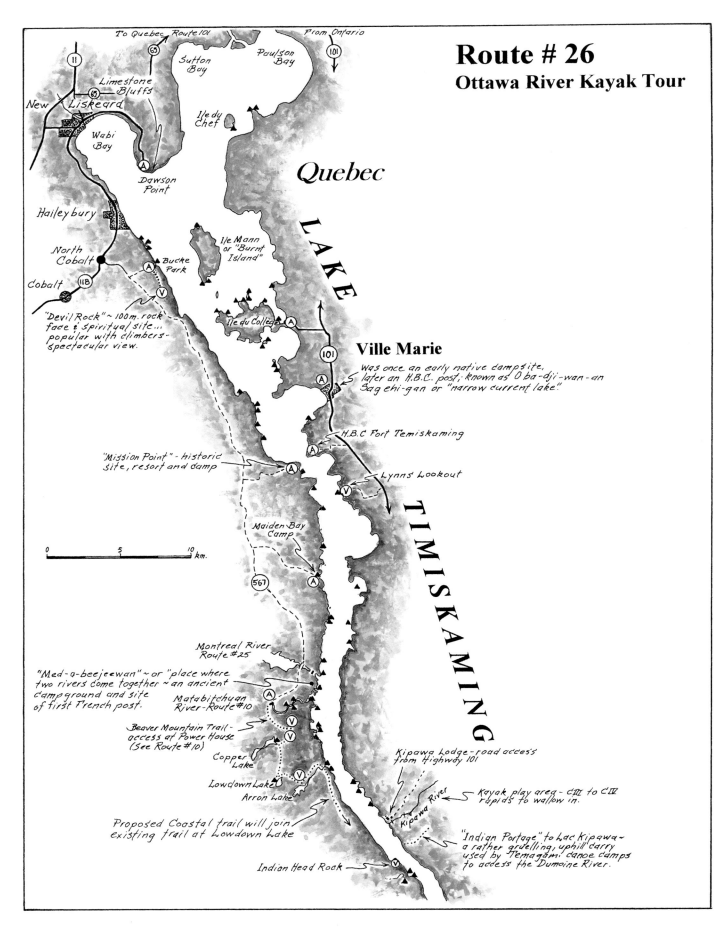

Route # 26
Ottawa River Kayak Tour

To Quebec Route 101

From Ontario

Sutton Bay

Paulson Bay

Ile du Chef

Limestone Bluffs

New Liskeard

Wabi Bay

Dawson Point

Haileybury

North Cobalt

Bucke Park

Cobalt

Quebec

Ile Mann or "Burnt Island"

Ile du College

"Devil Rock" ~ 100m. rock face & spiritual site... popular with climbers- spectacular view.

LAKE

Ville Marie

Was once an early native campsite, later an H.B.C. post; known as O ba-dji-wan-an Sag ehi-gan or "narrow current lake".

H.B.C Fort Temiskaming

Lynns Lookout

"Mission Point" - historic site, resort and camp

Maiden Bay Camp

TIMISKAMING

0   5   10 km.

Montreal River Route #25

"Med-a-beejeewan" ~ or "place where two rivers come together ~ an ancient campground and site of first French post.

Matabitchuan River- Route #10

Beaver Mountain Trail - access at Power House (See Route #10)

Copper Lake

Kipawa Lodge- road access from Highway 101

Lowdown Lake

Arron Lake

Kayak play area - CIII to CIV rapids to wallow in.

Proposed Coastal trail will join existing trail at Lowdown Lake

Kipawa River

"Indian Portage" to Lac Kipawa ~ a rather gruelling, uphill carry used by Temagami canoe camps to access the Dumoine River.

Indian Head Rock

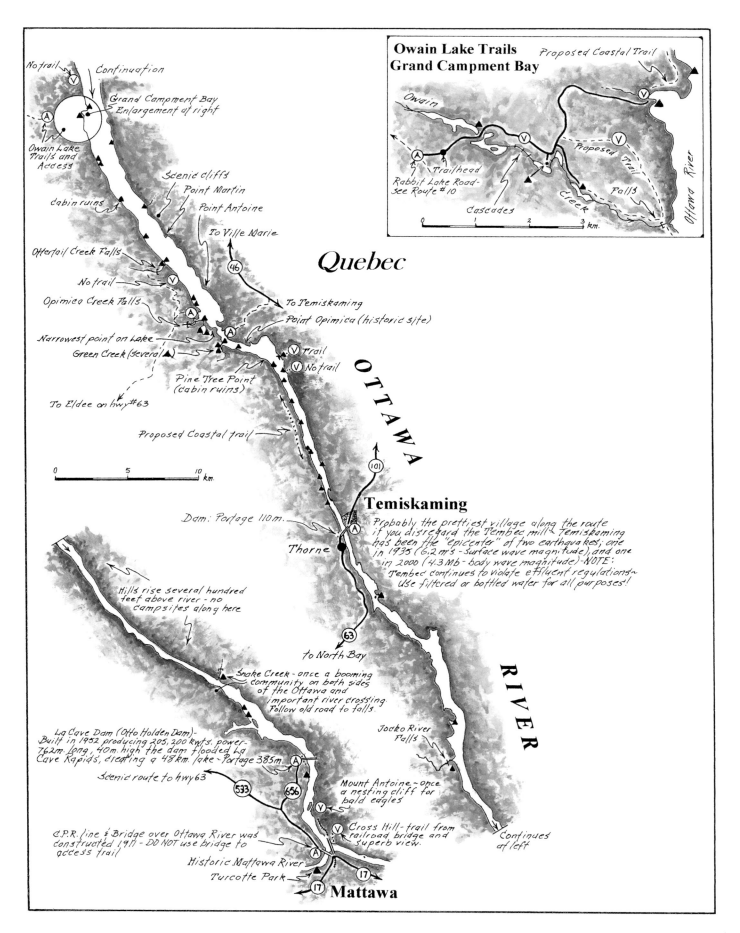

Owain Lake Trails
Grand Campment Bay

Proposed Coastal Trail

Owain

Proposed Trail

Trailhead
Rabbit Lake Road—
see Route #10

Cascades

Creek

Falls

Ottawa River

0   1   2   3 km.

No trail

Continuation

Grand Campment Bay
Enlargement at right

Owain Lake
Trails and
Access

cabin ruins

Scenic cliffs
Point Martin

Point Antoine

To Ville Marie

Otterlail Creek Falls

No trail

Opimica Creek Falls

Narrowest point on Lake

Green Creek (several)

Pine Tree Point
(cabin ruins)

To Eldee on hwy #63

Proposed Coastal trail

Quebec

To Temiskaming

Point Opimica (historic site)

Trail

No trail

OTTAWA

0   5   10 km.

101

Temiskaming

Dam: Portage 110 m.

Thorne

*Probably the prettiest village along the route
if you disregard the Tembec mill~ Temiskaming
has been the "epicenter" of two earthquakes; one
in 1935 (6.2 m/s - surface wave magnitude), and one
in 2000 (4.3 Mb - body wave magnitude)-NOTE:
Tembec continues to violate effluent regulations~
Use filtered or bottled water for all purposes!!*

63

to North Bay

Hills rise several hundred
feet above river - no
campsites along here

Snake Creek - once a booming
community on both sides
of the Ottawa and
important river crossing.
Follow old road to falls.

Jocko River
Falls

La Cave Dam (Otto Holden Dam)-
Built in 1952 producing 205,200 kwts. power-
762m. long, 40m. high the dam flooded La
Cave Rapids, creating a 48km. lake- Portage 385m.

Scenic route to hwy 63

533   656

C.P.R. line & Bridge over Ottawa River was
constructed 1911 - DO NOT use bridge to
access trail

Historic Mattawa River

Turcotte Park

17   **Mattawa**

Mount Antoine ~ once
a nesting cliff for
bald eagles

Cross Hill - trail from
railroad bridge and
superb view.

Continues
at left

RIVER

17

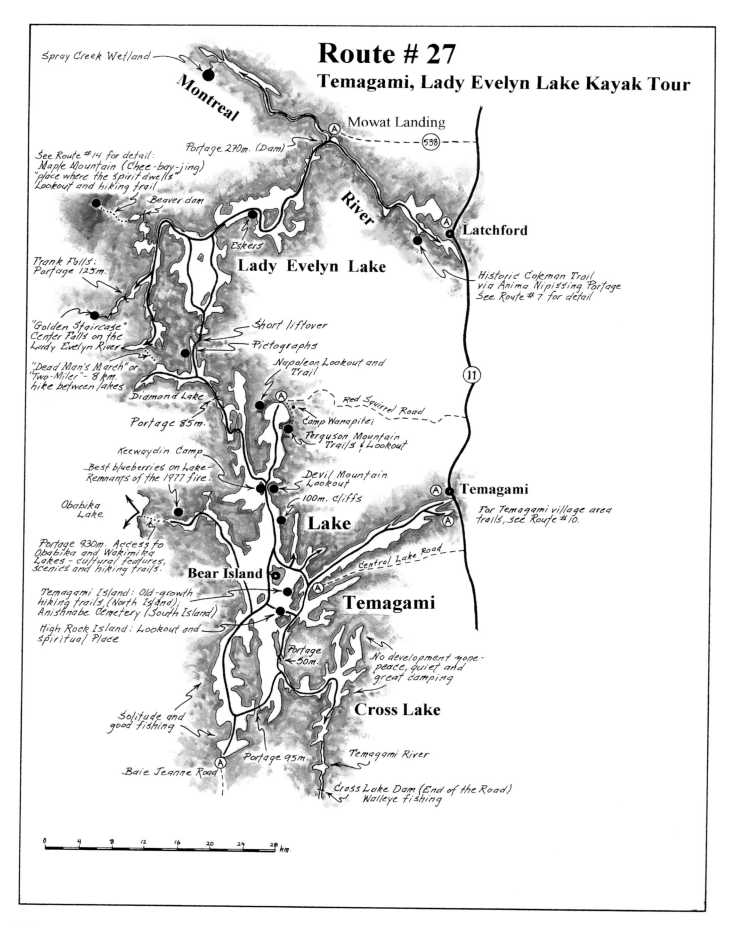

Route # 27
Temagami, Lady Evelyn Lake Kayak Tour

Spray Creek Wetland

Montreal

Mowat Landing

Portage 270m. (Dam)

538

See Route #14 for detail:
Maple Mountain (Chee-bay-jing)
"place where the spirit dwells"
Lookout and hiking trail

Beaver dam

River

Eskers

Latchford

Lady Evelyn Lake

Frank Falls:
Portage 125m.

Historic Coleman Trail
via Anima Nipissing Portage
See Route # 7 for detail

"Golden Staircase"
Center Falls on the
Lady Evelyn River

Short liftover

Pictographs

11

"Dead Man's March" or
"Two-Miler" - 8 km.
hike between lakes

Napoleon Lookout and
Trail

Diamond Lake

Red Squirrel Road

Portage 85m.

Camp Wanapitei

Ferguson Mountain
Trails & Lookout

Keewaydin Camp

Best blueberries on Lake-
Remnants of the 1977 fire.

Devil Mountain
Lookout

100m. cliffs

Obabika
Lake

Lake

Temagami

For Temagami village area
trails, see Route #10.

Portage 930m. Access to
Obabika and Wakimika
Lakes - cultural features,
scenics and hiking trails.

Bear Island

Central Lake Road

Temagami Island: Old-growth
hiking trails (North Island);
Anishnabe Cemetery (South Island)

Temagami

High Rock Island: Lookout and
spiritual Place

Portage
50m.

No development zone-
peace, quiet and
great camping

Cross Lake

Solitude and
good fishing

Portage 95m.

Temagami River

Baie Jeanne Road

Cross Lake Dam (End of the Road)
Walleye fishing

0   4   8   12   16   20   24   28 km.

TEMAGAMI, LADY EVELYN LAKE KAYAK TOUR

As an interior, coastal-type tour, this route may well be one of Canada's finest. As an undeveloped shoreline, it surpasses even Lake Superior or Georgian Bay for distance. One of the enduring features is the fact that it's a safe traveling environment, especially for novice kayakers. There is no threat of lay-ups due to the strong winds that are often a problem on coastal trips such as Lake Superior or the West and East Coast of Canada. There are more campsites available per kilometre of travel, and the option to explore an endless variety of lakes and hidden bays, climb high ridges (including the famous Maple Mountain) and enjoy the personality of such a treasured near-wilderness environment. Short portages between lakes pose little problem for even the largest touring boats. With over 3,000 km of undeveloped shoreline and over 250 campsites, there are endless possibilities here.

SUGGESTED TRIP OPTIONS

1 Fly-in to Hobart Lake. Maple Mountain tour, explore the "Golden Staircase Falls" (portage 120 m at Franks Falls), south to Diamond (easy pull-through), south to Sharp Rock and Lake Temagami (70 m portage), various route options back to Temagami village.
2 Leave Temagami village, head north to Diamond, Lady Evelyn, Sucker Gut to the "Golden Staircase" and Maple Mountain, continue on to Mowat Landing. Arrange with a local outfitter to have your vehicle shuttled to Mowat, or book a return ride back to Temagami.
3 Fly-in to north Obabika Lake to hike the Wakimika Triangle Trails, return to Lake Temagami via Obabika Inlet portage (two-person carry for 950 m), and return to Temagami village.
4 Loop tours can be organized from either Temagami village, central Lake Temagami access point, Sandy Inlet (north Lake Temagami), or Mowat Landing. Part of any of these loops will require retracing of a section of the route.

CLASSIFICATION novice

DISTANCE & TIME 2 days to 3 weeks

PORTAGES refer to map for detail

MAPS 1 P/1, 41 P/8, 31 M/4, 31 M/5, 31 L/13, 31 I/16

FEATURES & ECOLOGY There is just too much to relate, although most of the information can be gleaned from the other route descriptions. Temagami is known for its clear water, rock and pine vistas and old-growth forests of international importance. It is recommended that you visit Bear Island Reserve and Camp Keewaydin, where you can browse through local histories and archival information. There are several hiking trail options and viewpoints, including the famous Maple Mountain hike up to one of the highest points in Ontario. Vegetation Site Code: UCF, UMF, C, TS (Willow Island Creek), RB (Maple Mountain summit).

Part Seven

Afternotes

Afternotes

Campfire Muse

I push the coals around and new flames come to life; just enough fire to burn the last log. I have about five minutes left of ambient, protracted light before night's opaqueness absorbs my tiny mantel of granite. I'm down to the grounds in my coffee mug, so I thin out the sludge in the bottom with a bit more scotch. I light my pipe. The smoke lingers as if reluctant to leave and then gets caught in the updraft from the fire, curling skywards through the canopy of pine boughs in trailing wisps. It's cool enough that a ghost mist hangs over the lake in weird sheets, mixing congenially with the blue smoke of my fire. A thumbnail moon appears on the eastern rise of pine, silhouetting their outstretched wings. I lean back against my pack and draw up my collar to deflect the encroaching chill. I'm tired and it feels great. Everything fits together in an accidental organic unity.

> *Only once in these long Canadian wanderings was the deep peace of the wilderness savagely broken. It happened in the maple woods about midnight when I was cold and my fire was low.*
>
> JOHN MUIR

It's a sentimental moment for me; I want to both cry and sing at the same time. A quarter century later and this campsite can still conjure a sense of sacred place. For now, the space belongs to me and my thoughts alone. And those thoughts flow by, carried by the current of those years, and like the pages of a book I read the abstract chapters of my life with amused contentment. The adventure, the freedom, the battles won and lost, the romance and the bitter tears. I regret only one thing . . . that we were not unified enough, or devious enough I suppose, to protect more of this precious wilderness. I sit comfortably at this fire, at a campsite that falsely evokes a sense of calm in the region. Where other trails and camps have been lost to the ever-intruding machine, I fear that complacency or acceptance of these intrusions will instill a passive disposition among today's paddlers. Somewhere in the distance a loon calls.

I've witnessed a lot of changes in the past twenty-five years, changes in the outdoor accoutrement, changes in the politics governing Ontario parks and wild spaces, and in particular a change in the way we easily accept resource management policy that contravenes logical and sustainable use of the forest. A forest, I might add, that dramatizes an ancient culture by its unique Native nastawgan, attracts an international paddle-sport population, and is the heartland of Ontario's provincial tree — the white pine. In the 1980s, the state of the environment was Canada's number one concern. We made terrific gains in the environmental forum, including forcing the province to adopt a policy regarding old-growth pine forests. In the 1990s, public anxiety focused on job security and standard of living, and needless to say, environmental groups either faded into oblivion or came upon hard times. Many key activists burned out or were hired by industry. The new millennium brought about patent fears surrounding global issues compounded by terrorism, war and depleting resources. It is most unfortunate that it takes such drastic measures and events to get people refocused on what's important. As Thoreau noted about the complexity of the American Dream: "Simplicity, simplicity, simplicity! I say, let your affairs be as two or three and not a hundred or a thousand." American outdoor nature writer and philosopher Sigurd Olsen, who seems to have perfected a savoury lifestyle that blends the best of both worlds, implies that we should learn to live simply and all will go well. I couldn't agree more.

There are but a few embers remaining. The cold seems to have taken hold of some aching joints that remind me of the miles I've paddled and the portages I have walked. I stand up and shake the stiffness from my legs and breathe deeply of the piney fragrance. I can't help but smile. How lucky I have been to find sanctuary here. And even though I know the fight is not yet over, I revel in the opportunity to have participated at all, to possibly have made even a small contribution to the preservation of the Temagami wilderness. I'm tired and it feels great.

Trip Log

Checklist

BASIC

_____ Menu completed (calculated per person/day plus 2 extra days)

_____ All food packed in waterproofed & labeled dry bags

_____ Two sets of maps/map case and this book

_____ Fishing/travel licences purchased

_____ Medical/dental check-up

_____ Itinerary/trip schedule left with family or friend

_____ Outfitter services double-checked & verified

_____ Toilet seat up and kibble left for dog/cat

_____ Note to spouse

SPECIFIC LISTS

PERSONAL SAFETY ITEMS

First Aid Kit – A good one must include various adhesive-strips, gauze and tape, butterfly closures, antiseptic cream or ointment, pain medication such as Advil, antihistamine such as Benadryl for allergic reactions, antacid tablets (almonds, dried papaya, and fennel tea also work well), scissors, tweezers, razor & new blades, burn cream, lip balm & sunscreen, eye patch & eye flush, finger splint, 2 tensor bandages, blister patches, foot powder, aluminized rescue blanket, and first aid manual. Suggested reading: _Official Wilderness First-Aid Guide_ by Wayne Merry/St. John Ambulance.

CEREMONY

Pouch or plug of tobacco. A gift offering of money & tobacco is often standard etiquette required to secure the services of a medicine healer or shaman for personal ceremony. Tobacco offerings should be done at the beginning of your trip and at places of special prominence such as rock-art sites.

RESCUE AND SAFETY

_____ PLB/ELT: Cell phones will soon make these obsolete

_____ GPS unit & waterproof case

_____ Rescue throw-bag for each canoe

_____ Extra rope: 2 painters per canoe plus 100-150 ft. of climbing rope

_____ Handy prussik lines & carabiners for quick Z-drag set-up

_____ Good insurance policy if none of the above works

EQUIPMENT PARTICULARS

_____ Paddles (plus one spare per canoe)

_____ Appropriate canoe(s)

_____ Knee pads (affixed or slip-on type)

_____ Padding for yoke(s)

_____ Bailer & sponge per canoe

_____ Flotation bags and/or spray-deck

_____ Quality tent(s)

_____ Kitchen fly and/or bug canopy

_____ Rope bag for tarps

_____ Ground sheet for tent(s)

_____ Stove, fuel, funnel, fire-irons or grill (for open fire cooking)

_____ Reflector-oven (optional for baking)

_____ Pots, dishes, cups & cutlery

_____ Dishtowel, scrubber, bio-degradable soap & wash basin

_____ Compass, whistle per person

_____ Water purifier or tablets

_____ Dromedary bag or water bucket (collapsible)

_____ Sleeping-bag(s) & Therma-rest

_____ Toilet paper

_____ Daypack with water bottle & goodies

_____ Waterproof matches/lighter

_____ Folding saw and axe (no hatchets)

_____ Garbage bags & Zip-Lock bags

_____ Gear packs, dry-bags, kitchen wannigan checked out

PERSONAL ITEMS

_____ PFD (personal flotation device)

_____ Clothing: 2-piece Gore-Tex rain suit, paddling gloves, bug-jacket/headnet, hat or bandanna, canoe shoes & boots, wool socks, long underwear, briefs, T-shirts, fleece or wool sweater, baggy pants & shirts (quick-dry), bathing suit

_____ Sunglasses & skin protection

_____ Belt knife

_____ Whistle

_____ Toiletries, towel & facecloth

_____ Personal medication/vitamins

_____ Insect repellent (avoid DEET and use natural types)

_____ Cards/games for rainy days

_____ Mouth harp/musical instrument

_____ Diary or journal pad & pens

_____ Camera, waterproof case, extra battery & film

_____ Compact fishing kit & lure box

EMERGENCY REPAIR KIT

- Roll of quality duct tape
- Multi-tool
- Tent-screen patch kit/Therma-rest patch kit
- Sewing kit/extra buttons & heavy-duty waxed thread
- Self-tapping screws for quick canoe repairs
- Extra Snap-X fasteners for packs
- Waterproof adhesive
- Roll of copper wire

Please Note

These are only suggested basic checklists; you may wish to add or delete items listed according to personal preferences.

Menu Chart

BREAKFAST	LUNCH	DINNER
	DAY 1	

BREAKFAST	LUNCH	DINNER
	DAY 8	

BREAKFAST	LUNCH	DINNER
	DAY 2	

BREAKFAST	LUNCH	DINNER
	DAY 9	

BREAKFAST	LUNCH	DINNER
	DAY 3	

BREAKFAST	LUNCH	DINNER
	DAY 10	

BREAKFAST	LUNCH	DINNER
	DAY 4	

BREAKFAST	LUNCH	DINNER
	DAY 11	

BREAKFAST	LUNCH	DINNER
	DAY 5	

BREAKFAST	LUNCH	DINNER
	DAY 12	

BREAKFAST	LUNCH	DINNER
	DAY 6	

BREAKFAST	LUNCH	DINNER
	DAY 13	

BREAKFAST	LUNCH	DINNER
	DAY 7	

BREAKFAST	LUNCH	DINNER
	DAY 14	

Trail Cookery

Food is an essential part of our daily existence, and packing a healthy menu that replaces burned calories during the day not only replenishes our body but helps maintain our general spirit and positive outlook, especially when the going gets tough. Packing too light in order to make the load easier over portages will compromise a wider range of food types that you can add to your food pack, like real vegetables. I don't mind taking an extra trip over the portage if it means being able to have the occasional green salad, or fried potato with my morning egg. There are always compromises, but a good menu could mean the difference between wilderness survival and outdoor living! Here are a few tips and recipes you may find handy.

Bannock (fried bread) One of the easiest ways to pack your daily staple of bread is to mix the dry ingredients for bannock. It packs well, is easy to prepare and tastes great. Figure out how many days you'll be out and mix all dry ingredients together and pack in a Zip-lock bag. Pack this in a cloth or nylon ditty bag for protection. You need a good frypan that won't burn the food you're trying to cook, and you need a lid to put over the bannock while it's cooking. If you're cooking over a campfire, keep one side hot and scrape the coals over to the other side — this is where you want to medium-bake your bannock. If you bake over a portable stove, you'll have to rotate the bannock often, and make sure there's plenty of oil in the pan. Avoid cooking over direct flame unless you like your bannock raw on the inside and cinder black on the outside. Flip over once the bannock is brown on the one side (about 12–15 minutes) and bake for another 10 minutes. I like to prepare the day's bannock on the breakfast fire, allow it to cool and pack it in tin foil or a paper bag and put it in your wannigan or barrel, so it won't get crushed.

Here's a recipe for one bannock that will feed four people and keep them smiling:

1 cup organic whole-wheat flour   -
1/4 cup cornmeal
1 cup unbleached, organic flour
1/4 cup oat flakes
1.5 tablespoons aluminum-free baking powder
1/2 teaspoon of sea salt
1 tablespoon brown sugar

To make: Add water to make dough (can be sticky but not tight or like pancake batter); flatten onto a greased pan and brown slowly over medium-low heat. Put a lid on it to help it bake. Variations: try adding oregano, caraway or fennel to spice it up, or chunks of cheddar, bacon bits or sun-dried tomatoes.

Sunrise Salad There's no reason why you can't enjoy a green salad every day of your trip. Stephanie and I have managed to keep certain vegetables fresh for over four weeks if properly cared for and packed. The secret is not to put your food pack in the sun — always keep it shaded, even in the canoe. Air dry the veggies each day and remove or use those that look like they're ready to turn on you, rewrap in paper towel and avoid plastic bags. After your tomatoes and romaine have gone, here's a list of ingredients for a salad that will rock your tastebuds (using items that will keep longest):

sliced carrots	diced apple
chopped onion	minced ginger root
chopped garlic	
raisins	
diced cabbage	
sunflower seeds	

To make: Mix well with balsamic vinegar, olive oil, brown sugar (or maple syrup), and add a pinch of salt, pepper, basil, oregano or fennel seed. Pack liquids in plastic Nalgene bottles and label. (Packed in a Nalgene, olive oil looks a lot like scotch!). Try adding oxe-eye daisy leaves, sheep sorrel or dandelion to your salad. These can be found in several areas in Temagami, especially in grassy clearings.

Preserving Bacon (or other meat) Fewer people pack meat for their trips these days, but there's nothing like the smell of frying bacon to perk the nostrils in the morning. Look for double-smoked meat products and make sure they're fresh. Slab or sliced bacon should be removed from its plastic liner, rubbed lightly with vinegar, and packed in cheesecloth. Store it in a Tupperware box. Periodically wipe the meat with vinegar (a preservative that won't flavour the meat) and rewrap with fresh cheesecloth. You can keep meat for three weeks or more this way. The downside of bringing meat is that you have to be particularly careful about the smell. The used cheesecloth should be well bagged and sealed, and once meat has turned you have to get rid of it, as bears can pick up the scent even if you can't. Dry salami also keeps well as long as it stays dry. When you buy meat at a deli, ask them to vacuum seal it for you. This is good for about a week, but then you'll want to remove it from the plastic, wipe it down with vinegar, and pack it in cheesecloth.

Freezing and Pre-cooking Food For most of my trips I like to prepare some meals ahead of time. Chicken doesn't keep well unless it's smoked, so it's best to cook it well and then freeze it. You can do the same with beef. I like to cube it before freezing so it's ready to throw into a rice stir-fry. Put the meat into a Zip-lock or Nalgene before freezing. When you leave home, wrap the frozen goods in newspaper or bubble wrap and keep in a soft cooler pack. When traveling, keep the cooler out of the sun — on the bottom of the canoe while paddling or in the shade at the campsite. Frozen, cooked meats will keep up to a week if properly maintained.

Deep-Water Thai Stew
You can't beat this for a one-pot meal. You'll need:

    carrots
    dried apricots
    parsnips
    lemongrass
    potatoes
    onion
    garlic
    curry paste
      (canned or bottled curry paste
      can be packed in a Nalgene)

To make: Dice the veggies and boil them in a big pot. When they're cooked, do not drain. Add garlic, onions, lemongrass and dried apricots and curry paste. To thicken: using a small Nalgene, fill halfway with cool water and add 2 tablespoons of flour, shake well and pour into the bubbling pot, stirring constantly. Simmer over medium-low heat for 15 minutes. Serve over a bed of rice. Add cooked beef, chicken or tofu.

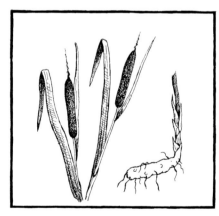

Cattail
(roots and fruit).

Hap's Bush Salad

Left: dandelion; top right:
sheep sorrel (contains oxalic acid
and may cause allergic reactions);
bottom right: oxe -eye daisy.

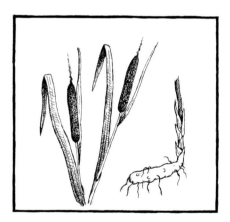

Spruce Tea
(brewed needles & shoots)

Wintergreen
(wilderness breath freshener)
and tea (both high in Vitamin C).

River Notes

Acknowledgments

As with any such undertaking, and without exception, the success of this guidebook over the last twenty-five years can be attributed to the support of many individuals and sponsors. Support manifests itself in many ways, be it emotional, assistance in the field, professional criticism, offering of in-kind services, or financial contribution. I'd like to thank the following people for their support: Firefly and Boston Mills as publisher and my editor, Jane Gates, my agent, Lynn Thompson, Living Legacy Trust for their financial support, Kirk Wipper for his wisdom and relentless aphorisms, Earthroots, Brian Back at Ottertooth.com, Richard Munn of Canadian Canoe Routes, the Canadian Recreational Canoeing Association as publisher for ten years, all of my corporate sponsors as listed in this edition, Ted Krofchak, Frances Boyes, Les Wilcox, Gord Lomax, Vicky and Murray Muir, David and Larry Wewchar, John Kilbridge, Alex Mathias, Craig Macdonald, Stephen Hurlbut, Bob Hunter, Ron Waters, Doug Hamilton and the Ministry of Natural Resources. Thanks also to Lands and Parks Supervisor, OMNR Temagami District, Reg Sinclair, who in 1976 hired me to map out the Temagami canoe routes for the first edition. Most of all, thanks to my wife, Stephanie, for her love, patience and hard work, and for sharing the journey.

Bibliography and Suggested Reading

BIBLIOGRAPHY

Back, Brian. *The Keewaydin Way — A Portrait: 1893-1983* (first edition). Published by Keewaydin Camp Ltd.

Cassidy, G.L. *Arrow North: The Story of Temiskaming*. Cobalt: Highway Book Shop Publishers, 1976

Speck, F.G. *Family Hunting Territories & Social Life of Various Algonkian Bands of the Ottawa Valley*, Ottawa: Geological Survey, Dept. of Mines, Government Printing Bureau, 1915.

Ministry of Natural Resources, Temagami District, Sensitive Features Report, archives, Vol. 1–2, 1980.

SUGGESTED READING

Callan, Kevin. *Further Up the Creek: A Paddler's Guide to the Rivers of Ontario and Quebec.* Erin: Boston Mills Press, 1999. (Temagami and Sturgeon river information).

Mason, Bill. *Path of the Paddle: An Illustrated Guide to the Art of Canoeing.* Key Porter Books, 1995.

Mason, Bill. *Song of the Paddle: An Illustrated Guide to Wilderness Camping.* Key Porter Books, 1988.

Meyer, Kathleen Meyer. *How to Shit in the Woods: An Environmentally Sound Approach to a Lost Art.* Ten Speed Press,1994.

Mitcham, Allison. *Grey Owl's Favourite Wilderness Revisited.* Penumbra Press, 1991.

Muir, Vicky & Murray. *Discovering Wild Temiskaming — One Day Adventures by Booklet.* Call to order: 705-648-3310

Books by Grey Owl: *Men of the Last Frontier, Tales of an Empty Cabin, Sajo and the Beaver People* Macmillan Canada

Ruffo, A. G. *Grey Owl: The Mystery of Archie Belaney.* Coteau Books, 1998.

Smith, D. B. *From the Land of Shadows: The Making of Grey Owl.* Western Prairie Books, 1990.

Theriault, M. K. *Moose to Moccasins: the Story of Ka Kita Wa Pa No Kwe.* Natural Heritage, Natural History Inc., 1992.

Wilson, H. *Rivers of the Upper Ottawa Valley.* Erin: Boston Mills Press, 2004.

Appreciation to the following sponsors for their support.

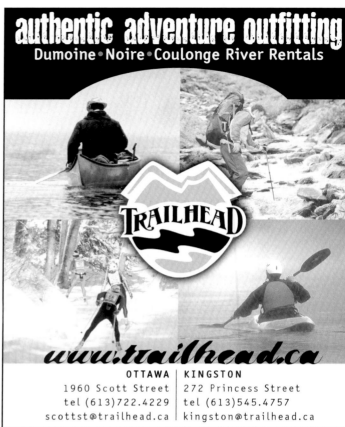

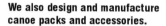

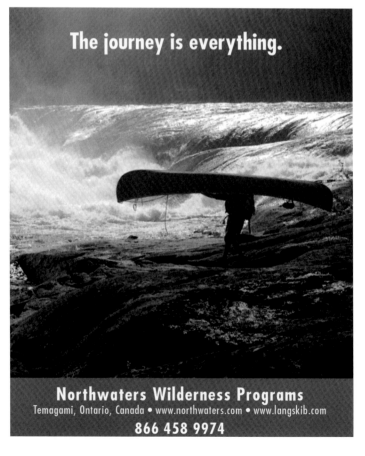

Chum Television is proud to sponsor Hap Wilson's work.
As a guidebook it is invaluable, but beyond that it is rich source of
regional history and a celebration of the beauty inherent in our natural world.

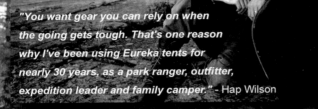

"You want gear you can rely on when the going gets tough. That's one reason why I've been using Eureka tents for nearly 30 years, as a park ranger, outfitter, expedition leader and family camper." – Hap Wilson

photo courtesy of Stephanie Aykroyd

Eureka!
Made to Meet The Challenge
www.jma.com

photo courtesy of Hap Wilson

Johnson Outdoors Canada Inc.   4180 Harvester Road, Burlington, Ontario L7L 6B6